LETTERS TO THE LONDON "TIMES," AND NEW YORK "COURIER AND INQUIRER"

Published @ 2017 Trieste Publishing Pty Ltd

ISBN 9780649631742

Letters to the London "Times," and New York "Courier and Inquirer" by Edward Vernon Childe

Except for use in any review, the reproduction or utilisation of this work in whole or in part in any form by any electronic, mechanical or other means, now known or hereafter invented, including xerography, photocopying and recording, or in any information storage or retrieval system, is forbidden without the permission of the publisher, Trieste Publishing Pty Ltd, PO Box 1576 Collingwood, Victoria 3066 Australia.

All rights reserved.

Edited by Trieste Publishing Pty Ltd.
Cover @ 2017

This book is sold subject to the condition that it shall not, by way of trade or otherwise, be lent, re-sold, hired out, or otherwise circulated without the publisher's prior consent in any form or binding or cover other than that in which it is published and without a similar condition including this condition being imposed on the subsequent purchaser.

www.triestepublishing.com

EDWARD VERNON CHILDE

LETTERS TO THE LONDON "TIMES," AND NEW YORK "COURIER AND INQUIRER"

Trieste

LETTERS

TO THE

LONDON "TIMES,"

AND

NEW YORK

"COURIER AND INQUIRER."

BY A "STATES'"-MAN, *i.e.*

Edward Vernon Childe.

———•••———

BOSTON:
BAZIN & CHANDLER, PRINTERS, 37 CORNHILL.
1857.

U.S.5095,7,2

1861, Jan.18.
Gift of
Charles Eliot Norton,
of Cambridge.
(Class of 1846)

LETTERS
DEDICATED
TO
A. H.
BY
E. V. C*hild*
1857.

CONTENTS.

LETTERS TO THE "LONDON TIMES."

LETTER I.
PAGE.
Resources and Debts of the United States,.....................9
LETTER II.
Mississippi Bonds and Exchequer Bills,......................15
LETTER III.
Corn and Free Trade,. 18
LETTER IV.
Exchequer Bills,......................................20
LETTER V.
President Polk's Policy,................................22
LETTER VI.
President Polk's Message,...............................25
LETTER VII.
Remonstrance and Defence,..............................29
LETTER VIII.
Strength and Consistency of the United States' Government,....34
LETTER IX.
Insolvent States of America,.............................38
LETTER X.
Mr. Webster and Mr. Dallas,.............................42
LETTER XI.
Defence of the Mexican War,.............................46
LETTER XII.
The delinquent States of America,........................48

CONTENTS.

LETTER XIII.
English and French Sympathies,......................51

LETTER XIV.
The Spanish Marriages,............................56

LETTER XV.
To Lord Palmerston,..............................59

LETTER XVI.
Defence of the preceding Letter, ...62

LETTER XVII.
Expulsion of the National Assembly foretold,........67

LETTER XVIII.
Men and Means wanted to make a Republic in France,..71

LETTER XIX.
Suppression of National Work-shops,................75

LETTER XX.
The French Republic,.............................77

LETTER XXI.
The French Republic,.............................81

LETTER XXII.
Louis Napoleon, his Family and the French Generals,..84

LETTER XXIII.
The State of Paris,..............................92

LETTER XXIV.
M. Thiers and his Political Economy,...............94

LETTER XXV.
The State of France,.............................96

LETTER XXVI.
The two Republics—France and the United States,....99

LETTER XXVII.
Louis Napoleon's Chances,........................104

LETTER XXVIII.
To the Prince President,.........................107

LETTER XXIX.
The Condition of Parties in France,..............111

LETTER XXX.
The Presidency of France,........................115

CONTENTS.

LETTER XXXI.
The French President,..................................121
LETTER XXXII.
Cuba and the United States,............................125
LETTER XXXIII.
Slavery in the United States,...........................130
LETTER XXXIV.
Slavery in the United States,...........................136
LETTER XXXV.
Russia and the Allies,..................................138
LETTER XXXVI.
Slavery in the United States,...... 143
LETTER XXXVII.
Russia and the United States,...........................147
LETTER XXXVIII.
Great Britain and the United States,.....................152
LETTER XXXIX.
The United States,......................................155
LETTER XL.
Anglo-American Relations and Mr. Crampton,...............161

LETTERS TO THE NEW YORK "COURIER AND ENQUIRER."

LETTER I.
The Spanish Marriages,.......... 165
LETTER II.
The City of Cracow,....................................169
LETTER III.
An American in Europe, and the State of Europe,............173
LETTER IV.
King Louis Philippe's Speech,...........................178
LETTER V.
Queen Victoria's Speech,...............................180

CONTENTS.

LETTER VI.
Prussia — Famine — Free-Trade,............................184

LETTER VII.
Fast-Day in England. France — Spain — Portugal,..........188

LETTER VIII.
Aspect of Paris after the Revolution of 1848,................191

LETTER IX.
The Revolution of February, 1848,........................195

LETTER X.
"May 15th, 1848"..199

LETTER XI.
The Troubled State of France,............................203

LETTER XII.
National Work-shops,....................................207

LETTER XIII.
Timidity and Weakness of the National Assembly,............210

LETTER XIV.
The "Four Days of June" and the Provisional Government,....212

LETTER XV.
The Great Movement in Europe,...........................214

LETTER XVI.
France in a State of Transition,............................217

LETTER XVII.
The Republic near its End,................................219

LETTER XVIII.
The Internal Administration of France,.....................221

LETTER XIX.
What can be substituted for the Republic?..................224

LETTER XX.
The *Coup d'Etat* of December 2d,........................229

LETTER XXI.
Will Mankind go backwards?..............................252

LETTER XXII.
The "Value of the Union,"...............................255

LETTERS

TO THE

"LONDON TIMES."

LETTER I.

It is frequently remarked by English writers, that the inhabitants of the United States "hate them," and would on the slightest provocation, or with no provocation at all, be glad to rush into a senseless war. This is not true, but it is so generally believed by them, that a very short time since, I was requested to write a letter, demonstrating the contrary, to be put into the hands of one of the leading men in your country.* We do *not* hate you, but all the actual wrongs you could heap upon us would hardly stir up such bitter blood as the venomous outpourings of the *Quarterly Review* and other periodicals have done. Should you not rather seek for good than for evil in those of your own blood, and have you not much more to lose than to gain by exciting our evil passions, and by keeping us just at that point of irritation where you yourselves ought to be answerable for any act on our part which may eventuate in war?

*Lord Chancellor Lyndhurst

I am a man of peace, and I cannot but think that the responsibility of those who strive to set brethren at strife, is awful in the extreme. If, therefore, my poor persuasion can induce you or others to put less gall into your anathemas against my country, if not for our sakes and our children's sake, then for the sake of human happiness and civilization, endeavor to preserve that peace which God loves and man should not despise.

In order to preserve it between two powerful nations, it is of some consequence that their respective resources be not mutually undervalued. I admit that my countrymen, to judge from their frequent self-glorification, are either stupidly ignorant of, or grossly indifferent to, the immense numerical superiority of your war marine over ours; but, on the other hand, our own means of annoyance in case of hostilities are vastly underrated by you. It is thought in England, because our public ships are not as one in ten to yours, that therefore our mercantile marine might be swept from the ocean, while yours remained almost unharmed. But you well know that a lancet can let life out as surely as a broadsword, and it needs no ghost of rich Indiamen, long sunk, to tell many a ruined family that a paltry privateer can do the work of destruction as effectually as the mightiest man-of-war with its hundred cannons. And, taking into consideration the myriads of private armed vessels which would swarm from all our ports in spite of blockades, and the immense extent of your commerce, considerably greater than ours, I hazard nothing in declaring, if war should come, that, ship for ship and man for man, we should have no reason to fear the last "dead reckoning."

In your leading article of the 30th ult. you say, that "the effects of a state of war would be equally injurious to the interests and to the liberties of the (American) commonwealth." To the interests, yes! but only temporarily and partially.

Temporarily, because the States are yet too young to feel for any length of time the effects of a blow, however heavy, and are possessed in a rare degree of that elasticity which youth alone possesses.

Were you to raze every town on our seaboard, (a thing impossible, as New York and Boston, not to mention other ports, I know, are so strongly fortified that no enemy could enter them,) but for the sake of argument, were you to give our cities to the flames and our ships to the waves, do you think the effects would be so durable as in an older country suffering under a like calamity? Do you believe that, a few years after earth's direst curse had passed, a vestige of it would remain?—that a people who, in less than the ordinary duration of human life, have turned thousands of barren spots into habitations which the heart of man delights in, would allow a second sun to shine upon the encumbered streets where their infant steps first trod?—or, that those who within the memory of middle age have distanced most competitors in the commercial race, and are now close upon the heels of the merchant princes of their parent isle, would leave their timber, their hemp, and their iron, for a single hour, while they straightened their backs beneath the blow that had bent them? No, Sir! The injuries to our interests would be but the history of a day. A young man can lose with impunity a pound of blood, while a single ounce from the veins of an old one, like the last ounce upon the camel's back, will kill.

Nor, while the storm lasted would its effects be more than partial. You seem to forget that foreign sources of luxuries and necessaries once shut up, our manufactures, no longer in a rude state, as at the commencement of the last war, would be pushed into more dangerous competition with your own— an affair of life and death to no small portion of your population, but of wealth incalculable to millions of ours.

I have not the presumption to crowd your columns, even if permitted, with reasons why I think you are mistaken in supposing that our "liberties, too, would suffer," and will merely say, if you mean our liberties in relation to our own rulers, that they are secured to us not by traditions, nor precedents, nor *dicta*, but by a written Constitution, which, though, from time to time, it may be violated by ignorant or rash or vicious men, can never be systematically perverted to private ends, because the people in their general intelligence know too well its value to let it be lost.

If, however, you mean our liberties as they relate to foreign nations, ask, I pray you, the first American you encounter, no matter of what party or of what politics, and he will tell you that at the least sign of war all the States would join with one accord, regardless of the justice of the cause, and defer till a more convenient season the discussion of their local animosities. You would learn, moreover, that whenever an anti-war cry has arisen in the midst of hostilities, it has been as instantly stifled by the universal voice of the people. So far, indeed, is it from being believed among us that war would endanger the Confederation, that not a few are heard openly to express the opinion that if it were to come every twenty years, it would serve to bind us more closely together, to knit up our ravelled sympathies, somewhat damaged by our ever occurring elections, and to open our eyes to the value of the Union. Some, in their fear of a separation, even pray for a national debt. But, for my own part, I am firmly convinced there is not a cabin on the remotest skirts of our borders, nor a dwelling in our most populous cities, where the necessity of union requires to be taught by any such extraordinary means as these.

With respect to the Oregon dispute, I think with you, that the sooner it is settled the better will it be for all honest men in both countries, though it may disappoint a host of army contractors, speculators, and adventurers, greedy for their prey. I agree with you, too, in the opinion, that a refusal to submit one's claims to arbitration, when negotiation fails, is *primâ facie* evidence against the party so refusing. But has negotiation failed? I believe not, and I have just learned from a most intelligent source that there are yet good grounds for trusting that it will not. For this reason I do not, like you, "ground all hopes of a settlement on arbitration," though, as a *dernier ressort*, I can conceive of nothing more desirable on the score of interest or of honor, especially where territory is concerned; and, notwithstanding a prevailing notion among my countrymen that their claims, being the claims of republicans, would not stand a fair chance beside those of England if submitted to the award of a crowned King, I am quite sure, could any thing like unfairness enter into the decision, that England herself — rich and powerful England, the object of envy to the European world, would be the more likely victim.

Your correspondent "A. B." asks, "If the degradation of the Republic" (a thing taken for granted) "is not caused by the conduct of the Americans themselves, who by deliberate and public frauds, have excluded themselves from the community of civilization?" and gives as a reason for the affirmative of the proposition, an answer which would raise a smile, were it not for the sympathy one feels for the unfortunate. He says that in 1839, he loaned a sum of money to one of our States, which in 1845, it cannot or will not repay. So then, because Illinois, an individual of our vast Confederation, rashly, but not in bad faith for aught that appears, made to "A. B." a promise six years ago which she cannot now redeem, (for, be it remarked, her willingness to pay has always been manifest), our Republic, forsooth, is "degraded" and we, in the mass, as under an excommunication of old, are "excluded from the community of civilization." Verily, even if Illinois were as bad as "A. B." would make her, it is hard that all our teeth should be set on edge for sour grapes, which others — not "our fathers" — have eaten.

But let us put the case more strongly than "A. B." has done. Not Illinois alone, but nearly one half of our States are, as every body knows, in the same predicament, with one exception, which I will presently notice, They borrowed money, meaning and expecting to repay it, and they cannot at present. This is the "head and front of their offence, no more." Their liability they never denied, and even if they had, I do not see how the Republic, the nation called the "United States," should any more be degraded by the misconduct of some of its constituent parts, over whose money affairs it has no control, than England would be if several of its richest and most powerful corporations were to become fraudulently bankrupt. The government of the United States, which is the sole representative of the Republic at home or abroad, never pledged its faith for the States' individual solvency, nor did it ever plead unwillingness or inability to meet its own engagements. A truce, then, to such nonsense as "A. B." in his angry mood puts forth. He is sore, and well he may be, after having so foolishly squandered his money; for I can tell him that, had his means or his patience permitted it, if he had waited yet a little, he would have received "his own with usury." But angry as he is, even though it be against himself, it does seem to me that one "who once loved that land," and therefore placed his money there rather than with "despotic Russia" or "drowsy Austria," if influenced, as he says he was, by love for us and not for our high rate of interest, even under a still greater provocation, might have shown a more Christian, if not a more gentlemanly, spirit, in his reproaches, especially as he is "unwilling to irritate a people sensitive to shame, but dead to honor."

The State of Mississippi is the exception I above alluded to. Strictly and technically speaking, she is not liable for that portion of her bonds which she has repudiated. A fraud was committed upon her in the negotiation of them, by persons for whose agency she was not accountable. But there is no doubt that in refusing to acknowledge her liability she has committed an enormous blunder — and a blunder I now find the more to be lamented, that it has enabled "A. B." *ex cathedrâ* to declare that "he is as much startled on meeting an American in (his)? society as to hear of Robert Macaire at Almack's."

Paris, Nov. 3, 1845.

LETTER II.

I should not reply to your correspondent, "X. X.," not even to point out his errors, were it not for the hope that the few lines I venture to intrude upon your indulgence, may reach, through your universal journal, the eyes of some of my countrymen at home.

Though brief in his epistle, wherein I will strive to imitate him, he has had the misfortune to commit several slight mistakes. I did not say that New York and Boston were "impregnable,"—a place to be impregnable must be able to defy attack both by land and by water, — but I said that the "ports of these two cities could not be entered by an enemy," and this I learned within three months upon the spot from the best engineer authority in the country.

In comparing the Mississippi and Exchequer-bills cases together, a parallel is sought for where none can be found. In the former the now repudiated bonds, before the law which gave them being had been consummated in the manner prescribed by the constitution, and, moreover, contrary to the terms of that law, were thrown into the market by that "fittest imp of fraud" knavishly self-christened "Bank of the United States," whose rightful sponsor was Pennsylvania; and, as law recognizes no such plea as ignorance, the deluded purchasers became the victims. But still I think that the State is in honor bound to pay them; and I doubt not that every honest man amongst us blushes at its short-sighted political criminality. In the latter case — that of the Exchequer-bills — the English Government had not a peg to hang a doubt upon. Honor out of the question, not a single point of law, thanks to the Chancellor himself, could be urged in extenuation.

The amount of the Mississippi debt is not as "X. X." supposes, 12,000,000 dollars, but, to be exact, only 7,600,000, of which 2,600,000, called the "Planter's Bank's bonds," are acknowledged to be due, while 5,000,000, the "Union Bank's bonds," are repudiated; and by referring to my letter of the 3d inst , it will be seen that I did not commit the blunder of speaking of the "whole debt as subject to a legal quibble."

In saying that the non-paying States, with one exception, have never denied their liability, but merely declared their inability to fulfil their contracts, I adopted their universal plea of pauperism, without making it entirely my own. For I believe that certain of them, if they would put their shoulders to the wheel, could, without the aid of any Hercules, extricate themselves from the mire, cleansed from the pollution which now covers them; and, moreover, that could they feel a tithe of the shame which we, their countrymen abroad, do on their behalf, they would pay to the uttermost farthing, though it left them as poor as the first tillers of their soil. But there are others, Illinois and Indiana, for example, which I know to be for the moment physically incapable of meeting their engagements. Would you, however, the English, with true wisdom throw open your ports, and allow their corn, their sole produce, to come in, whereby their railroads and canals, constructed as you say with British capital, would rise many fold in value, instead of asking, without receiving your due, you would reap a rich harvest from what is now but fallow ground. But, your rich landed aristocracy resist the repeal of the corn laws, though all wise men, and lovers of their country, with Sir Robert Peel at their head, see the necessity of it. *He would lend head, hand, and heart to carry the measure to-morrow, if he dared to do so.* But though he "bide his time" believe me, he is not the man to shrink from cutting off even a right hand to save the whole body politic from what is akin to hell-fire. Would you but open your ports, the cry of "Oregon" would die in the distance.

Abuse then, if you please, certain of our defaulting States — abuse them as much as you think your interests will sanction; but when you assail a whole nation — a nation which one glories in calling his own, a nation, too, that may, perhaps, carry the fame of England to ages which will seek in vain for the landmarks of her glory, — at least be just in your wrath.

Paris, Nov. 13, 1845.

LETTER III.

I am far from being sure that any thing one of my countrymen can say will be of the slightest service to yours, however true his words and however important the occasion, because, as we all know, uncalled-for counsel, even from a friend, is generally contemned, and too often, even if followed, rendered worse than useless by the drag-chain of unwillingness, which clogs its good intent. But, if it be lawful to be taught by an enemy, why should it be less so to receive useful suggestions from those who, after their own country, regard in the bottom of their hearts yours with a pride and an affection not unworthy of a fatherland?

From some of the late English papers, it seems to be a general impression that the American supply of wheat but little exceeds the home consumption, and that therefore it would avail you nothing to open your ports and let it come in on reasonable and certain conditions. Assuming, without admitting, this to be true, there is no intelligent countryman of mine but will tell you, that with trade less shackled than it is, our labor being free from every municipal vexation, a demand, however great, upon an almost boundless territory, a grateful soil, and an industrious people, could never be made in vain. Whence comes it that we have not more wheat if, after satisfying our own wants, only little remains for exportation,—we who, by every law that can apply to the case, are pre-eminently an agricultural people, and would have willingly kept, in the words of Jefferson, our workshops in Europe for ever, had you not forced us by your high-pressure policy to become manufacturers ourselves? It is because we have too much of your own calculating Saxon blood in our veins, not rendered more sluggish by a burning sun, to waste our strength in sowing where we cannot reap an ample fold. It is because we find it more profitable to raise tobacco, cotton, rice, and Indian corn — the last in such abundance that neither man nor beast can need — than to fill our barns and our ware-houses with that whose sale depends upon a scale so barometrically slippery that we dare not trust ourselves to its sliding mercies.

Were you to set a moderate and fixed duty on corn, (and what moment like the present to do it, when the American Government, almost beyond a doubt, will in a few months reduce their own tariff to 20 per cent. *ad valorem*) ? the cry of starvation would soon become as strange to your ears as it is to ours ; your manufacturers in their turn would permanently enjoy the fruits of your wisdom, and the moral effect on the American States would be almost incalculable. They would see at once that their pecuniary interests imperatively dictated an amicable settlement of every disputed question, and the thing would be done. Then, where one bushel of wheat is now raised by us there would be one hundred, and, if that did not suffice, more would be forthcoming. Indian corn, which under our summer sky grows, as it were, spontaneously, would fill up any deficiency at home, and that without hardship even to the poor, if poverty can be said to exist where alms are never asked, except by the wandering emigrant from Europe's overcrowded shores. Even at our richest tables the hot gold colored maize-cake at all times, and the luscious green corn in its season, have, like our crystal-ice amidst summer's parching heats, ceased to be luxuries, — they have become the necessaries of life.

There being, as you are aware, no impertinent legal interference in the cultivation of our lands, all we want is a market in England that can be relied upon, and thousands of acres, now producing the "filthy weed," which neither feeds the hungry nor clothes the naked, would be devoted to supplying the real necessities of man, and thousands upon thousands, now lying in sterile virginity beneath the wasted influences of a genial heaven, would not send forth a single leaf that did not tell in living characters of man's good deeds and God's beneficence.

Paris, Nov. 21, 1845.

LETTER IV.

Owing to the late arrival of the English mail yesterday, I did not see " X. X.'s " letter in your number of the 20th, till the hour was passed for answering it. And now that I send a reply on a subject not germane to any other either of immediate consideration or present interest, I would respectfully leave to your discretion whether to publish it or to forward it to his address.

He seems anxious to know of me, "if the State of Mississippi did or did not receive the proceeds arising from their now repudiated bonds?" To the best of my belief, if she did not actually receive them, which I have been assured is the fact, she profited by them directly or indirectly; and it is my conviction, therefore, that, though she might by some technicality escape in a court of law, in no court of equity or of honor could she fail to be condemned. After this I need not add that I believe there can be no half-way house between right and wrong, and that dishonesty is an unprofitable article of traffic, which will return to "plague its inventors." He then, with just feelings of pride, demands if his countrymen "urged legal objections to the payment of the forged Exchequer-bills?" I am not aware that they ever did. But, whether they did or not, what law and honesty and honor dictated, that they performed.

When one quotes, the least that can be done is to quote correctly. Your correspondent gravely puts these words into my last letter but one, which I search for in vain: — "The Chancellor of the Exchequer stated that we (the English) were legally bound to pay the forged bills." Without citing any authority, it was my own assertion that "you had not a peg to hang a (legal) doubt upon, thanks to the Chancellor himself." Nor had you, notwithstanding the pretence that " the law did not require the bills to be paid ;" for, begging " X. X.'s" pardon, the law did require them to be paid, just as it requires the notes of a bank to be paid, whose president, recklessly signing, as did the Chancellor, in blank, all the paper which his villainous underlings may see fit to present, is made the unwitting instrument of a fraud which the proprietors of the institution must expiate.

His argument, that, " if the law had required the payment of these bills, then all the parties holding them would have been entitled to payment," is bordering somewhat upon the absurd; for in that case the fraudulent holders would have been able to avail themselves of their own wrong, which is contrary to one of the first maxims of English law. "The power to discriminate the circumstances under which they (the bills) were received," he says, " proves that there was no legal right to payment." It follows, then, by consequence, that had a legal right to payment existed, "the power to discriminate," even in cases of palpable fraud, would have been wanting, — a position which " X. X." will hardly find tenable.

He admits that you "enabled" — these are his own words — "your agent through neglect to deceive innocent holders of bills," and if he knows any thing of the law of his own country, he need not be told that in awarding civil damages — damages touching property alone, I mean, — it makes no distinction between the commission of the *malfaisant* and the omission of the *négligent;* and that the acts of an authorised agent, though his intent be fraudulent, so that he exceed not the letter of his instructions, are those of the principal. If, as he says, "no one can sue on a forged bill," I can tell him that every innocent holder can sue on an Exchequer-bill, duly signed and executed, but fraudulently issued by its legal fabricators, and moreover, that he can recover upon it.

He rather plaintively exclaims in conclusion, that "England gained nothing while Mississippi received the proceeds of her bonds." What then? does he reckon for nothing the conservation of his country's honor, or does he envy Mississippi her paltry gains at the expense of her reputation?

Paris, Nov. 23, 1845.

LETTER V.

We have the high authority of Dr. Johnson, if we needed any, that there is a world of moral difference between one who "lies unwittingly" and him who "knows that he lies;" and, although I am far from thinking that some of your weekly newspapers, deliberately, and with malice aforethought, put forth on American affairs what they know to be false, yet my conviction is that they commit an offence scarcely less heinous in *foro conscientiæ*, when like the stabber in the dark, carelessly searching for his foe, they let off their random shots in the direction of my country, wilfully reckless whether they "hit or miss."

They are "still harping on my daughter" I find — still fumbling at the Oregon question — at Mr. Polk and his policy, like an ignorant machinist, with monkey-like mischievousness, affecting to scrutinize what surpasses his powers of comprehension. According to them, Oregon is but a "quarry," out of which our President's "temple of fame" is to be hewn, if England will only "stand like a sheep to be shorn, as did Mexico;" Mr. Polk is a "villager who never wagged the tongue or wielded the pen;" and his policy is to make a "hero of himself," cost what it may to his country.

Now, all this is doubtless very convenient to fill a column or two, which, it would not be consistent with a paper's healthy circulation to blacken every day with tamer stuff. It is "fun" too for the "groundlings," though, like the venemous insect's sting to the hunted stag, it may help in a small way to hurry into death-breeding confusion the higher tiers of society. But, is it true? Is it true that we are the arrogant swash-bucklers which they describe us to be; that our President is the god of his own imagination, in the "temple of whose fame" his country, if necessary, must be sacrificed; and that his policy is war to the knife, unless that deity be propitiated? I think not; and, if I be mistaken, then have these writers stumbled upon the truth in a most "miraculous manner." And I believe not, because their information can hardly equal in accuracy that which is within my reach, coming as it does from those who, with reason, speak as men, "having authority and not as the scribes."

On the day of the arrival of the United States' mail by the last steamer, I received a communication from a gentleman, inferior only to our Chief Magistrate in rank, and inferior to no one in honesty, to whom I had freely expressed opinions, held by me at a former period, in common with many others no better informed than myself, respecting the apparently warlike disposition of our Cabinet, and its novel claim to the whole of a territory hitherto admitted, on all hands, to be a "debateable land." As he is of the Administration party, and a man incapable of wilfully deceiving any one, his words, though never intended for publication, may not, perhaps, be deemed unworthy of a place in your journal. "Mark me," was his reply, "whenever the President's message shall arrive in Europe, you and all men will clearly see that it is not we, but the English, who have been exacting and unreasonable; that it is they who have always thrown obstacles in the way of an amicable settlement of our difficulties; and that the justice of our cause will be made manifest to all the world, as well as the probity and courtesy with which it has been maintained; and this will delight you." And it did delight me; for though I dread an unrighteous war as much as any man, especially with England, from whom we have so much to apprehend, still, with our "quarrel just," I entertain no fear as to the results, seeing that it would be a war not of party but of principle, and one which would enlist the sympathies of not only all the American States, but of all the countries of Europe in our favor.

It seems, too, that the proposition lately made by our Secretary of State, as a new basis to treat upon, was not a mere repetition of former offers, but that it comprised a concession of greater extent than had ever been made by us before, and one quite sufficient for your Government at least to entertain, especially just at this moment, when it evidently cares much less about territory than it does about the national honor, supposed to be at stake. But Mr. Packenham did not consider it to be admissible, whereupon it was instantly withdrawn, much to the dissatisfaction, as I understand, of his Government, which is far from being pleased at his so abruptly closing a door which might have conducted to a quiet adjustment of a difficult, and hitherto, in some respects, an ill-managed affair.

> " But I know not how the truth may be ;
> I tell the tale as 'twas told to me. "

For I would carefully, and even conscientiously, avoid that presumptuous style of certain writers of the day, who seem to think, "Sir Oracle"-like, that when they "ope their mouths no dog must bark;" while I will tell them, if they do not already know it, that even in the hands of a fool a firebrand is a dangerous missile, which once thrown may not at will be gathered up again; and that my countrymen in usurping the soil of the red man, did not leave that peculiar attribute of his unappropriated, which never forgets or forgives an unprovoked and unexpiated injury.

Paris, Dec. 10, 1845.

LETTER VI.

That "nothing good could come out of Nazareth," was a no more self-evident proposition to the Jews of old, than that nothing but evil can spring from American parentage, is a matter of faith to certain countrymen of yours, who, I doubt not, had they flourished in the time of our Saviour, would have lived and died, in spite of miracles, the victims to their exaggerated self-esteem. And I verily believe, that, could the embodied spirit of Wisdom itself descend in the shape of an American Presidential Message, these carping gentry would contrive to pick a hole or make a rent in even such a "divine perfection," while striving to tack on their churlish commentaries to its skirts.

Two[*] of your leading journals — the one Whig, the other

[*] Chronicle and Standard of the 23d inst.

Conservative — in dealing with our President's late communication to Congress, remind me strongly of a fellow I once saw cuffing a pugnacious mastiff with one hand, and holding out a tempting bone with the other — balancing between his hopes and his fears, and undecided as to the wisdom of coaxing or bullying the unmanageable brute. In like manner, and almost in the same breath, they call his counsels "intemperate, insane, blustering and threatening gasconades," and then throw him a Corn Law repeal sop to soothe what they are pleased to term "their most dangerous and impracticable opponent." But in the midst of their hot though fluttering displeasure, I must admit that they pay, however unintentionally, the highest possible compliment to the "American people, who," in their own words, "will sacrifice the passion nearest and dearest to their hearts, if they can thereby gain a truly national object." This is indeed praise greater than we ever dared to covet for our "Anglo-Saxon character," though attended by the drawback, according to them, of that "character's being marked with degeneracy from the parent stock."

I have carefully read several times that portion of the message which relates to the Oregon territory, and I am constrained in the spirit of fairness to declare that it appears to me manly, modest and firm, and not unbecoming the exalted station which, unsought for by him, its author now occupies. The first five paragraphs of it are taken up with a simple narrative of what had been done by his predecessors in office; the sixth, with what were his convictions and consequent measures on assuming the responsibilities of the Chief Magistracy; and the rest, with what he proposes to do, provided that it can be effected without violating, "even in spirit," the mutual occupation convention, to which he almost reverentially alludes no less than four times in tones of warning too serious to be mistaken. He concludes this part of his subject by throwing himself "with deference" upon the wisdom of Congress, whose suggestions will be met by him with "hearty concurrence."

Now, nothing can be gained but merited ill-will by attempting to distort and vilify language like this; for even among foes, and much more between two nations bound by ties of blood and interest to friendship, honesty is the wiser policy; and sure am I that these very writers themselves, would have been the first to twit, as crafty and pusillanimous, the man who could shrink from declaring and acting up to opinions, whether right or wrong in their eyes, which he once formally enunciated, and which, it is evident, he yet in all sincerity entertains.

In your number of the 24th inst., though you courteously allow that the "President's style is unusually readable, simple and clear," yet you find fault with him for "taking great credit to himself for having made an offer which he acknowledges to be less than what the British Government has repeatedly declined." But in my humble opinion, even without considering the high motives which induced him to propose more liberal terms than he would have done had he had the initiation of the negotiation, he is fully entitled to take credit to himself for the offer, whatever it was, since it is now known to me, on still better authority than it was when I wrote my letter of the 10th inst., that Mr. Pakenham rejected the said offer without consulting Lord Aberdeen, and received but niggard thanks from his employers for his injudicious precipitation.

Whatever may be Mr. Polk's sins of omission or commission, it cannot be said that he has been other than frank in the exposition of his views and intentions; nor can he or his countrymen, in their foreign relations, be accused of the least tincture of cunning, but much rather of that rash disposition to "cut the knot" and "throw away the scabbard," perchance before the sword be ready, which, if it gain not your love, must at least command your respect. Nor can it be pretended that he has curried favor with that Power whose creeping policy in the Texan affair, so signally defeated, has just received at his hands a rebuke, which it would feel the more keenly were it convicted, as I have been assured more than once that it well might be, of, while holding out the hand of good-fellowship to England, having attempted, at the time of the insurrection in the Canadian possessions, the same game which it had so successfully played at an earlier period in the history of the North American colonies.

Notwithstanding all the magnificent promises made by the preachers of the *entente cordiale*, you will one day find that the French dread and dislike you, as much as you, in your secret souls, undervalue — I had almost said despised — them; and whether their most wise Sovereign (who would sacrifice every thing to peace, save his own dynasty) live or die, you will learn at the eleventh hour, should a war arise between our two countries, that not even he, except at too dear a cost, could prevent them from rushing into it, to take vengeance on you for mortifications, under which they have never ceased to writhe. Do not build any hopes of sympathy from them on the shallow devices of the Guizot Administration; for there is here as all the world knows, but one lord and master, who is Louis Philippe, with his velvet colored gauntlet; and he said not long since to one of my countrymen in high station, "Why do you not increase your navy? It is that to which you should direct your attention. And as to the Oregon territory," he added, "the English might as well lay claim to New Orleans as to any part of it."

It is very convenient, doubtless, for the King and his

Prime Minister to play fast and loose between two parties, as did the rich land-owner and his heir-at-law in your civil commotions, to avoid a confiscation whichever side went to the wall; but it is not less convenient, I apprehend, and quite as safe, for you to be confirmed, in what cannot but be your misgivings as to their double-dealing, by one who is upon the spot and a "looker on" in Paris.

Paris, Dec. 29, 1845.

LETTER VII.

For weeks past, it has rejoiced me much to see that an honorable peace between your country and mine, has been the professed object of leading articles such as appear in your journal, and in no other; but I am so fully aware that it needs not my poor testimony to procure their due praise for high talents, so nobly exercised in the noblest of all causes, that I would have remained silent, had it not been for the hope of being listened to for a moment, while I remonstrate with you on the sudden change of sentiments manifested in your number of the 26th inst., wherein, having first discussed Mr. Pakenham's proceedings at Washington, you indulge in one of your tirades of former days against us, with a gusto akin to that with which we return to our first love. Instead of maintaining your former high, but conciliatory tone — the offspring apparently of honest intention, and conscious strength, you descend to personalities, such as our "nasal jargon, bad grammar, and worse principle;" and you condescend to act the part of one, who, fearing that his dignity has been compromised in the eyes of an antagonist by too gentlemanly a bearing, without waiting the result, strives to redeem his imaginary error, and to demonstrate that he was not under the influence of fear, by redoubling abuse once deliberately rejected as worse than useless. Why you rejected it I cannot say, unless it was that you perceived there was a certain sort of blood in our veins, which, though not English, is sure to boil at an insult, while it remains lukewarm at an injury; nor can I tell why you did not persist in such a wise rejection, when, to quote your own words, you knew that "a spicy article in a newspaper is sufficient to kindle a flame, which the blood of thousands can alone quench," and must have known too, that such an effusion as yours might perchance furnish materials to the mischievous, wherewith to light a conflagration, by whose lingering embers ages to come would trace with shame and tears the blight upon civilization that it had left behind.

Do you on reflection really believe that "the war policy against America would be supported by men of liberal views, of disciplined minds, and of intellects refined by thought into the most repulsive fastidiousness?" [*] If you do, I pray God

ANSWER OF THE TIMES.

[*] We consider that the gist of the complaint, no less than the courteous tone of a letter addressed to us by a Citizen of the United States, demands from us a few words of explanation. He has taken umbrage at some expressions contained in our leading article of the 26th ult., expressions which we think must have been severed from their context almost for the purpose of misconstruction, but which, if taken in conjunction with, and interpreted by it, cannot be pronounced intentionally offensive.

It was our object to show that it would be no difficult matter to light the torch of a savage contest between the United Kingdom and the Republic of the United States. We did this by a reference to the passions and prejudices which influence different classes amongst ourselves. We know that it is a common thing for American rhetoricians to lay great stress on what they imagine to be the republican tendencies of our middle ranks, and the liberalism of our political enthusiastics; that the American war party reckon too much on the inertness of our pacific, and the parsimony of our economical, legislators; and that they are completely ignorant of the tone of feeling prevalent among the young and ardent members of our more educated

to save me from such self-delusion, and to protect the world from the effects of such "liberality, discipline, and refinement," which if they exist except in fancy, must be the bastard produce of that " unnecessary luxury, a regal government, and that expensive metaphor, a crown;" and at the best can be but a poor set-off, however ready to leap to a bloody conclusion, against the decaying affections of the Irish people, and the decayed state of their sole means of subsistence.

I have reason to believe, and my sources of information are not bad, that the English Government just at this moment is in the awkward predicament of a man, who, having made a

orders. Knowing this, we thought it right that they should know it too; we therefore cited in continuity the particular feelings and prejudices which, whether reasonable or not, would actuate men of different conditions in the contingency of an American war. Of these sentiments we spoke, and could speak, neither in terms of justification nor encouragement. We merely asserted their existence as a fact which ought to be known by those ready to rush into a hazardous struggle from a reliance on ill-founded premises. And if, in describing the particular bias of classes or persons, we used language likely to wound the pride of a kindred nation, we used it simply as an exponent of their feelings, such as they themselves would make use of; not as that which we would willingly suggest or unprovokedly adopt. We have too clear a perception of the miseries consequent upon any war, and too sincere a dread of those which might follow an American war, to add to the knotty difficulties of diplomacy the petty stings and exciting annoyances of newspaper abuse and scurrilous nicknames. But we do not think we are transgressing our public duty in communicating to our opponents the sentiments of those with whose country they are at issue. Less baneful consequences are likely to flow from a consciousness of the spirit and determination with which Great Britain would engage in a war, than from a pacific acquiescence in the delusive insinuations that her Ministry can be frightened, or her people bullied, into any dishonorable capitulation or any ignoble concessions.

Having premised thus much in vindication of a course which has been misrepresented, and in explanation of phrases which, perhaps, ought to have been more minutely illustrated or more specifically appropriated at the time they were written, we may now repeat our expression of a hope that the great difference between the two countries is capable of a peaceful and honorable adjustment.

claim in the dark upon a neighbor, in the beginning no better informed than himself as to their mutual rights, now that truth has fairly dawned upon both parties, finds it rather difficult to extricate himself with credit from the false position into which his unfounded, but not dishonest, pretensions have hurried him ; and that, if negotiations respecting the Oregon territory were now to be entered upon for the first time, a boundary line could be run as fast as it could be travelled over, and that, too, without the intervention of an umpire to decide, when the commissioners were not of accord.

Will you permit me to express my regret and astonishment, that a person of your far-reaching sagacity should join in O'Connell's peevish cry about slavery ? — that bane which the English themselves forced upon us years ago, in spite of our earnest remonstrance, and which they now revile us for without even suggesting an antidote for eradicating it from our Constitution. When the " Thirteen States " became a nation, it was by a compromise among conflicting interests, which, had it proved a failure, would have left them a set of disjointed links, and a scoff and a by-word for those who contend that man is unfitted for self-government. And the only means of avoiding so great a calamity — for calamity it would have been to the human race, notwithstanding the passion of your countrymen for "expensive metaphors" — was to tolerate the curse which their English ancestors had bequeathed to them. To this end a solemn compact was entered into, that not the general, but the State governments should, within their several limits, have power to legislate on a subject so hostile, I admit, to the spirit of our institutions, and by this compact is the government of the United States still bound. Your would-be philanthropists had much better look to their own laborers than to our slaves, who are better fed and lodged than the white serf, their decrepit parents and helpless children better cared for, and themselves better protected against the vicissitudes of life. Or, if they will meddle in a matter which they can nowise benefit — if they will persist in doing evil that good may come out of it, I would fain entreat them — I, who am from an Eastern State, where there are no slaves, and look with undiluted disgust on slavery, whether it assume the shape of physical bondage, as with us, or of moral servitude, as with you — to propose one feasible scheme for ridding ourselves of the plague-spot, without ruining the land and its owners, and entailing worse than death on its black cultivators; and if we do not adopt it without delay, then may they go on with their vituperations, and we will forever hold our peace. No one in his senses, I presume, would counsel the same experiment which you made in your West India Islands, even if it had not signally failed, as no two cases less parallel to each other could be found.

You twit us, too, in the article above alluded to, with the administration among us of what is termed Lynch law, when such a thing is neither justified nor excused by any American, nor has ever had more than an occasional existence in distant and infant communities, where the arm of inchoate justice was too short to save the dearest of all relations from being violated by the lusts and passions of lawless invaders. To charge us with being subject to such a monster, is as absurd as to call Englishmen assassins, because murder is rife in Ireland — a country on your very threshold, when compared to our western borders in relation to the Atlantic States, — and because now and then a man is shot down at mid-day in the streets of London.* You judge and condemn a whole nation on the presentation of isolated facts, and yet you will not pur-

---

* Sir Robert Peel's secretary, mistaken for the baronet himself, had, shortly before this was written, been assassinated in a crowded thoroughfare.

chase a dwelling-house on the mere inspection of individual bricks. "Fair and softly go far," is a wise saying; and if you are sincere, as I believe you to be, in your love of peace, you should recollect that rough grooming, where not the blood but the skin is thin, is apt to render the steed restive at times, and is always a dangerous experiment.

Paris, Jan. 30, 1846.

LETTER VIII.

*Among other reasons for thinking our government "too feeble to restrain bad impulses, and our population too excitable to be conscious of consequences," a "moonstruck madman's" speech, and the manner in which it was listened to in the United States House of Representatives, seem with you to rank among the foremost. Without stopping to inquire whether it is his "much learning that has made him mad," if Mr. Quincy Adams be really mad, (for learning, even if his wits be disordered, he possesses to a degree seldom equalled in Europe or America,) and without uttering a suspicion that the superstructure, reared on such a professedly crazy foundation, may be unsound, allow me to ask in what, and on what occasion, the general government at Washington has exhibited feebleness, and wherein has our population betrayed an excitability which is regardless of consequences?

*The plain principle of *audi alteram partem* has induced us to publish a letter on the political institutions of the United States, which will be found in another place, over the signature of a "States-man." But without this, the letter itself has intrinsic merits, both of thought and style, which make it well deserving of a place in our columns. The writer has studied with effect the history of his country; and with no little art concentrates into one focus the scattered rays of light that shed a lustre upon the general government of the Union.—*Times.*

Since we came into being, which was but as yesterday in the history of nations, it can be said without a boast, that there is not a quarter of the globe that will not bear witness to the strength and energy of our Executive in its foreign relations. Were we not the first to refuse tribute to the Algerine, while all Europe was laying its black mail at his feet? Did we follow or lead in declaring and making the slave trade subject to the penalties of piracy? — which was at least one step towards purgation from the black plague inherited from our ancestors. Was our claim upon the kingdom of Naples for indemnification suffered to grow weak through age? Had France any repose till the 25,000,000 of francs were paid? And, in these latter days, was not Texas annexed in spite of foreign interference?

But perhaps the feeble nature of our government developes itself only at home. Well, then, at home. Did it not quell a most portentous insurrection in Pennsylvania, and that, too, while its powers were in their infancy, without shedding a single drop of blood? Did it not, in its full strength, stifle South Carolina's nullification scheme with a menace? Did it not easily crush a monster bank conspiracy? And finally, has it not recently, in scorn of domestic opposition, added a new territory to its own?

Should weakness in the art of defence ever be charged against it, the voices from English graves throughout the country, honored wherever found, would be far too many not to gainsay the slander. And if its power of offence be doubted or forgotten, not the wide ocean alone, but your very channels, whose waves almost kiss the lintels of your doors, could, if their records were not written in water, bear witness to its reality. The smoke, too, from many a richly laden convoy, was wafted too often, with a not sweet smelling savor, to the nostrils of their armed but too distant guardians, to convict the aggressors of inoffensiveness.

As to the excitability of a population, no part of which corresponds to the English mob, or the French *canaille*, and to few of whose members the common rudiments of education are strange, it is vain to speculate on its evil results; for intelligence goes hand and hand with it, and the cool, calculating spirit of my countrymen, is a sufficient guarantee that it will never lead them into danger.

Tried by the Procrustean standard of Europe, I doubt not that we should often be pronounced out of measure, and that even upon the floor of Congress certain scenes might be curtailed to advantage; but that " one branch of the most important legislative assembly of the new world, should listen with interest and excitement" to our "lunatic" ex-President's most original exhibition, ought no more to raise your wonder, than that the House of Commons should be amused by a ludicrous description of a noble lord's coal-hole escapade,* or that it should now and then uproariously cheer on " Young England's" champion to badger a man who is to him like Jupiter to a rejected satellite.†

As, in common with my countrymen here, I no longer regard the Oregon question as a war question, with your permission I will add a line or two respecting what is described by you to be "the threatening state of our relations with Mexico." Your intelligent correspondent in that unhappy country might have told you that, as against a powerful antagonist, it is more helpless than a wailing child, whether for offence or defence, because it is like a " house divided against itself;" that it can no more prevent the flood of emigration from the States into California, and its consequences, be they what they may, than could the red man close his forests

---

*A noble lord, to escape voting took refuge in the coal-hole.

†Sir Robert Peel and Mr. D'Israeli. The latter had been refused office by the former.

against the inundation of the whites; and that, though it may declare war till it is "hoarse with calling," it can never make it, unless, perchance, which I do not suspect, some European nation come to its aid, and then, without time even to see the forecast shadow of coming events, one universal howl of war, on both sides of the Atlantic, will for many a year be heard, smothering in its death echo the voice of peace.

Our "democratic pretences," I sincerely believe, are entirely misunderstood in Europe, especially as they regard territory. We want none of your possessions, and Canada we should be much less thankful for, than you yourselves would be to get honorably rid of a colony, which is ravenous as a horse-leech and ungrateful as its own soil.

No! pretences, unjust pretences, if they have an existence, time will show that they are not on our side. But in the eyes of some, because we are professed Republicans, and having power, choose to use it as to us seems best, we therefore and our claims are arrogance itself; and, because we will not that kings or nobles should have dominion over us, we are for that reason "of the earth earthy," and on the high road to anarchy and confusion. And what is most "strange and unnatural" is, that it is not those who are divinely hedged about and stand in high places that are in general our self-deluded or malicious traducers, but mere men, unnoble and untitled men like ourselves, who, having sucked in with their mother's milk an overweening reverence for rank, cannot bear to see others, void of sympathy for their weakness, asserting and maintaining the dignity of their common nature.

Paris, March 18, 1846.

LETTER IX.

I did not intend to intrude again upon your thickly serried columns, at least while they were teeming with messages of glory from England's Indian Empire, but your correspondent of the 1st inst., "M. J. H." seems so sad amid the general rejoicing, when dwelling on what "Republican integrity was twenty years ago," that I have not the heart to let his touching murmurs go by without an attempt to administer consolation to his perturbed spirit.

He is a "large holder," he says, "of American securities." Fortunate man! I would that I too could assert the same of myself; especially if, as was the case with him for aught that appears, I had purchased them before they rose from their first fall. And still more fortunate will he be, if he can afford to hold them for a while longer, when, unless the most sagacious among us be mistaken, he will receive his wept-for treasures, with something better as an accompaniment than he of the "folded napkin" was able to render up at the bidding of his lord.

But, as he may wish to know the grounds of my belief in the goodness of these securities, which, according to him, are most "facetiously" misnamed, I will inform him that in my humble opinion there is more than one upon which his anxious and angry heart will find a resting place. The bankrupt States, it must console him to know, will, if they remain defaulters a moment longer than stern necessity demands, have public opinion throughout the Union to contend against — no mean antagonist, when it is considered that its sway is more powerful with us than with any other people under the sun; then, in a very few years their rapidly increasing population, added to their incalculable sources of wealth, will make the payment of their debts so easy, that there will not be room to assume to themselves even a virtue in doing it; and the last, though not least firm ground I go upon is, that their interests, about which they are so "careful," will imperatively demand that justice to their creditors be done. In a single word, they cannot afford to be dishonest.

I am accused of "omitting to touch upon the fraudulent insolvency of many of the States of the Union." But my pen must have been long indeed could it have touched what, so far as fraud is concerned, a resentful fancy alone has conjured up. One State alone has repudiated, and that only a part of its bonds. Its reasons for doing so, whether good or bad, are before the world; and you were so obliging a few months ago as to publish my poor views upon the subject, to which I beg leave to refer "M. J. H." since he demands them, but without venturing to repeat what I then said. If, however, he be really bent upon informing himself as to public delinquency, I would advise him, while about it, to look into the records of the Bank of England, and inquire for the number of years[*] during which, by act of Parliament, it strove to cover the nakedness of its credit with depreciated rags; and he will learn that when the people asked for specie, though stones were not literally substituted for bread, they received a paper currency, which not even a tyrannical law could prevail on them to accept as an equivalent for what had been promised to them. Perhaps, then, he will admit, that if the fourth of a century was required by the richest country in the world to redeem its plighted faith, a little space may well be allowed to a few infant States, with nothing but broad lands and brawny arms to depend upon, wherein to collect their "hundred pieces of silver."

[*] 25 years.

Should he again converse with his "many honorable and respectable American friends," I would bid him beware of ascribing to them an "admission" of their countrymen's want of probity; for they know, as well as he himself ought, that it is the temporary poverty of the defaulting States, and not their will, which consents to the duration of their present embarrassment. And if, as he declares, they allege, in extenuation of State defalcation, the "deplorable weakness of the Executive," he may give the lie to their intelligence, with a salvo to their honor, if it suit him, by telling them that the weakness or the strength of the Executive of the United States has no more to do with State liabilities than with the election of the Lord Mayor of London.

I am next charged with vain boasting, though nothing was said by me, except in defence of my country and of truth. And no less than three paragraphs are devoted to a pretended quotation of my words, which are so "lamely and unfashionably" put together in their new estate, that I verily believe the dogs would bark at their halting pace, could they be made to listen to them. Why did not your correspondent, when honoring me with his notice, rather betake himself, like one endowed with reason, to answering my questions and meeting my arguments, and why did he not try to demonstrate the feebleness of the United States' Government abroad and its imbecility at home, if such things be, instead of peevishly putting into the mouths of grave legislators the puerile bravado of "preferring war with all the world to the payment of their debts?" Unless a blind as well as a deaf devil has possessed him, he might have much better employed his time in ascertaining whether his debtors are really fraudulent, or merely unfortunate, before bedewing them with the stingless venom of an angry man.

If he be a "great holder" of American securities, let him,

for his own sake, become also an intelligent one, and no more indulge in idle prating about "some" of the States repudiating, and "others" doing it with "indignation." And let him give himself no solicitude respecting our "honor," for we know what is due to it, equally well with what belongs to our creditors; and he, with all his tribe, may sleep in conviction tenfold strong, that the claims of neither shall be neglected. He cannot, I think, be so maliciously obtuse as to persist in the belief that a debt contracted with the expectation and probable means of repayment, and always acknowledged to be due, is in itself a subject of disgrace, however much it may be a source of regret to all parties concerned.

He may "assume" without fear of contradiction, "that a fraudulent bankrupt is considered as infamous by Americans as he is by Europeans," and out of his own mouth will I convict him of inconsistency. For never have the defaulting States, though blamed as rash and imprudent, been despised or esteemed infamous by their more fortunate confederates, nor indeed, by any European, unless his passion blinded him, or his ignorance led him astray.

You will observe that I do not choose to mix up the solvent with the insolvent States, any more than I would calumniate the English and the Scotch, because Ireland is a hot-bed of assassination. Nor will I admit the liability of our General Government for State debts, unless, by parity of reasoning, you too will allow that your own is responsible for all bankrupt corporations in the kingdom, that of Edinburgh included, and for every broken-down county bank.

If "M. J. H." never took the pains, as his present benighted condition would imply, to ascertain the extent and strength of the securities on which he loaned his money, to whom does he owe thanks for his losses but to himself alone? He affects to "despise, dislike, and laugh at us," but we have not leisnre to listen to the hysteric giggles, or the unmanly complaints of a victim to his own greediness and negligence.

Paris, April 4th, 1846.

LETTER X.

A London daily paper of this week "disputed the propriety of (your) insulting so great and so good a man as Mr. Webster, by placing him in rivalship with such a false and shabby creature as Mr. Dallas."

Now, without wishing, even if I had the power, to detract one jot or tittle from the high and well-won reputation of the "great and good" Whig leader, and without stopping to make a single comment upon the extreme delicacy and refined taste exhibited in the above quotation towards the American Vice-President, I would gladly continue in juxta-position, only for a moment, the names of these two distinguished individuals, so gratuitously brought together for the purpose of extolling one at the expense of the other. For if it can be shown, that in the most important passages of the political lives of these gentlemen, one has done what the other has not left undone, it necessarily follows, that either of the two having been "false and shabby," his fellow must be so too, and that either having been "great and good," he cannot stand alone in his glory. Mr. Dallas was a protectionist, and is become a freetrader; Mr. Webster was a federalist, and is now a democratic Whig. But mark the difference between their coats when they were turned, and draw what conclusions you will. The former found his rough to the touch, and though serviceable, an object of ridicule and censure, while the latter felt no surprise at discovering his to be richly lined throughout, though of no fixed color.

In this working-day world, however, we have hardly time for splitting hairs about the comparative moral qualities of this or of that public man, since it is by their works, and not by their motives, that they must be judged, as it is with their works alone that we, the "mob," the "many," have any thing to do. The protective system well tried in England, was found wanting, and Sir R. Peel, who rode into office on it, preferred catching a fall himself in securing its overthrow to journeying upon an easy road, which, however long, he saw must infallibly end in ruin. The same suicidal system, bolstered up in America by golden arguments and highly feed advocates at Washington, has at length met with a Curtius ready to make the plunge fatal to it, and, notwithstanding all that is said and done against the self-sacrificer, many a fellow senator who once stood by, "letting I dare not wait upon I would," if the vote were to be taken again upon the tariff question, would be found by his side, shoulder to shoulder, in support of the common interests of their common country. For there is no more chance of the American people, once emancipated, becoming a second time hewers of wood and drawers of water to those who were the protected "few," than there is of the galled jade's yearning for the collar which has worn its neck to a raw. And so slight is the probability of the high and noble workers in the liberal cause, though under a temporary shade, eventually falling before their less enlightened opponents, that, New Englander as I am, and with all my interests dependent on New England's prosperity, I have no fear lest the scales should not fall from the eyes of the monopolists, convinced, as they will soon be, of the wisdom of contenting themselves with a profit that shall feed their own households without impoverishing those of others.

But facts are more valuable than opinions, however numerous or plausible the latter, if the facts cannot be gainsaid, and the opinions want the sanction of a name. And the first to be mentioned which will defy all contradiction is, that the American manufacturers, so far from needing protection, have for some time past been underselling their English competitors in one of your East India markets, even with a duty of 12 per cent. to contend against, which has lately been raised to 15, while the net returns upon their capital have for years been between 20 and 40 per cent., which, of course, could come from the pockets of the consumers alone, and in 19 cases of 20 the home consumers. And another fact, not less incontrovertible and important, is the physical, to say nothing of the moral, impossibility, of the tariff of the many being metamorphosed back into the tariff of the few. During nearly three years, at least, the present President of the United States will have a large majority in the Senate, and, even setting this aside, still two thirds of both Houses at Washington can alone suffice to render his *veto* of no effect. Then, after the expiration of these three years, and when the light of experience has had full time to cheer and comfort both the interested and benighted, who can believe that the proverbial sagacity of the Eastern Yankee will not discover how much more desirable is a certain profit of 10 and 15 per cent. for all time to come, than heavy gains whose own weight must sink them in the end?

That Mr. Dallas was burnt in effigy, as the journal alluded to in the commencement of my letter so triumphantly avers, is no more a disparagement to him than was Galileo's suffering in the cause of truth to him, or the fiery ordeal in their proper persons to many a reformer who was in advance of his age; but should your contemporary be again beguiled into descanting upon "uncompromising integrity," when its existence in the individual whose exaltation turns upon another's abasement, is all a matter of guesswork with him, — or, should be another time rejoice his readers with a "counterfeit presentment" of American statesmen, — I would advise him, before renewing his instruction of others, diligently to seek out a teacher for himself.*

Paris, Dec. 12, 1846.

*The "STATES-MAN," to whom we have been indebted for many valuable communications, has kindly contributed his testimony, in a letter which appears in yesterday's impression, to the truth of our comparison between Messrs. WEBSTER and DALLAS. The difference between these two gentlemen is exceedingly simple. Mr. DALLAS, having for a long time taken the protectionist theory on trust and gone with the stream, has recently had his eyes opened with the rest of the rational world. It is no discredit to partake of a general conversion all but miraculous in its extent, rapidity, and depth. No one need be ashamed to be taught by nature and convinced by events. But in the case of that noble federation, of which, in all its oneness Messrs. WEBSTER and DALLAS claim to be statesmen, the destiny of the whole, and the relative duties of State to State, conspire with the interests of mankind against the petty spirit of monopoly. That an empire of serfs, that a bureauocracy, that a nation of contrabandists, or any other perverted form of society, should deliberately injure the whole for the supposed good of a few, is too customary a thing to be wondered at. But in the United States a monopolist statesman is in as false a position as the man who should propose to invest Mr. POLK with the insignia of royalty, or claim for the elder States of New England a veto on the internal elections and government of the Southern and Western States. The wonderful combination of causes which has in this country convinced every candid opponent, and stopped the mouth of every other, ought to tell with tenfold force in the free atmosphere of the American Republic. It is Mr. DALLAS's crime in the eyes of a few interested men that he has yielded to these mighty teachings. It is Mr. WEBSTER'S glory that he can still defy them.

As for the comparative consistency of the two men, as "a STATESMAN" reminds us, it has been the fortune of both to change. Mr. DALLAS was a Protectionist, and is now a Free-trader; Mr. WEBSTER was a Federalist, and is now a Democratic Whig." Mr. DALLAS has enlarged his sympathies to the breadth of the Union; Mr. WEBSTER has contracted them to the proverbial prejudice and narrowness of a New England manufacurer. Mr. WEBSTER is the more remarkable man. He has long been distinguished for information, astuteness, eloquence, versatility, and, above all, for his intimate acquaintance with the law and institutions of the mother country.

LETTER XI.

Whenever an American President's message to Congress arrives in Europe, a hue and cry against the length of it is invariably raised by a set of carpers, which would lead one, unaccustomed to the false notes of their sweet voices, to suppose that there existed a dire necessity for each one of them to read the offending document from beginning to end. I have heard too, in like manner, some dainty dames, whose appetites were delicate and patience slender, indulge in affected lamentations at the many courses of a ceremonious dinner, from which they might have staid away without loss to any one except themselves. But these highly sensitive, not to say pharisaical, scribes ought to know that the Chief Magistrate of the United States is not paid $25,000 a year merely to occupy a palace and clothe himself in purple and fine linen every day. They should be informed that he is not only a working man among working men, and as such expected to administer his stewardship, and give an account of it too, but that if he were to venture to intrude upon his constituents such an insult to their understandings as would be a composition akin to what is here called a "King's speech," he might with reason calculate on being hooted from the capitol to his home by the very boys in the street.

The gentleman who at present fills the first office in America, has lately published, for the instruction of his country-

He has been called the BROUGHAM of America. Whether such qualities are the most favorable to the growth of political honesty, candor, and self-sacrifice, we will leave to ethical writers. It is a vulgar opinion that they are very compatible with selfishness and prejudice. Mr. DALLAS has not been so distinguished — that is, till his recent elevation. If, however, his recent reply to the Washington Committee is to be the test, he not only possesses great talents, but he is pre-eminently a man to be trusted and believed.

men, and doubtless to the edification of others who will not acknowledge it, an explanation of the Mexican war and its causes; and though from my knowledge of his personal character, I believe him to be incapable of wilful misrepresentation, still I am constrained to declare that, according to my humble notions, he has completely failed to prove the necessity of it. The whole affair therefore, I regard not only as an iniquity, but a blunder. The war was unnecessary, for a while at least, because whenever two antagonists, one of whom is rich and the other poor, commence negotiations, nothing but glaring injustice or peevish impatience can prevent a peaceful issue. It might have been avoided too when troops were sent into the disputed territory, had a sufficient number been ordered there — volunteers, if regulars were not to be had — which would have saved the deluded Mexicans from their first fatal essay in arms. But I speak now as a christian man, an abhorrer of strife, and a lover of peace. If, however, it be allowed me to declare my conviction as an American, unbiassed by those religious considerations which should weigh as heavily with nations as with individuals, I would fearlessly assert that for the last two hundred years not a single war has been waged in Europe with a juster cause of quarrel than that in which my countrymen are at this moment engaged.

Let no one on this side of the Atlantic dare to "cast the first stone" at us. The Russian should rather call on the mountains of the Caucasus to cover his own shame: The Frenchman must begin by rendering an account to God and history, of the mass of life[*] and means of sustenance that have been turned into worse than a dead loss in avenging a thoughtless rap of a fan. And you yourselves confess, "that

[*] 100,000 French soldiers have perished in Algeria.

to govern in India you must conquer, and that to prevail you must continue to advance." You did not hesitate an instant to declare war against Spain when the ears of an obscure Englishman were cut from his head in that country: Within a child's memory France has been murdering on a wholesale scale in the Pacific, because a poor half-savage Queen saw fit to wave a flag whose colors did not suit its fancy: And shall we, "the great and kindred nation treading in your steps," whose force, like yours in the East, must ever be preeminently a moral force — shall we listen unmoved to the cries of our countrymen rotting in Mexican gaols, and of their bereaved and beggared families imploring redress?

Paris, Jan. 6, 1847.

LETTER XII.

Owing to accident I did not see *The Times* of the 5th inst. which contained "A G.'s" letter upon "the delinquent States of America," till more than twenty-four hours after its reception in Paris, or I would have taken an earlier notice of it. Not that its writer, when he thought "it would meet the eye of some honest American," had the least right to expect any answer to a communication so querulously and rudely shaped; but that I am desirous of suggesting to him, and others who have been wronged, and deeply wronged too, the unprofitableness of trying to right themselves by means of abusive language, indiscriminately employed. Even the stupid fellow who put his head in the lion's mouth had the good sense to remain quiet till he could withdraw it in safety; and the simplest of American backwoodsmen never yet ventured to "raise a cry till he was well out of the wood."

We are told on the highest authority, "Not to answer a fool according to his folly, lest we also be like unto him." But as in the following verse we are allowed to "Answer a fool according to his folly, lest he be wise in his own conceit," I trust your correspondent will not take it amiss if I prove by his own words, and others not less worthy, that the term "collective roguery," when applied, as it is by him, to the people of the United States, is as indiscreet on his part as it is unfavorable to "the profound respect entertained for your paper in America," to which "an author of great talent and accuracy" bears such undeniable testimony.

"A. G." confines himself, at least nominally, to four of the delinquent States, which must therefore be considered as preeminently criminal in his opinion; and, as he had his choice among them all, it cannot be expected that I, who would avoid prolixity, should travel out of the record in search of others to refute him, if reference to these alone will answer my purpose. In the first instance, cited by him, the whole country is condemned, because in receiving Florida into the Union, its debts were not adopted at the same time. But there was no more reason for doing this, than there was for assuming the responsibility of all the obligations of every defaulting State. It is true that Florida had been a national territory, and as such, had borrowed money on bonds, but the faith of the "States" was never pledged for the validity of these bonds, nor ever understood to be so by the lenders themselves. And every one who took the pains to inquire, might have ascertained that all responsibility with respect to them ended where it began — that is, in the territory itself, unless the approbation and registry of them by Congress had been first secured. Add to this, that the debt of Florida as a State is of more value than the debt of Florida as a territory, and the charge of "collective roguery" against the whole nation falls, in this case to the ground.

Pennsylvania is next subjected to the ordeal of your correspondent's censure. Having premised that a large portion of the inhabitants of that State are Germans, who can with difficulty be induced to submit to direct taxation, and that four fifths of the rest of the population were always ready to do their duty, I will, for the moment, content myself with quoting the words of another correspondent, " Θ," in your number of the 2d inst., whose correct information goes hand in hand with "even-handed justice." He says with regard to the State under consideration, that "what she has done has proved that she is earnestly endeavoring to pay, and each successive year shows an improvement in her position, such as to give a rational ground for believing that she will fully restore her credit in a short time."

Of Maryland, which is the third defaulter on whom "A. G." in just but ill-directed wrath descends, he himself declares, that "she has paid part of her arrears in specie, and has not, at present, attempted to fund the remainder at a rate of interest inferior to that paid on her original debt." And of Illinois, the fourth on the black list, he adds, that she "will be honest when her means permit her."

What, then, becomes of the charge of "collective roguery?" And if the individual States be pronounced guiltless of fraudulent intent, how can the United States be condemned?

It ought to be made known that, while no efforts are wanting to redeem State honor, the warmest and most general sympathy is felt for foreign creditors by all "American gentlemen of private worth and public honesty," who "A. G.," in unpardonable ignorance, or most inexcusable ferocity, says are "*rari nantes in gurgite vasto.*" And he should have blushed at the miserable sarcasm flung at American ancestry, when even his schoolboy reading must have taught him that " the convicted and fugitive outcasts of the Old World" were honored martyrs to religious and political opinions.

To show that I do not speak at random, when I talk of "efforts and sympathy," I will briefly mention, that in Mississippi, the frailest of the fallen sisterhood, numbers of the best and richest citizens have offered to subscribe their respective shares towards paying off all debts, repudiated and not repudiated, principal and interest; and that in Massachusetts, owners of State stocks have voluntary agreed to defer their own claims till creditors in other lands have received their due.

In extenuation, but not in justification, of the greediness and improvidence with which many of the States contracted loans beyond their present means of repayment, I would remark, that their over-weening and disastrous self-confidence grew out of the eagerness that foreigners showed to lend them money, and the facility with which two not inconsiderable debts had been paid off by the general government since its short existence. But do not understand me as defending, much less advocating, repudiation in one State, or the pitiful approximation to it in another. Shame, unmitigated shame, belongs to them both. It is their rightful portion, and should rest, like the brand of thrice-heated iron, upon their brows, but on theirs alone, until self-purgation has entitled them to assume their former high position, from which, alas! a contaminating relationship has dragged down the innocent in a disgraceful descent.

Paris, January 10, 1847.

LETTER XIII.

You will regard it, perhaps, as very supererogatory on the part of one who is neither of French or English birth, to express an opinion upon the relations subsisting between two leading nations of Europe — its self-constituted high constables and the would-be supervisors of the American continent. You may so regard it, because of the apparent uselessness of adding a single touch to the comprehensive and masterly-drawn views so often furnished forth by you of late, to the delight and instruction of your many readers. But, as the judge on his bench does not disdain the testimony of an eye-witness to a transaction submitted to his decision, provided no dishonesty is suspected, however humble be the intellect of the speaker, so you may possibly not turn a deaf ear to the result of my experience during a long residence in France, as there can be no motive on my part for deception.

Far be it from me, even if it were within my power, to plant or water the smallest seed of discontent among individuals, and infinitely further from me be the will, as is the power, to set communities at strife. From such audacious iniquity I should shrink as I would from the responsibility (enormous as it must be in God's sight) of the gratuitious slaughter in war's unholy name which is now going on in different parts of the globe, whatever be the flag under which it is perpetrated. But, just as I would avoid evil doing, and, on the contrary, would help to establish, as far as in me lies, a good understanding wherever practicable, sparing no pains to maintain it when once confirmed, so I should hold myself deeply criminal if, perceiving at any time in the very foundation of such understanding a principle fatal to its duration, I were wilfully to keep silence.

The French Minister for Foreign Affairs, a few days since, said, " Policy is founded on the sentiments, the instincts, and the wants of the soul; and the mechanical system, that relations between nations result from material influences, is false and to be deprecated." But what, I should like to know, is to be done when no such community of sentiments, or instincts, or wants of the soul can be found? when there is nothing to appeal to except material interests, and influences? What better can be done than to avail one's self of these despised interests and influences, whereon to construct an unaffected good fellowship at the least? It was because more than this was attempted that the late *entente cordiale* between England and France broke down. Too much was expected from it on the strength of a supposititious sentiment. An exotic, the product of a factitious soil, was deemed capable of sustaining the rough breezes which none but a plant of natural growth can withstand, and the consequence was, that a breath, even from the *south*, destroyed it.

As I have before said, France is not a strange country in my eyes, nor are its parties unknown to me for lack of representatives of them among my acquaintances. I can hardly, therefore, be accused of superficiality, when I remark, that there is nothing here but material influences on which the English can rely, as a permanent base of friendly relations. I have taxed my memory severely, and I speak the truth when I declare, that never was uttered within my hearing by a Frenchman, a single sentence which indicated favor or affection towards your countrymen in the mass. What mockery is it, then, to talk about what has no reality!—about "instincts and wants of the soul!" especially when it is remembered that there are other all-sufficient influences, ever operating on both sides of the Channel, to keep the two rival nations on neighborly terms,— the only terms that promise any lasting security! A proper apprehension of the great common cause in which, as representatives of constitutional rights, they are engaged in eternal opposition to absolutism, is a better bond of union between them than the most cunningly-devised fable respecting instinctive and sentimental wants; and the recollection, that rogues are never so happy as when honest men fall out, should save them from stultifying themselves a second time by giving to Russia another opportunity of plucking, with impunity, amid their dissensions, the long-coveted fruit which she dare not otherwise touch.

But, after all, what interests or influences, material or sentimental, has England in common with this country, worthy to stand alongside of those which exist, and must forever exist, between her and her Trans-atlantic kinsmen? Cover every acre of France with the salt sea tomorrow, and England would be no worse off the day after than she is now. Not one of her myriads of wheels would be stopped, not a workman would cease from his labor, and not a mouth the less would be filled. But let that country, whose productions supply her factories with materials wherewith to employ and clothe her people, and help to keep starvation at bay, be washed into nothingness by some mighty convulsion of nature, and she might, with good reason, fold her arms in dismay and become a "waiter upon Providence."

There is no sympathy between Englishmen and Frenchmen. Your blunt bearing is taken by them for rudeness, just as their solicitude to please is mistaken by you for hypocrisy. Your plain speaking argues, in their opinion, an indifference to the feelings of others, while their anxiety to avoid giving offence, convicts them in your esteem of insincerity. Even to language, the same importance is not attached by you and by them; and a slight infraction of truth is not so severely judged here as in England. But this arises from an habitual looseness of expression, and a lighter reverence for truth itself, perhaps, rather than from a spirit of mendacity. By their own standard then, and not by yours, should they be acquitted or condemned. Still, the fact is incontrovertible, that there is no community of feeling between you, and that in France an Englishman is looked upon as an alien in every sense of the word, and treated as such, except so far as the influence of money acts upon his condition. He is *in* society without being of it. His table is filled if it be well covered, and his saloons are crowded if the eye, the ear, and the mouth have been luxuriously catered for. But look at his fire-side, and there you will see neither friends nor intimate associates, save those of his own race. His wines are drunken, his good things are eaten, and his guests go heedlessly away, in perfect indifference, barring what is yet to be got out of him, whether their host shall be found the next week on his way to *Père la Chaise*, to the *Rue de Clichy*, or to Australia.

In contrast with all this, now let me ask, what is an Englishman's reception in the United States, when proper credentials are not wanting? I was upon the point of asking what it *was* before the slander-market of London had created a supply equal to the demand? But, notwithstanding all that has come and gone, I will still inquire what it *is*, even now? And I fear no contradiction from any of your countrymen, who have crossed the Atlantic, when, without waiting for a reply, I say it is such as the native of no other land than that of our fathers will meet with, even though he present himself under the most favorable auspices, for the simple reason that it is dictated by "sentiments of the soul," to which "material influences" hold a very secondary place.

Paris, February 8, 1847.

LETTER XIV.

Everybody knows there is Quixotism in politics as well as in religion, and though I am not aware that the one or the other belongs peculiarly to your countrymen, yet my observation has led me to believe that when an individual of the island race is fully possessed of the spirit of either, not red-hot iron is more disagreeable to handle, nor the cold metal itself more difficult to bend; and this M. Guizot may find out to his cost, when experience teaches him that the stiffness of the Puritan, and the wiliness of the Jesuit united, are by no means an equal match for it.

If, as is proverbially said, Truth lies at the bottom of a well, the well where she has taken refuge at the present moment must be profoundly deep; for, notwithstanding she has been assiduously sought for, on both sides of the Channel, to clear up the mystery which envelopes the much-fretted question of the Spanish marriages, she has hitherto so effectually eluded pursuit, that, beyond the simple fact of two princes having espoused two princesses in spite of England's remonstrances, every thing is as problematical as the French King's good faith, his Prime Minister's political honesty, or the Spanish Queen-mother's innocence.

Fortunately the quarrel, which is like to prove a "very pretty" one, belongs as yet exclusively to the Governments of the two countries, while the English and French people care no more about it, or the cause of it, than they do about the rupture of the peace of Amiens, or the fate of last year's snow. But Lord Palmerston very naturally feels sore at having been overreached, and the more so, because bent as he is on recovering from his bad reputation of being the first fire-eater in Europe, his hands, it may be, are to a certain extent tied. Nevertheless, as no one need be told, neither he nor his subordinates at Paris and Madrid have been slow or undecided in announcing by word and deed his thorough disapprobation and condemnation of the course pursued by his adversaries. It is asserted, and as I believe truly, since no denial on worthy authority has ever been made to it, that an understanding was entered into, while the monarchs of France and England were holding high holiday at the Chateau d'Eu —an understanding more binding from its very nature than any written compact among gentlemen could be—to the effect that, provided the British Ministry refrained from urging the Coburg claim at Madrid, the French, on their side, would not press the marriage of the Duke de Montpensier till a certain time had elapsed, or a certain event taken place, subsequent to the espousals of the Spanish Queen; that in the face of such agreement not only was the offensive act complained of done, but done cunningly and clandestinely; and that now a perfect right exists in the wronged party to exact an indemnity against the mischievous consequences which may grow out of such faithless proceedings.

But the French King, having secured a princess and a princely dowry for his son, turns a deaf ear to all this; though I cannot help thinking he sometimes regrets what has been done, or, at least, the manner of doing it; since, if my information be as correct as from its source it ought to be, he is far from being tranquil at heart for its possible results. And with good reason, too, for the English being by tradition a people fond of "a word and a blow," giving precedence often to the blow over the word, he cannot but be apprehensive lest he receive an unwelcome remembrancer of his sins of omission and commission, without even the prophetic words — " Thou art the man ! " — once thundered in a Royal ear, to put him on his guard.

And yet it seems that the Dowager Queen Christina was the sole immediate exciter of so much bitter blood, for the English and French Governments, it would appear, were of accord on most points involved in the marriageable condition of the Spanish Queen and her sister, when their mother, taking fright, perhaps, at certain ultra-liberal demonstrations connected with the popularity of the unmanageable Don Henrico, instructed her agent in London to acquaint the English Ministers with her willingness to give her eldest daughter to a Coburg Prince, if they would further such a scheme by their instant support; for, as she told them, it was her fixed determination to marry her to some one without delay. It has been suggested that she did this in order to entrap them into a false step, which would have released Louis Philippe from his promise, and allowed him and her to do what they had long since agreed upon; but better informed persons believe that she was playing her own game, independently of her French ally, under the mistaken notion that others were as void of honesty as herself. For her sole and selfish fear was lest, a son-in-law being found capable of appreciating her at her just value, he should unite himself with the true friends of Spain and its liberal institutions, and she be thrust out of the kingdom a second time, to be henceforth a wanderer from the scenes of her former grandeur and her base intrigues.

Lord Palmerston's answer was quick and resolute,—" England's honor could not be violated even to advance the family interests of England's Queen." Post haste was this message carried to Madrid, and hardly was it delivered before another in still hotter haste was despatched to Paris, which astounded the Spanish Minister, took even Louis Philippe by surprise, and awoke M. Guizot from a state of complete ignorance as to the advanced stage of the negotiation. But the astonishment of the first and the ignorance of the last were of little import to the Royal juggler, who, on receiving the Queenly missive, after a moment's reflection, exclaimed, "Be it so!" He hesitated; not that he disapproved of the proposition it contained, but that he doubted if it were the fitting hour for carrying it into execution; and the amount of this proposition, which we now know, was, that the writer, having resolved at every cost to put an end to an uncertainty which might terminate in her banishment, and chosen a suitable husband for her eldest child, would give to Louis Philippe, if he took part in such arrangement and broke troth with the English, a Royal dowry, and almost a Royal bride, for his son. Whereupon, the temptation proving too strong to be withstood by a man whose heart has been for years a stranger to every feeling but a passion for accumulating riches, and an anxiety to perpetuate his dynasty, the regal sanction required was hurried off by a return courier, and things have come to the pass where we now find them.

Paris, Nov. 13, 1846.

LETTER XV.

As a stranger I have no claims upon you; as a foreigner, and that foreigner an American, still less; yet, in the possibility of meeting with indulgence at your hands, I venture, through the only journal that cannot escape his notice, to address the enclosed note to Viscount Palmerston, Her Majesty's Secretary of State for Foreign Affairs, M. P., &c.

My Lord, — You are, or are supposed to be, a statesman, a Christian, and a gentleman. If it were otherwise I would not take the liberty or the trouble of referring to a speech made by you in the House of Commons on the 6th of July last. But, believing that the world renders to your character no more than is its due, I would fain ask, if it was not your bounden duty, on that occasion, when you so unnecessarily dragged into debate the concerns of a third nation, thoroughly to acquaint yourself with the affairs about which you discoursed, that you might not, through sheer ignorance, transgress the laws of peace, prudence, and courtesy?

In reply to Lord George Bentinck's motion respecting Spanish bonds, you saw fit most gratuitously to arraign the United States of America, and to threaten them, at least by implication, with the strong hand of coercion, unless, forsooth, certain defaulting members among them "wiped away from their history that blot which," according to you, "must be considered as a serious stain upon their national character."

I am unwilling to insult your intelligence by presuming you to be ignorant of the fact that the Government at Washington never participated in State debts, by consequence never incurred any responsibility, and, therefore, can in no way be held accountable for a single dollar of them. But wherein the General Government neither could nor would act, individual governments have not been heedless or inactive. Premising that two-thirds of the United States, containing more than four-fifths of the entire population, either never contracted a debt, or never committed a default, it should be known that all the rest have resumed payment, or are upon the point of doing so, with a few exceptions, one alone of which has ever repudiated any portion of its bonds. Nor is Mississippi, the repudiator, wholly without the show of justice on her side; for she has offered, through her constitutional organ, the Legislature, to waive all objection to jurisdiction, and to abide the issue of a trial at law. What can be fairer than this proposition, which her creditors should immediately avail themselves of, to carry into the Supreme Court of the United States a single case that would be decisive of all others, and at a very trifling expense?

While obscure and isolated sufferers gave vent to their just but ill-directed indignation, silence, it may be, best became the calumniated; but when a gentleman in your high station enunciates sentiments like yours, it is well to inquire whether higher, nobler, and more philanthropic ground could not have been taken by him; and whether God and all good men would not have more approved you, had you been guiltless of bravado, and not forgotten those great common bonds of interest (blood and religion) which should forever "grapple with hooks of steel" the hearts of Englishmen to the hearts of Americans?

Were European communities composed of "people of the ballot-box," as those of the "model republic" are truly, but in tasteless mockery, described by you to be, every body knows that their public debts would not be worth a day's purchase. What wisdom was there, then, in flouting a nation which, by the ballot-box itself, and universal suffrage too, has incontrovertibly demonstrated a saving popular virtue to exist within its limits that is to be found nowhere else? You yourself, I doubt not, regretted as soon as it was spoken the speech that fell from your lips; for, even without the excuse of occasion, it breathed the spirit of war — unnecessary war, that concentration of all crime, and its burden was menace — empty menace, disparaging to your reputation as a statesman and a man.

Menace, my Lord, is unworthy the mouth of an Englishman, or the ears of his countrymen; and still less is it an argument fit to address to the Transatlantic descendants of Englishmen. What! England make war on America because a few poverty-stricken States cannot for the moment pay the interest on their bonds! I would not be guilty of disrespect towards your lordship, but surely it was not in earnest that you gave countenance to such an impossible extravagance. Or, if it was, let me entreat you to forbear in future from such untoward earnestness, unless you are perfectly disregardful of the rights both of foreign and domestic State creditors; for, though "Paul may plant and Apollos water," God alone (not to speak it profanely) can give an increased value to depreciated stocks in this country, if they who are responsible for their payment are to be dragooned into doing what is right by English dictation and denunciation.

Boston, U. S. A., Aug. 16, 1847.

LETTER XVI.

As the remarks which it pleased you to make upon my letter of August 16th were not published till after the steamer's departure from Liverpool on the 4th of September, they necessarily could not reach me before the arrival here of the next mail — that of the 19th of the same month — and consequently the present is the first regular opportunity I have had of returning an answer, which, brief as I shall try to make it, will not, I trust, be refused the privilege of appearing in the columns of the *Times*.

If you have any recollection of my communications, so flatteringly received at your office until now, you will do me the justice to acknowledge that in none of them have I ever favored either the principle or the practice of repudiation; but, on the contrary, have unreservedly condemned them, though at times repeating the excuses made by repudiators themselves, but never adopting their sentiments, while I stated what is the opinion of most intelligent and honest persons in the States, that through legitimate means, judiciously used, this land will eventually be cleansed, and at no distant day, from the stains both of bankruptcy and repudiation, without being "put to its purgation" by the threat of foreign interference.

To accomplish so desirable an end — an end devoutly to be wished for by every American who has a heart to feel for his country's honor, or to sympathize with the victims of State delinquency — I have added my feeble influence to that of many other men far more powerful than myself; and you, Sir, need not be informed that the work has prospered, since you admit, that "a portion of those (States) which had stopped payment have begun to pay dividends anew," — thanks (you might have continued) to those much-despised ballot-boxes, which, in anti-republican fervor, you would fain "cast into the Mississippi amongst the snags and sawyers." Yet with such a fact as this — the resumption of payment by mere force of popular suffrage — and that, too, in more than one instance — staring you in the face, and with "no wish to rip up old sores," as you say, you have, to my regret and astonishment, in your article of September 6th, run directly counter to your own declared purpose.

In my letter of March 18th, 1846, I remarked, that "to no part of the people of this country were the common rudiments of education strange;" and, arguing upon this undisputed truth, as well as upon the good degree of intelligence pervading the community, I thought it a fair conclusion, and it is one which, according to your own confession, results have not falsified thus far, that the worldly wisdom and practical virtue of my countrymen would not permit a continuation of non-payment of debts any longer than stern necessity required it. I claimed for them a superiority over the common people of England, large portions of whom, for lack of moral and intellectual culture, are known by every traveller in the two countries to be below the lowest standard of humanity in America, and masses of whom your own reports of Parliament describe to be so grossly ignorant that the names of Jesus Christ and Pontius Pilate are confounded together in their thoughts, while the existence of a God is hardly entertained by them as a possibility in which they have any concern.* But I never was presumptuous enough to pronounce them so enamoured of justice in the abstract that they would immolate themselves upon its altar though the heavens were about to fall. I thought them in the main more than "indifferent honest," but I never imputed to them that sublime virtue which is made more virtuous by kicks and buffets. It was therefore that I entreated you not to "o'er leap your custom of choice terms," lest you should defeat your own intent; and it was therefore that I said, and said advisedly, that though Paul may plant and Apollos water, if you persist in dragooning and denouncing your debtors, you will do more harm than good — you will tear down faster than the best of us can repair the shattered fabric of State-credit. But because in all truth and friendliness I gave you this warning, sincerely pitying the victims of American bankruptcy, and feeling no less shame for imprudent defaulters on one side of me, than disgust for reckless repudiators on the other; and because I advised the creditors of Mississippi how, at the expense of a few dollars, they might knock the paltry prop of law from beneath her in a court of equity at Washington, (which, by the way, could not be attempted without her legislative sanction,) my "pleading is disgraceful" in your eyes — "more disgraceful than the knavery of my client." But, thank

* Laborers in the Mining Districts are here alluded to. See Parliamentary Reports.

Heaven, as there was an appeal from Philip drunk to Philip sober, so is there, I hope, one also from the Editor of the *Times* misconceiving my words, to the Editor of the *Times* convinced of his error.

Whatever may be the authority on which you declare, that in the United States "public opinion is busy to palliate, to excuse, to applaud, and not to censure and condemn acts, for which, in Europe, a bankrupt would be refused his certificate," it is utterly worthless. Upon no spot on earth is public opinion more powerful for good than it is here. If it works slowly, it works surely, as is proved by the solvency of several bankrupt States, of which you formerly despaired. But recollect that Rome was not built in a day. And when you, impatient at the little visible progress made, not only withhold due credit from those who have redeemed the error of their ways, but unscrupulously term "non-rascality" the admitted honesty of four-fifths of a mighty population, putting it, more wittily than wisely, "upon a par with not forging a check, or not embezzling an employer's money," you tempt me to inquire, whether you think that in so doing you render more honorable the high mission to which you are called, as the foremost journalist in the world, whose responsibility at the present critical moment is such as should make a conscientious man tremble.

You believe that "the American name will not recover for half a century the slur that has been cast upon it." It is a long time, fifty years, for the convalescence of a nation in its first youth, having all Europe before it for a guide and warning. But long as is the term which your imagination fixes upon, and accurate as is your judgment in general, I doubt not that you and I will yet survive to witness the fallacy of your prophecy. Not fifty years were necessary, but less than fifty months sufficed the Bank of England to recover from the slur of its legalized bankruptcy, though it had wantoned in its depreciated rags for the fourth of a century; and as for your Northern Capital, though its honesty, or "non-rascality," as you have christened the thing, is long past praying for, we never hear of your "having an uneasy feeling in your breeches pockets whenever a 'sandy-haired Scotchman' passes you in the streets."

From my "exquisite probity and reasoning" you draw these three "conclusions," which, barring all offence, are "most lame and impotent:" — "first, that the repudiating States (State ?), and those who countenance their repudiation" (a countenance more strange than true), "upon the showing of their advocates" (I know not such), "are doing what is dishonest and wrong" (never by me gainsaid), "with the most perfect knowledge of the fact" (whch I deny as inference from my words, seeing that I spoke of *right* as I, not they, regarded it) : "secondly, that there must be a special interposition, a miracle worked, before such words as good-faith and fair-dealing are admittted into the vocabulary of the Union": (Even had the Union, instead of a remote fraction of it, been the subject-matter of my comment, still I could not rightly be held accountable for misconstruction like this): and, "thirdly, that the attributes of Providence are absolutely limited in the case of the American debtor, should his dormant tendency to non-payment be roused into vitality by the most distant hint from his creditor:" Not "distant hints,' but direct threats, and that, too, from the English Foreign Secretary, were the provocation to the criticism which has been so highly honored by you.

I cannot accept, Sir, the distinction of being ranked among "American statesmen," so gibingly conferred upon me; but while helping, within my limited sphere, to smooth down the asperities which have occasionally risen between your country and mine, it seemed to me, native-born as I am to the States, a not unsuitable signature to assume, that of a " States man."

Boston, U. S. A., Oct. 16th, 1847.

LETTER XVII.

Without regarding my opinion — the opinion of an American and Republican — upon French affairs as " rich," you may possibly look upon it as " rare," and consequently give a place to it in your otherwise better filled columns.

When the late revolution took place in Paris, or, as it should rather be called, accidental eruption and evident revelation of the spirit of regeneration that has now been working in the bowels of Europe for years, I was at once convinced of its ultimate usefulness, end in whatever way it might. I knew from long personal observation, that things here had been for a great while in the worst possible train, as must always be the case whenever the real interests of the ruled are made subordinate to either the real or imaginary interests of their rulers. I knew that, as with individuals, a State which systematically exceeds its revenue to a large amount must by necessity, sooner or later, fall into bankruptcy and anarchical confusion. And I knew, too, that the late King of the French had, for a counteracting force against such hostile influences, wilfully provoked by himself, neither a political party, personal adherents, nor attached friends. To have maintained him, therefore, longer on the throne — him, upon whom the experience of many years and extraordinary vicissitudes had obviously been thrown away — would have been, it is true, to defer the evil day, but it would have been also to increase in frightful progression the amount of the evil itself. It was in consequence of reflections like these, that I was rejoiced at the Revolution of February, being well assured, that a great, a generous and a deceived people, could not but be the gainers by it.

And now comes the question, what is to happen next, and in what is the present confusion of parties and politics to end? For my part, I am persuaded that Republicanism, or man's self-government, will, like truth, prevail at last, wherever the blessings of civilization are felt; but I am also and equally persuaded, that Frenchmen are no more fitted for its appreciation and enjoyment now, than they were in 1830, when even the brave and sanguine Lafayette, shrank with honest distrust from setting up the cherished idol of his youth, his manhood and his age. That a Republic — a bad, a bastard Republic — is, and for a time will continue to exist here, I do not doubt; but that a good, a well-proportioned and a durable Republican form of Government can be adjusted to this disjointed people, seems to me as impossible, as for the most skilful tailor to fit becomingly a well-made garment to the distorted limbs of a humpback.

Had Louis Phillipe faithfully fulfilled the mission to which he was called by God and man — had he labored night and day to educate the masses of his subjects, so that an immense proportion of them, should have been no longer unable to read their prayers and write their names — had he, after that, sought, in judicious kindness and with prescient wisdom, to extend the right of suffrage gradually and according to the increase of knowledge — had he discarded bribery, diminished taxation, adopted a free trade policy, and striven to augment the income of the State — had he, in a word, served his people with a tithe of the intense fidelity with which he tried to serve (not served) his family and himself — France of the present day would have been more than a Republic in name, with a beloved monarch at her head, and twenty years hence, she would have become a Republic in very deed.

It may seem to you presumptuous, and perhaps it is, for me, a stranger in Europe, to criticise the deeds or misdeeds of the Provisional Government of France — self-constituted lords paramount since the 24th of February. But there are some things so "plain, that the wayfaring man, though a fool, need not err therein;" and is not this one of them? M. de Lamartine and his coadjutors were literally, as you know, mob-chosen. They were, therefore, less the rightful representatives of their country and its power, than mere temporary and volunteer agents to keep the wheels of State in motion, till such time as the nation at large could express its will and act for itself. They were like sub-officers on the deck of a ship, with only just so much delegated authority as the stern necessities of the safety general demanded. Whence comes it, then, that they have dared to exercise more than imperial authority, — have gratuitously tampered with the rights of property, — have dabbled beyond their depth in matters of finance, and even stooped from their high functions to the prescribing the fashion of a coat?* It is that, in a pitiful propitiatory spirit towards their mob-creators, they were willing, nay, anxious, it would seem, to commit the future Representatives of the nation to a course, the adoption of which is very likely to drive the nine hundred members out of doors and windows, some fine morning, at the point of the pike and the bayonet.

But in answer to the suggestion of this possible event,† it is said that the *bourgeoisie* of Paris are too strong to be successfully resisted by the populace, however enraged it may be at

*Costume of Representatives.

†The Assembly was expelled by a mob in less than a week after this letter was written.

the disappointment of its unreasonable expectations, which have been so recklessly excited. Sheer nonsense! One man of the barricades, is worth, in action, ten of the *Garde Nationale.* Besides, this *bourgeoisie,* this National Guard, of which we hear so much, are no lovers of Republicanism, except as for the moment they think it the synonym of order; but are instinctively, and by their dearest interests, bound heart and soul to courts and drawing-rooms, to costly equipages and aristocratic *faubourgs,* and to all those who wear purple and fine linen and fare sumptuously every day.

Below the *bourgeoisie* are found the unambitious workmen, who very sincerely advocate a Republic, for the simple reason that they have been taught to believe it the only means whereby their hands can be provided with work and their bellies with bread, and the *canaille,* who are rampant in a cause which promises to their imagination immunity in licentiousness. But above the middle class, are the capitalists, the gentry, the Royalists, the aristocrats — call them what you will — in short, the men of knowledge and intelligence, who see clearly that the time has not arrived in France for the "lion to lie down with the kid,"— for St. Germain and St. Antoine to embrace each other; and who, if the word Republic is by a palliating sort of *force majeure* upon their lips, have garnered up within their hearts the image of a King — a puppet king if you please, and of a Court that shall forever keep in mind the remembrance of their past glories.

Men here, then, are at sixes and sevens as to their ideas of Government, and parties are at daggers-drawing, though with unruffled composure of look and demeanor; and I verily believe, that thousands who are shouting for a Republic, shout in the fear or falseness of their hearts, and in entire unbelief of its possibility, for they must know that it is founded on a lie — a pretext, the pretext that it is the nation's wish, and that, therefore, it cannot stand.

The very persons who wrought the revolution in Paris, were identical in class with those against whom the National Guard and troops of the line in Rouen and Lyons have since been fighting to the death. At one moment it was the toss of a copper whether the Duchess of Orleans should be appointed Regent to the infant King, her son, or be chased away. Who, then, will venture to predict stability in the present state of things? France in its entirety is a grand enigma; may the solution of this enigma not prove a miserable dream.

Paris, May 6, 1848.

LETTER XVIII.

. It has been said that great occasions always bring forth great men, and certainly the English, the French and the American revolutions would seem to corroborate the apothegm. Is it, then, that the present is not a great occasion in France, or that its abortions are as yet only the precursors of a Cromwell, a Bonaparte or a Washington? I am aware that it is impossible for me to escape the condemnation of many persons, when I say that in my eyes the occasion does not appear great, because there is no honest and high-wrought enthusiasm in the contest now going on, which is not between mighty principles, as those of Monarchy and Republicanism, but between men and their own convictions — between men, rashly, yet fearfully seeking for what they neither love nor comprehend — convictions which are contradicted by words and works whenever these are open to the world's inspection.

By your courtesy, I was allowed, a few days since, to declare through *The Times*, my unbelief in the existence here of *matériel* adequate to the constitution of a good and lasting Republic; and I would now gladly avail myself of the same medium to inquire if, so far as has yet been shown, any reasonable confidence can be placed in the *personel* depended upon for attaining the desired end? Have the prominent actors on the last three months' scenes been wise and consistent in counsel — discreet and brave in conduct? or have they, by the tendency of their legislative acts, rather impoverished the upper and middle classes without bettering the condition of the humble, and leveled down the mass of millions without leveling up any portion of it? Government, or, more properly speaking, its fantastic shape, has been in France, nothing but a fiction since the 24th of February. The national machine has been going on from that date through the momentum previously imparted to it. But the momentum is fast dying away, and who shall breathe into the collapsing body the breath of life? The late Minister for Foreign Affairs, and I need not say, the ablest member of the present Executive, was, and perhaps still is, the centre of most men's hopes; but what proof, I would like to know, has he thus far given of being the man of his day — the man upon whom a great occasion, if, as some say, it be great, calls to turn its exigencies with a master's hand to his own account and his country's good? He can charm the ear, it is true, with brilliant periods, but has he ameliorated, in jot or tittle, the condition of France? Nero, too, could fiddle in exquisite fashion, but did he thereby lessen the horrors of burning Rome? History does not say so; and history will tell, or I am much mistaken, that M. de Lamartine, in his poetical inaptitude for important political emergencies, has let slip unimproved one of those glorious, and almost heaven-sent, opportunities to save the body politic, which rarely occur more than once in the career of the most fortunate of public men.

Poeta nascitur non fit; and I am almost persuaded that the same may be said with equal truth of a statesman. M. de Lamartine seems to be a *grand homme d'état manqué;* and not being a man of the sword, what detracts from his usefulness is, that he lacks the early drilling, so common, and thought to be so necessary, to politicians in general. He showed that he was not up to his work, when, on the famous 16th of April, he would have passively succumbed before insensate Radicalism, and suffered himself to be destroyed, had it not been for the presence of mind and prompt decision of General Changarnier, who — and not M. Ledru Rollin, as that gentleman has repeatedly boasted — caused to be sounded the *rappel général,* by which many a life was saved. He came into the National Assembly with an astounding popularity, on the strength of which he might, in the strictest honor, have permitted events to float him clear off, and far above the false position where several of his colleagues had planted themselves; he might, without an effort, have allowed the skirts of his virgin executive mantle to become cleansed of the stains cast upon them by decrees and circulars, which everybody knew, notwithstanding his declarations to the contrary, he disapproved; and, instead of joining in the false and feeble but frequent cry, "There are no parties!" he might, by mere force of circumstances, have been the leader of a powerful party, which would have smothered every other long enough to ensure success to the Republican experiment, if present success had been within the compass of human means. But, in place of this, what has come to pass? The people's choice — their first choice — trembling for a popularity so suddenly achieved, has "loved his own barn better than their house;" untrue to himself, timorously or deceitful, he fell upon the neck of men whose Radical toils will embarrass or choke him in the end; he feared, lest he might not be able to draw it back again, to thrust out his arm to its full length, unless supported by those that, already tried by him, had been found wanting; in a word, he shrank from making himself the strong head of a strong body; and the first instalment of his reward he instantly received from the hands of those who, in creating an Executive, justly preferred others before him. Hence I conclude that the man has not yet arisen who is sufficiently stout of heart, honest of purpose and wise withal, to drive and check betimes the spirit which sways the million, while it is to be lamented that so many miscreants are daily turning up, whose labor of love it is to precipitate or retard, as the fiend of mischief may prompt, the course of events which might conduce to internal order and external peace. So that it must be avowed that the hearts of many fail.

Marat, who was no fool whatever else he might have been, thus wrote in a paper called *L'Ami du Peuple*, under the date of May 17th, 1792:— "There is nothing under the sun so ridiculous as folly and boasting joined together; and, unhappily, this is the indelible characteristic of Frenchmen, who are incapable of foreseeing or appreciating anything, and whom nature appears to have destined to be the eternal dupe and victim of a silly credulity." Napoleon, too, no ordinary observer of mankind, it will be admitted, in his *Maximes et Pensées du Prisonnier de Ste. Hélène*, spoke of his countrymen as follows:— "They cannot have a Republic in France. The sincere Republicans there are idiots — the rest are intriguers."

And does it not seem that those two men said what at least looks like truth, when we are told that, in the order of things contemplated, opinion tends towards a hydra-headed Executive — a monster, both in nature and art, and to a one-sided Legislature, which, for want of the counterbalancing power of an upper house, its own popular violence will infallibly destroy?

I had written thus far for yesterday's mail, when at 4 o'clock, hearing the *générale*, I repaired to the spot where I knew that the next act in the play, whether tragical or comical, would come off. I will not intrude details upon you, but, by your leave, will transcribe in a few words the impression made upon me by the scene I witnessed. The decent persons of all classes, I thought, looked heartily weary of things as they are, and as though they would soon be in the humor to hail with joy any one, whether of Royal or other blood, by whose agency order and industry might be restored; and I was the more convinced of this because the better I am informed the surer I feel that though there are Republicans here enough to do much harm, there are not enough to do any good now; and that a Republic without Republicans, good and many, is at all times just as impossible, as is Paris at the hour wherein we live, without its princes, its palaces, and its countless other gewgaws, which must yet for years fill up the gap between the visionary hopes of its changeful inhabitants and their reasonable expectations.

Paris, May 16, 1848.

LETTER XIX.

Traditionally speaking, it is very easy to raise the Devil, but somewhat difficult to lay him, and the experience of the last few days in Paris has not belied the time-worn saw.

Who caused the insurrection which openly declared itself on Friday morning, and who were the occasion of it, is very well known. The former call themselves pure Republicans, and are as correct and definite in their ideas of a Republic as are Brazilian monkeys in their notions of a steam-engine. They are nothing more or less than pure revolutionists, whose fancy always sees a higher steep, and is sure to "fall on the other side." The latter went by the name of Executive Government, and simply did what they ought not to have done, leaving undone what it was their duty to perform.

The national workshops had been established. They were an accomplished fact, bad as it was. How to get rid of them was the question. No one denied that there were within their walls hundreds of *forçats liberés*, and hundreds upon hundreds of *mauvais sujets;* but then there were also among these outcasts of society many honest workmen, who, with their families, had been flung upon the *pavé*, not for want of will to work, but for want of work to do. Now, was it the part of wise men — nay, was it not the act of fools, to throw some thousands of desperate, though involuntary, paupers into the arms of double their number of unscrupulous vagabonds, to be used according to the pleasure of a few designing knaves? And yet this has been done; and, without a figure of speech, blood has in consequence of it been made to flow from human fountains, like waste water, through the streets of Paris.

It is well ascertained that large sums of money have been at the disposition of insurgent leaders, and hence I have heard it argued again and again, that it was not poverty which drove their followers to arms. But it is no less certain that by the rash and sudden attempt of the Executive Government to disperse the occupants of the workshops, good and bad, the people were excited to rebellion; and there is no evidence to show that these secret funds were forthcoming in the shape of bread before the moment for devoting them to the work of destruction had arrived.

All Frenchmen of honor and sentiment, deeply as they deplore the frightful loss of life, are still more humiliated at the barbaric mutilations, hangings, and decapitations of prisoners which have taken place; and it is with shame they acknowledge that even poison has not been wanting among the instruments of death.

Religion has often suffered in the name of religion; Liberty has had its turn; why should Republicanism hope to escape a similar fate?

Paris, June 26, 1848.

LETTER XX.

As the present is a moment of general, and more than ordinary, disquietude throughout France, and as something like a crisis seems approaching, it appears to me not impossible that a few observations upon the actual state of things here, from the pen of an American looker-on may be acceptable to you.

The time has been, and that not long ago, when indignant Europe set its armed heel upon the very heart of this glorious but distracted country, when her territory was torn from her like the limbs from a traitor to the common good, and when her throne was disposed of as if everybody except her own children had a right to a voice in the matter. But still there was then an obvious way of escape. Now, however, although no strange legions are at her gates, either to curtail her proportions or bid her bow before a sovereign of foreign dictation, yet are there within the limits of the land such elements of strife and confusion, so faint is the spirit of self-sacrifice, and so wrapt in darkness is the future, that I sometimes picture to myself the prelude to the springing of a mine.

Because manufactories are not all at a dead stand, as they were, and because the *générale* is not sounded night and day, as it was, some fondly hope that commerce is reviving and that tranquillity will endure. But such persons seem to forget that men cannot go naked now-a-days, as they would have to do if woollen-mills were closed and tanneries abandoned, and that even in the worst of tempests there are sometimes intervals when the sun may shine and the grass will grow.

I need not say that now is one of those perilous hours in which the man of his age, if such there happen to be — the creature of occasion — springs from the ranks, and all men hail him master. But alas! no one has yet answered to the pressing call, and the ill-modelled and improvised Republic is tolerated only as a flimsy raft is clung to by the helpless fugitives from a sinking ship. France will not emerge from her present troubled condition till, the reign of false ideas over, a religious spirit, joined to an iron will and a mighty arm, comes to the rescue.

In one month's time from this, as you know, a President is to be chosen by the French people, and the two most prominent candidates for the highest office in the country are Prince Louis Bonaparte and General Cavaignac — the former acknowledged on all sides to be a man of very ordinary talent, and the latter accredited in no quarter as possessed of commanding excellence. To one or the other of these, probably, is the fate of liberal institutions in France, and, by relation in some sort, throughout the Continent of Europe, to be confided for several years. *If the nephew of the Emperor be the successful competitor — and his chance is not the worst —*

nobody, as I have ever heard, dreams of his contenting himself with a simple Presidency of four years, to give place at its termination to some rival of less pure blood. He will make his chair a throne, say his partisans openly, or, at least, will try to do so. And with four-fifths of the army to lean on, not to mention one-half of the National Guards, with majorities in most of the Departments, — disgusted, as they are, at experimental governments, — to sustain his pretensions, and with many of the Legitimists (be their motives fair or foul) to bolster him up the steep of power, what, it is asked, can stand between him and greatness? Nothing, literally nothing, I fear, if the election were to take place tomorrow; but with thirty days to work in, with every arm brought skilfully to bear, and with political existence, if not something else quite as dear, upon the issue, General Cavaignac's party, if it die, will die, I doubt not, " with harness on its back."

Should universal suffrage put the princely aspirant at the nation's head, he being the younger, and therefore more favored exponent of popular power, his position in regard to the Assembly would be decidedly a vantage ground. Hence evil is apprehended, for it is no secret that between the two there exists neither sympathy nor love. But failing a choice by the people, should the name of Bonaparte be presented to this same hostile Assembly, backed by a number of votes far exceeding any given to other candidates, the curious question then would arise, " Will the Representatives of the people reject the nominee of a majority of the people?" They dare not, I suspect. But whether they dare or not, their situation will be painfully awkward; for in one case they must bid defiance to their constituents, and, in the other, their constituents' last choice will bid defiance to them as soon as he feels himself at home in his new place. A second Chamber then, would not be amiss, I ween.

On the other hand, supposing General Cavaignac becomes President of the Republic, whether by the votes of the people or by those of the Assembly, wherein does the future assume a brighter aspect, except it may be, by the deferment of the evil day? To create for any good purpose, one must have suitable materials wherewith to work. But, saving the red or rabid Republicans — a race of men whose creed in all countries, in America as well as in Europe, is subversion, and whose religion is revolution, who scoff at opposing majorities, however legitimate, and laugh at every knot which the knife can cut — all here that are not enemies to a Republic, are friends to it by persuasion only, and not by conviction. I speak advisedly, for, besides the best information to be obtained in the capital from all classes of persons, the facts which have reached me through trustworthy channels from the Departments lead to the belief that the people put no heart, and less faith, in the present attempt at self-government. They are willing to let the thing run its course, whether it come to an end in four years or in as many months or days; but that they are nothing more than willing, and in many instances hardly that, is evident from the indifference, not to say reluctance, with which they go to the polls. Notwithstanding this spiritless humor, however, there are serious apprehensions, that the triumph of no party will effectually secure the blood of a deluded populace from being again vainly shed upon a soil, which, till now, has brought forth scarcely any fruits worthy the cause of rational liberty.

The twenty-second Constitution having been pompously *fêted* the day before yesterday, we are now to see if it will answer the purposes for which it was designed better than its predecessors; we are now to learn if its saving virtues be sufficient to preserve from anarchy a nation "two-thirds of whose population are in a state of complete ignorance, and only one fourteenth part capable of reading and writing correctly."* It is now to be decided how one Assembly alone, which is sovereign, and a Chief Magistrate, who is subject to none, can get on together. One of them must certainly go to the wall; and which of the two it shall be, the character of the individual first raised to the presidency will determine. But what sort of a Republic does this suppose?

Paris, Nov. 14, 1848.

LETTER XXI.

Since last February Paris has never been so tranquil in appearance — perhaps in reality — as it is at present; but, at the same time, never has it been in a state of more perplexing uncertainty, politically speaking, as to what the morrow is to bring with it. Seldom will any one now venture an opinion of the future, so constantly has the unforeseen forestalled the probable; whereas till very lately the whole world seemed turned into political prophets. Men, too, like events, have belied every guess. From the poet-revolutionist, who, notwithstanding his words of fire and deeds of daring, fell from his full-blown popularity flatter than ever did he of the waxen wings from his ambitious soaring, to the General Dictator, who owed his rise and fall to two of his nearest kinsmen's memory — from one to the other, including all the intermediate mote-like existences, which revelled in the sunshine of their little hour, all have come in such quick succession, and so departed, that one can hardly fancy he

---

* *France, her Governmental, Administrative, and Social Organization, Exposed and Considered.* James Madden, publisher, London, 8 Leadenhall-street, 1847. 2d edit., part 2d, chap. 2d, page 3d.

has witnessed other than the representation of a play, and, too, of an ill-played play, no single actor having been fully equal to the part assigned him or by him assumed.

Occasion then having called in vain for some one to shape it to wise ends and purposes, for lack of the reality a name has filled the void — a great man's name, a solitary heritage, which has swayed more votes by millions than its gigantic owner ever enticed or wrung to meet his proud demands, when life, and rule, and royalty were his.

A few months gone by, the people delegated their sovereign power — so the phrase went — to some hundreds of representatives — a power which it is not denied still subsists in all its sovereign integrity, and which, logically regarded, renders the President incapable, except as a mere subject, of either good or evil action. His election was evidently premature, or his masters have outstaid their time. And it is this ill-defined position of parties, and consequent incertitude of rights, even more than unskilfulness and impetuosity, that caused the late lamentable derangement in the Cabinet, the details of which, as they came to me from one of the Ministers, I am able to give you with perfect accuracy.

It appears that the numerous reports respecting the occasion of M. de Malleville's resignation of office are for the most part fabulous, the sole difficulty between the President and himself having risen out of an inopportune demand unconstitutionally urged and insisted on by the former. The Minister of the Interior had received a letter from the *Elysée Nationale,* requiring him to confirm by his signature the appointment of prefects to two Departments, and of a director-general to the Musée; to which he replied, that as soon as the proposition had been entertained by the Ministry in Council, which would be in the course of a few days, he would hasten to return an answer. This took place on Thursday, the 28th, in the evening or late in the day — probably after dinner. The President, far from being satisfied with the result of his missive, immediately wrote a second to this effect: — "I am much surprised at the contents of the letter received by me from the Ministry of the Interior; I require that the nominations made by me be signed by the Minister himself within two hours: (*je l'entends et je le prétends*) — so I mean, and so shall it be." Whereupon a Council of Ministers being summoned, and the facts communicated to them, it was unanimously decided to send in a joint resignation, which was straightway done, the despatch reaching its destination at 11 o'clock, P. M. Instantly the high functionary to whom it was addressed rushed off to the assembled Council, *comme un homme effaré*, to use the words of my informant, made all sorts of excuses, pleaded his ignorance of forms and facts on account of his foreign education, offered to tear his offensive letter to pieces, and, in short, humbled himself completely, to induce the holders of the portfolios to retain them, or at least to defer their final decision till the next day. His prayer was successful so far as a postponement was concerned, owing partly, it is thought, to the vote on the salt-tax which had passed that afternoon, and on the morrow, as is now known, an arrangement was concluded. M. de Malleville, however, did not subscribe to it, because the President refused a condition which he would have imposed, that the three candidates for office, already rejected by himself personally, should never be again proposed to the Council, even for consideration.

The present aspect of affairs in France, though it can no more be relied on than can the face of the Atlantic at the autumnal equinox, seems to look towards the attempted permanent abiding of Prince Louis in the chief ruler's place during his natural life; yet those who voted for him through hate to General Cavaignac, and detestation of the Republic, are evi-

beginning to doubt the wisdom of their choice. The Bonapartists of the Morrow, agape with wonder at the facility of their victory, are stupidly inquiring, "What is next to come?" while those of the Eve are already struggling with might and main for the accomplishment of their hearts' desire — a Presidency beyond four years for their leader to begin with, and then, as circumstances may favor them, something with a brighter name.

Even now, daily deputations and petitions arrive from the provinces, praying that the Republic may be changed into an Empire; and as the candidate for his uncle's throne does not want ambition, it is very like that before long he will take some step or other which will eventually lead the way to the restoration of a Bourbon.

Paris, Jan. 3, 1849.

LETTER XXII.

I doubt much whether the following letter will meet with your approbation; but perhaps there is no better way of arriving at the truth, (at which all must aim, and which must come out sooner or later), than to allow every looker-on, who has no motive for perverting it, to speak plainly his convictions, provided he do so with becoming propriety.

The world, we know, is proverbially called ill-natured; yet it does not seem to have proved itself so in regard to the present Chief Magistrate of the French nation. Judging from its indulgence towards him, one may waste his youth in dreams, his manhood in folly, and, so that he avoid all forfeit to what is loosely termed the code of honor, it is never too late for him, should happy chance betide his steps, to draw forth plaudits from the mob, and take the place which favor, fate or fortune may assign him. This may be well or ill; but in the eyes of such as are not wholly strangers to the tortuous windings of worldly policy, doubt and mistrust must ever mingle with the brightest hope, whenever middle age's wisdom springs at once from infancy to maturity only upon the opportunity offering of some unexpected material prosperity.

I confess that I have no faith in Louis Napoleon's love, or fidelity or good intent, towards the new-born Republic over which he has been called to preside. I lay myself open to no charge of disrespect in saying that his oaths and protestations I consider as no more worthy of reliance than were those of his Great Uncle. On his advent to power he was no longer a young man, and the time past of his life more than suffices to fill me with dread for the future. That he aims, and has always aimed, at a throne, or something akin to it, for himself and his heirs, is universally believed; that the coveted prize has been invitingly presented to him by occasion more than once within a twelve-month is acknowledged on all hands; but that, grown cautious by having twice overleaped himself, he is content to go on steadily, instead of clutching at a leap the imperial gewgaw, is too clear to be questioned.

The close observation of months, added to what has lately come to my knowledge, induces me to believe, that the army is generally well-disposed, though it is no longer enthusiastic, for him, as it was last December; for, on finding that he employed himself in little else than making journeys and speeches, and in writing letters to subordinate agents of his own, unacknowledged by the French Government, instead of devoting his whole soul to measures of utility and vital importance within his proper province, its affection, so sudden in its rise, as suddenly subsided; and now, should a critical moment arrive, those on whom at all times must be his chief reliance are quite capable of demanding, "What has this man done, that he should reign over us, and what is the victory to which he has ever led us?" Still there is a portion of the Line which is said to be devoted to him. It is composed of those soldiers. who, having passed a long time in Africa, separated for years from their families, have lost in no inconsiderable degree the habits and ideas of civilized life, which very naturally change to blood-thirstiness and a wild manner of thinking, whenever there happens to be a too close and too long continued intercourse with half-savage adversaries of the Desert. And it is on the love of such, if of any, that the legal representative of a glorious name must depend in the last extremity.

As are the rank and file, so are the subordinate officers of all the African legions, and, with few exceptions, even the chiefs themselves. Among the Generals, emphatically denominated "Africans," Cavaignac is, perhaps, the only one who has not completely fallen into the Arab way of life. Lamoricière is a legitimist both by descent and antecedents, and by consequence is in heart the reverse of all that is republican. He lent himself, nevertheless, with all his energy, to the Cavaignac Ministry, and when it had fallen, though he indulged for a space in a sort of brooding discontent, yet, on presenting himself at the Elysée, having been received with open arms by its new occupant, he consented to forget his prepossessions altogether, or, at least, to forego them for a season. This general has great facility of speech, but his talents as a warrior are not regarded as super-eminent, and he has the reputation of not being sparing of blood. At one time he was even clamorous in his expression of republican opinions, and, previously to his flattering reception in the Faubourg St. Honoré, no terms were too strong for the utterance of his hatred to the Russian dominion, which he pronounced to be the eternal enemy of civilization. No sooner, however, was the mission to St. Petersburgh held temptingly before his eyes, than, much to the astonishment of everybody, he eagerly accepted it, and, on his presentation at that Court, equally surprised the monarch and all about him by the extreme adulation which he unsparingly lavished in the imperial presence. Bédeau, who is considered to be more capable than any other man of his own rank, is without political importance, and is, moreover, a partisan of the Count de Paris. He is, however, of too indolent a nature to be of much value to any one, and in his tastes is too literary ever to become a favorite with the soldiery. His passion is to remain secluded at home, and he loves not to be interrupted. Changarnier is simply a *bon sabreur*. As he did not go to Africa till his fortieth year, he is, with the exception of Cavaignac, the least savage of all his contemporaries. Yet he shrinks not at the sight of blood, and his own interests are the alpha and omega of his rule of conduct. Energy is the striking characteristic of this man, in whom dwells not a particle of scrupulosity. There is no command his chief could give which he would not obey, if obedience were called for by occasion, and suited his own proper views. He would not hesitate, for instance, to prostrate himself before His Holiness to-day, and remorselessly to send him to his last account tomorrow. Notwithstanding his temporary devotion to the Prince-President, however, General Changarnier would rather see the Duke de Bordeaux at the Tuileries, than the nephew of the Emperor at the Elysée.

Not one of all these generals has the entire confidence of the army, which has seen them fighting only against Arabs; nor is there one of them in whom it would unreservedly trust, were a European war to arise. Bugeaud alone, possessed the soldier's affection, and he alone heartily advocated the cause of Louis Bonaparte. But, unhappily for that cause, which has not many true friends, his course is finished. The recent conqueror of Rome, too, had a certain degree of influence in the ranks, on account of the *préstige* of his family name, but he was adroitly sent upon a worse than bootless errand, the execution of which, it is needless to say, has not increased his popularity. I am aware that an attempt has seriously been made to cast the blame of the Roman expedition from off the shoulders of the President by a supererogatory ascription to him of a most reluctant assent to that untoward measure; and thence it is argued that he could have taken little or no part in the appointment of the officer who was to command it. But it is labor lost to tell the world, that a Ministry which, at the moment of demanding funds to send troops to Civita Vecchia, was in opposition to a constituent, that is, an omnipotent assembly, could have accomplished its purpose, had it not been supported by the good will of its chief.

It is very possible, and by some persons thought highly probable, that by a timely modification of the Constitution the President will be allowed to remain where he is and what he is, even after the expiration of his present term of office; by many, too, it is believed that he will long be kept from falling by the counteracting forces of different parties, not one of which is, or is likely to be, strong enough to risk itself single-handed against all the rest; but if it be his intention to make himself Emperor, or ruler for life, whatever be the title preferred, it is in the eastern provinces of France that he stands the best chance of success, for in those of the west his reception, during the tour lately completed, was anything but flattering to his aspiring hopes.

If he were not a man who habitually feels his way, where,

to effect his purpose, he should take a bold bound at once, he might, perhaps, the time being well chosen, organize at Strasburg or Metz a plan for having himself proclaimed the legal heir of the Empire, and then, by telegraphic communication having produced a corresponding movement at Paris, his point would be gained, for the moment at least, provided the army could be induced to side with him. And this last condition, it may be, he could count upon with reason, for General Changarnier, whose influence on the military is not feeble, with a Marshal's staff within his grasp, and promised honors in perspective, would stop at no obstacle. But I doubt much, after having missed such occasions as those of January the 29th, and June the 13th, especially the latter, whether Louis Bonaparte has quickness and decision sufficient skilfully to play the part proposed. Yet an attempt of some sort or other on his part, and at a moment least expected, is not impossible, for his peculiar characteristic is a caution which, carried to excess, frequently changes to extreme rashness, taking the whole world by surprise. The Strasburg and Boulogne exploits are examples of this. Had he been elected in the first instance President for life, he might have gone on contentedly forever, as he is now a king in all but name; but, with old debts weighing on him sufficient to sink a Spanish galleon if turned into bullion, he must be more simple than the simpleton who attributes to him such patriotic disinterestedness, if he ever quits the Elysée without a struggle, to take refuge in a furnished lodging here or in London.

It must be admitted, even by his enemies, among whom I neither am, nor, being a foreigner, have a right to be, that the President is not without a certain sort of merit, and that his mettle is beyond question; but, like capricious coursers, whose bottom and speed are ill-proportioned, he requires no slight persuasives to spur him into action. If when heated by words and wassail, which are the tongue's familiars in the banquet-hall, he should take a leap in a blaze of light that men not less bold, but wiser far, would hardly dare even under the deep obscurity of a well-concerted conspiracy, I, for one, should in no way be surprised. Never forgetful of his one great object — self, the moment an office becomes vacant, be it high or low, one of his creatures is immediately thrust forward as a candidate, and such is his persistence in this course that his Ministers prefer keeping in their places old *employés*, though not exactly of their own way of thinking, rather than, by removing them, make room for new levies of Bonapartists.

Of late he seems to have preferred his own will, or that of those with whom he is the most intimate, to the counsel of his constitutional advisers. And his intimates, unhappily, are not such men as inspire with unbounded confidence his best friends. His *entourage* is composed of persons who are not tolerated by real greatness, except at a distance. His very family, indeed, is in itself a living proof that Heaven never intended mediocrity like theirs for the permanent governance of France. Napoleon, son of the ex-King Jerome, has never up to the present day, given in action any promise of future usefulness. Pierre, son of Lucien, has all the faults of the Corsican; his brother Lucien, though energetic and master of his passions, is fierce in temper, and "with liver burning hot." Lucien Murat is a *bon vivant*, and, lacking the means whereby to minister to his tastes, he has been in season and out of season, at his cousin's palace, crying "Give, give!" till at last he is not sent empty away.

It is evident, then, that no effectual aid from any relative of his own, can be securely reckoned on by the President, if a throne or a perpetual dictatorship be the goal he has in view. Upon the army, therefore, or the Assembly, or the general sympathy of the country, must centre his entire hope. The disposition of the army, as we have already seen, is a matter of the greatest doubt. That of the Assembly will be better understood if we examine its component parts. First, then, come the Legitimists, whose eyes and hearts are steadily fixed on the to-be-crowned head of another Henry. Next the Orleanists, who will listen to no change that does not benefit the Count de Paris. After them the Republicans — the sincere Republicans, of whatever shade, to whom all endearments of all parties are but sounding brass or a tinkling cymbal. Following in order are the Roman Catholics — the bigots, *par excellence*, I mean — who will support that man best, on whose favor their clergy can most rely. And last of all, the Bonapartists, who in number do not exceed three score. From among all these a large majority can always be obtained to resist every act of violence proceeding from the blood stained quarter of the Reds; but should imperial pretensions, or the like, ever be proffered for the Assembly's consideration, poor indeed would be the minority to save them from falling still-born to the ground.

The national enthusiasm for the Bonaparte dynasty is believed to have cooled down very much since the elections of last December; and in the National Guard no party, as a mere party by itself, can have any well-grounded confidence; for out of Paris it is powerless whenever rapidity and concert of action are necessary, and within the walls of the capital, to say nothing of the number of its legions which have been disbanded, the apathy of supreme indifference reigns throughout its ranks.

The present, then, is all uncertainty. The powers that be are only on sufferance, and the clearest sighted must feel confounded when he seeks for even the beginning of the end.

Paris, October 7, 1849.

LETTER XXIII.

The news which tomorrow's mail will convey to you may excite your curiosity, but hardly your surprise. Whenever a Government advisedly irritates a populace, already in a state of exasperation, its motive can seldom be other than a bad and selfish one. During the last ten or fifteen days we have seen the public hewers of wood engaged in cutting down sundry unseemly objects which occupied most prominently the best quarters of this city, and were called — for what reason I know not — *trees of liberty*. This gratuitous insult to the lower orders, or, to say the least, this graceless task, had it been necessary, might have been begun and finished between the setting and the rising of a single sun. But no; day after day has the work been going tediously on, till at last the planters of these very proper symbols of their factitious freedom have become — as it was perhaps meant they should be — seriously angered and willing to show their game. All this day long has the Assembly been in an unquiet state; grave and moderate men of the majority, with whom I have just been conversing, condemn, though in measured terms, the Executive; *attroupemens* have taken place, and wounds, if not worse results, have followed; General Changarnier has ordered every officer of the *Etat Major* to be ready to put foot in stirrup at a moment's warning; the garrison of the city is under, or ready to take, arms; and the morrow is big with menace. And whence comes all this? Is it that Frenchmen are more difficult to govern than other men? or is it that to misgovern them for a long time, and to keep them in the beaten track meanwhile, is beyond the power of any man living?

I know it is the custom to call them fickle, discontented, violent and revolutionary; but when did they ever have a fair chance to show their disposition and capacity to live in tranquillity under the fostering care of a wise, economical and paternal Government? Their adored Henry IV. gibbeted them without mercy if they happened to indulge in an unlawful passion for venery; their *Grand Monarque* ground them to the dust and used them like stubble to light the furnace of his ambition, while their nobles he chastised as though they had been so many grown up children; their first Republic bandied them about till the mind of France became but a confused mass of ideas jumbled together; their Emperor, on whose glory they still subsist, whipped and spurred them till their withers were so wrung that they had no strength even to wince; their two *restored* Sovereigns (Kings by the grace of the Allies and the Duke of Wellington) half a century behind time, would fain have taught the nation to go crab-wise; their own elected (a lie without the circumstance) but unannointed, of the barricades, gave them, instead of bread, a stone which, felled him as they sent it back; and now, for two years past, the Republic of their riper age, has been to them a plague and pother, leading them such a dance as to afford them neither time nor space for measuring their steps aright. And it is because they have not always, with saint-like simplicity, turned their cheek to the smiter—because while they struggled they struck, that they are, forsooth, disturbers of the public peace, and the world's pest.

Affairs were going on here passably well; commerce, external and internal, was daily gathering strength; the public securities, even if fitfully, were on the rise; and yet the powers that be, as though men's minds were not already in a sufficiently feverish state, must needs set their agents to raze a few scores of poplars, unsightly to be sure, but perfectly insignificant in the eyes of all till the police axes made them so many standards of revolt.

Some persons, wise as the world goes, do not hesitate to declare that the President, fearful of waiting till his turn of tide went by, himself directed this arborous foray, to make of it, and its probable consequence, an occasion whereby to serve his one great end—a perpetuity of office in his own proper person. But difficult as it is to account for causeless provocation, I can hardly agree in ascribing to him such fatuity as this supposition would imply; although it is no easy matter to calculate, with accuracy, on the motives or movements of a man whose deliberately laid schemes thirty minutes sufficed to defeat at Strasburg and a third of that time at Boulogne; and who, after going out on the 29th of January, to do or die, went only to the *place Vendôme* to return to his palace, unable, "like the cat in the adage," to seize the thing his heart most coveted.

Paris, Monday, Feb. 4, 1850.

LETTER XXIV.

Poets, they say, are born, not made; the same may be true of orators; but who ever heard of a political economist leaping, Minerva-like, ready for action into this working world?

If M. Thiers ever made political economy his special study, which may be, he skilfully concealed the fact in his late speech. Outwardly there was all the brilliancy, transparency, and brittleness, too, of the Crystal Palace, but inwardly what a contrast! The honorable gentleman descended from the tribune amid the plaudits of a host who, as M. Ste. Beuve remarked, in regard to his own free-trade propositions, had never heard, or were incapable of comprehending, what was said. The orator had it all his own way, for lack of an opponent worthy of his powers. But although he is not another Adam Smith come to judgment, still, as his intelligence is one not to be treated lightly, rather than set him down as a blind leader of the blind, I prefer attributing to him a conscience which, like that of Bailie Nicol Jarvie's, good, easy man! "never did him any harm." If, however, he really believed all he said, then is he another melancholy example of the dangerous use that a little knowledge may be put to by a large capacity. But I apprehend he knew perfectly well what he was about, while discoursing such eloquent fiction respecting free trade and protection, which are probably both to him as "leather and prunella." Far other matter occupied his thoughts, for the truth is he had long seen that the august body of which he himself makes no insignificant part, was faring as badly in public opinion as did the Government securities in 1848, that the glory of its head was departing, and that more than its extremities had been besmirched and bemired in its abortive struggles on a false and slippery ground. He knew, therefore, that a gentle fillip would not be amiss to the stricken Assembly — that his was the supple tongue which could best raise it from its low estate, and, what suited his book still better, that in so doing, and as he proposed to do it, he would be most effectually serving the interests of Rouen's representative, Rouen being, as you know, a hot-bed of protection, and its inhabitants M. Thier's constituents. Now, it so happened that these highly respectable, but most matter-of-fact fellow citizens of his, were beginning to tire of their Protean *protégé*, which you may be sure he was quite aware of, and here was an occasion for hitting two birds with with one stone, which the adroit self-made man was not likely to miss. This, then, is the explication of the antediluvian rhapsody lately administered to a congregation ever ready to seethe in their own humors, good or bad, when to a chronic fever within is applied an unwonted degree of caloric from without.

M. Thiers is, doubtless, a wise man, but he has yet to learn that it is not the dearness of bread, but the want of means to buy bread, which is at the root of all modern revolutions; and that an anti-protective tariff which shall mete out equal justice to all classes is the only means of insuring to France that internal tranquillity which strengthens the heart of domestic industry, and is the life itself of commerce with foreign lands.

Paris, June 30th, 1850.

LETTER XXV.

The internal commerce of this country is flourishing, and the foreign trade is not in a bad condition. Here, then, so soon after the events of 1848, is proof sufficient, if such were wanting, of the prodigious elasticity, the enormous resources, and the inexhaustible spirit of the French people. Yet, in the face of all this material prosperity, the shadows of the possible future becloud the political horizon, not through the fault of the population at large, who, if tradesmen, have as much as they can do, if manufacturers can give full wages to their men, if agriculturists, can, with one or two exceptions, easily find a good market, and if day laborers, lack not employment; but through the bitter hostility existing between the President and the Assembly, to which this country is indebted for the almost hopeless uncertainty which wastes the energy of man or turns it to desperation.

At the time that a Constitution was in the process of being fabricated here for the last time, I ventured to suggest in your columns the possibility of a strife between the two great Powers of the State, and the consequent convenience in such a case of having a second Chamber, which might throw its weight of wisdom into the juster scale. That strife has now fairly commenced, and, if I am not mistaken, we shall see that the President is playing the surer game. For what comparison can there be more striking than that between one sovereignty invested in a single man and another personified by seven hundred and fifty persons, heterogeneous, selfish, and discordant in respect to every condition of thought, wish and action? As well might we test against a given weight of metal compactly beaten into a handy shape the same quantity diversely tempered in its several different links and then inartistically jointed together. If we glance, however superficially, over the history of the last two years, it will be seen that, though the President of the French Republic has, in the eyes of the wise, been guilty of some imprudent words and actions, not to mention a gross political sin or two, yet that he appears to have risen high in the good graces of his countrymen, while the Assembly, worthy of great praise as it is, notwithstanding certain spots and blemishes defacing its fair fame, has sensibly fallen. The seven hundred and fifty-fold entity is thus most clearly proved to be no equal match against unity; and not less manifest is it that, without another active and efficient body entering into the political machinery, and serving as a compensation-balance, things cannot but go awry in France, whether Republicanism or Monarchism be in the ascendant.

Notwithstanding, however, the discomfiture of the multitudinous branch of national sovereignty, President Bonaparte's rise is rather imaginary than real, like that of an island which the retiring tide seems to elevate towards the sky, without its ever approaching the heavens by a single inch. True, the Elysée is weekly crowded with an armed host, that once regarded the Assembly, with General Changarnier for its right arm, as the fountain of strength; true, too, is it, that the clergy look with an eye of increasing favor on the elected of 6,000,000, — thanks to his pastor-like protection; and not less true is it that the magistrature, which at one time turned with cold decorum from the face of the Chief Magistrate, now smiles upon him, in remembrance of the real or apparent outrage committed against it by his rival in the Maugin affair. But all this is only a temporary shifting of the political sand. The Assembly, in itself or its successors, cannot die except with the Republic, but the Presidency is only for four years; and, if the present occupant of the Elysée would but recollect betimes that a greater man than he once paced its deserted floors, with none so poor as to do him reverence, he would not trust too much to his popularity, but, entirely confiding in his own honesty of purpose and the counsels of the wise, he would cease to fret himself with the phantom of a General Officer panting for an occasion to do him mischief.

At this moment, though tomorrow it may not be true, he can command a large majority in the Chamber, owing to the intestine feuds which, at the country's expense, disgrace that body. From good sources of information, I reckon that the representatives may be classed as follows: — For President Bonaparte, 180 Socialists, 20 moderate Republicans, the followers of General Cavaignac, in opposition to his fellow-General, and 280 Bonapartists of every shade, — amounting in all to 480; while for General Changarnier there are 160 Legitimists, 20 moderate Republicans belonging to his train, 20 devoted Orleanists, and 60 lukewarm friends of the lately fallen family, who go in the steps of M. Molé. These, in number

260, added to 480, and allowing for the usual absence of 10 members, make up the complement of 750; and if you think these *data* worth publishing, they may be referred to hereafter as a matter of curiosity.

Paris, Jan. 9, 1851.

LETTER XXVI.

The French people, as you well know, are not famous for constancy of affection to their political idols, which they glorify one day, cover with pollution the next, and the third cast out as unknown gods; nor for adamantine firmness in attachment to their political ideas, which they deify and discard with an alacrity that would do credit to the best ballet master of the Opera. And yet many grave and intelligent men believe, or profess to believe, that the Republic has taken such deep root in France that it must prevail, not merely eventually, which is not impossible considering that the elements of monarchy, seriously damaged during the last half century, are fast wearing away, but presently, and from this day forth, it will go on from strength to strength till its full development be attained. In combatting such a notion no argument drawn from the history of democracies long since extinct can be of much service; but a momentary reference to a democratic Republic, whose birth, it is true, some persons now living can recollect, may be useful in appreciating the vitality of the form of government in which this country now rejoices, though with tears.

It has never been denied that political institutions are healthful and durable only according as they have naturally grown out of the manners and wants of the population among which they exist. Thus, the inhabitants of the United States, inheriting from their English ancestors the habit of taking care of themselves, and needing nothing but to be left to the government of their own magistrates, have gone on prospering and to prosper in the work of their own hands. Every State, county, city and town in America, you need not be told, has always been accustomed to manage its own concerns without application to, or interference from, the supreme authority at the capital. And this self-controling policy is so habitual and ingrained wherever the Anglo-Saxon race has spread, that it will ever present an insuperable obstacle to the successful usurpation of undue authority by any individual. Even had Washington consented to be called King, he would have been King of nothing save a Republic in fact; and had an hereditary nobility, the necessary consequence and prop of Royalty, been created, it could never have maintained itself in the absence of the law of primogeniture, which universal public opinion — the offspring of equality in civil rights — repudiated. The people of the thirteen original Transatlantic States, in the construction of a commonwealth, had only to build upon a real and solid foundation made to hand; but in France the reverse of this was the case, when in the last century a Republic was proclaimed, and continues so now, without any material diminution of the rubbish which must be swept away before a trustworthy basis can be found for the most dangerous experiment in a nation's history.* The Ex-

*Perhaps it must be said that the French are not a free people. Perhaps the "fashion," to which it ever bows — that successive development of grand ideas of which it is pleased to be proud, is incompatible with the liberty of individual minds. That is not our present question. We are merely observing, that a tyrannical reduction of the whole mind of France to one formula for the time being, and an omnipresent, omnipotent administration — for such it affects to be — are almost insuperable difficulties in the way of a really free and constitutional government. On this point the testimony of an American observer, witnessing with his own eyes the political vicissi-

ecutive power, securely ensconced in central Paris, like a sleepless fly-catcher in the middle of his well-spun web, feels and responds to every vibration throughout the artfully organized system, which extends from channel to sea, and from river to ocean. Its aim has been to keep the Departments in leading-strings, and its success to prevent neighbors from leaning only on each other for mutual aid and comfort in every undertaking, great or small, and to drive them to the Minister of the Interior as the sole dispenser of patronage. Provincialism has hence become naturally associated with social inferiority, sliding easily into vulgarity; and as vulgarity is often carelessly taken for intellectual incapacity, the consequence is, that the many millions living at a distance from the factitious fountain of power, are regarded and treated as children even in matters that most deeply concern their daily comfort. If, for example, a river is to be bridged, a morass drained, or a church erected, more time is lost in negotiating at head-quarters for permission to commence the undertaking than would suffice in England or America to accomplish the same object twice over. Disgusted, doubtless, with all this, and, as too frequently happens, expressly educated by as-

tudes of France, possesses unusual value. The letter of "A Statesman" on the two Republics, which we lately published, deserves to be kept in record against the many evil days which French bureaucracy has still to bring forth. One passage, in particular, so exactly tallies with the complaints we have heard from every province and from every class in France, that we cannot forbear quoting it. After describing the habits of self-government, derived from this country, which have given such expansive and creative power to the population of the United States, the "States-man" proceeds:—"The Executive Power," &c., &c.

Hence that perpetual craving after power and position in France, that consciousness that a man must be *aut Cæsar aut nihil*, that division of society into officials and revolutionists, partisans of the Powers that be or of some other form of government or dynasty—that surrender of self, conscience, and intellect on the one hand, and that extravagance of political speculation on the other, which distinguish France above the rest of the civilized world.—TIMES.

piring parents for some official employment, most provincials of distinguished talents, instead of honorably addressing themselves for advancement, as is the custom in the United States, to their own immediate communities, hasten to the feast of good things, whether within the Elysée or elsewhere, at which they soon learn to take care of themselves, leaving their country, as the motto on their current coin has it, to the "protection of God."

No one ought to feel surprised, then, whenever a revolution happens here, and a Republic, the universal panacea which haunts the French brain, is announced, that the people out of Paris, utterly destitute of political training and without leaders, as they are, should stand agape and helpless as a shipload of passengers in a gale, whose ruthless violence has left them without captain or crew. Nor should their helplessness and apparent imbecility be a reproach to their natural intelligence, for the system of Centralization, so briefly alluded to above as a curse to the country, has in its long course benumbed their faculties and paralyzed their energies for every sort of action beyond the little circle of a material existence. Neither is this system likely to be soon abandoned, the present Minister of the Interior having very lately, to my certain knowledge, fiercely and firmly resisted every attempt on the part of the Council of State to modify its operation. In the absence, therefore, of the very groundwork whereon to create and sustain a Republic, how can such a form of government endure except while it is kept, as at present, from toppling over by the unwilling support of various factions, which preserve it from falling only to prevent an antagonist still more detested from taking its place?

If, however, a Republic has no moral base, not a whit more material foundation has a Monarchy to rest upon. For where is now to be found an aristocracy which, rich in ancestral names and title deeds, can present the only insurmountable barrier to the wave of popular violence that in our day so often dashes against the throne itself? And even if found, into what portion of the vasty deep of conflicting interests and insensate passions are we to look for that support of public opinion which alone can consecrate it in the eyes of the destroying Socialist?

It seems to me, moreover, that the absence of a disinterested public spirit, of an exalted patriotism, furnishes another argument against the present peaceful establishment either of a Monarchy or a Republic. In other countries we have frequently seen party distinctions melting away whenever national honor or safety were endangered, but here men appear to cling to their party with the passion one has for a paramour, while for the land of their birth the affection which animates them wears a much more legitimate aspect, guiltless of all enthusiasm. In the present interneciary struggle, in what quarter is a self-sacrificing spirit, an elevated love of country, to be discovered? Is it in the President, who dismissed the favorite General of the Assembly, from whom no harm could have come so long as his princely word remained inviolate; or in that General himself, who obstinately refused, when his mission in the cause of society had been accomplished, a voluntary resignation which he knew would save a world of trouble; or in the majority of the Assembly, which bootlessly insulted the Chief Magistrate in the persons of his Ministers; or in its minority, which gleefully exults over the mischief on foot, and would no doubt fiddle *à la Néron*, if the civil edifice were in flames.

The conclusion, then, to which I am forced, in spite of my prejudices and predilections, is that a wisely-conducted Republic is beyond the reach of the present generation of Frenchmen; and that as to a permanent monarchy, one might as well attempt to re-invest the nursery's phantom with its pristine horrors as to try to hedge about with his hereditary divinity a King whose predecessors have been treated like felons and vagabonds for the last sixty years.

Paris, Jan. 18, 1851.

LETTER XXVII.

It is probable that a legitimate substitute for defunct monarchy will be made to do duty here till better times arrive, for society revolts at anarchy as much as nature abhors a vacuum; and that this will be replaced by a permanent government of some sort or other, for it is not in the nature of things that eternal instability, like the brand on the first murderer's front, should forever exclude this people from the common lot of humanity — a certain degree of tranquillity in prospect, without which the Commonwealth must perish for lack of individual enterprise. What this substitute is likely to be, it now is, — a Bonapartean Democracy, and it will exceed in duration, if I mistake not, the expectation of most men.

We gain nothing by giving wrong names to things. That is not a Republic where an immediate appeal to the people, or the weight of a soldier's sword, are the only remedies in case of variance among rival sovereign powers of State. It is nothing more nor less than rank democracy, and is in constant danger of becoming something worse. England is at this moment more essentially republican than France; for in that country the people's good is never liable to be wantonly sacrificed to the caprice of a sovereign, the arrogance of a senate, or the fickleness of a popular assembly; because one at least of these three great estates can, even in its own proper interests, be always counted on as a conservative force, which, backed by the omnipotence of the press, needs no aid either from the mob or the army.

If to the continuance of the actual organization which I have supposed it be objected, on the one hand, that the Constitution forbids the re-election of President Bonaparte at the expiration of his present term of office, and, on the other, that an additional and more aristocratic legislative body may change the whole face of affairs, I answer, that never yet in France was a written instrument an insuperable obstacle to a State necessity, either real or imaginary, and that as to the creation of an upper house, under whatever name, it is the great mass of the common people, and not the middle or highest classes, who will oppose it; such is their inherited dread of an aristocracy, even in outward show, and so long does it take to root from the popular heart a sense of injuries inflicted on the fathers of those now living, by men whose gentle nurture should have taught them better things.

The Count de Chambord was once hailed as the *dieudonné*, and if God had saved him from his friends, he might have lived to be so hailed again; but if ever in this country any man could rightly be called a God-send, that man is the President of the Republic. Hardly is he wanting in a single requisite pertaining to the lofty place he occupies, now that the notion of empire seems less potent to disturb his wiser judgment. He is of imperial blood, and on the day of election no one of meaner lineage can stand beside him; for, oddly enough, the French, with all their horror of nobility, will suffer none of less than princely dignity to rule over them. Of well-tried courage and much passive endurance, he cannot but be respected, and yet, untrained to war, he can never be feared as a military despot. Of infinite *sangfroid*, he has very lately proved himself more than a match for the acutest among his countrymen. Older than the repreesntative of the Orleans dynasty, he cannot be kept in leading-strings; and, not a Bourbon, he is not incapable of improvement. Above all, to his name alone, throughout the length and breadth of the land, is there a tradition attached. Enter the meanest human habitation in the remotest Department, and upon the poverty-stricken walls some memorial, however slight, of the great Corsican's glory will be found. Of that glory he is the legal inheritor, while its attendant evil, so far as he is concerned, sleeps in the tomb of the *Invalides*. But the case is widely different with the two rival descendants of a long line of kings. Only within the faded halls of legitimacy, or the garish saloons of Orleanism, are the Count de Chambord and the Count de Paris spoken of or known. Talk of them to the common people of the provinces, and their reply will be, "Napoleon's fame is dear to us; the name of Bonaparte belongs to France; but as for those you tell us of — who, and what are they?" In one word, the President I believe to be the very man this country stands in need of during her troublous ordeal; and, more than that, he is the only man, I am convinced, whom, for the time being, she will tolerate.

Theoretically, and to a certain extent practically, that democracy which, with its senseless, because indiscriminating, companion, universal equality, originated even before the first revolution began in France, will be represented in the National Assembly; but Louis Napoleon, if clever as he is reported to be, will, like Cæsar in regard to the Roman Senate, adroitly turn this popular mania to his own profit by courting the common people and caressing the army. Not that he will ever seek to destroy the representative body, for it will occur to him, as a warning example, that even Cromwell, though unable to get on with any Parliament, could never do without one; nor need he even feel tempted to do so as long as he can subordinate to his will every Assembly, however chosen, through the magic virtue of the blood he has inherited, and the popularity he thereby enjoys. But, among a people who, nationally speaking, have no fixed ideas on government, or its best forms, and cannot, therefore, be relied upon for an indefinite time, let him beware of the imperial purple, and a life-long presidency, if he loves permanence of power and hopes to see days of happiness; or otherwise, if French history have any truth in it, his last state will be as bad as, and perhaps worse than, any he has yet experienced.

Paris, February 5, 1851.

LETTER XXVIII.

If I were his countryman, and could without impropriety address the Chief Magistrate of the French Republic, I would, with the most profound respect, do so in some such words as these:—

The position of your Excellency is certainly not an easy one, but it is less difficult than that of any other man who can aspire to the Presidency of this country at the next election; because, to accomplish your purpose—a prolongation of power,—nothing is required of you but to wait, and instead of active courage, to exercise a patient forbearance. While Monarchists, Republicans, and Socialists cannot cease from agitation without relatively losing ground, and while they are consequently in continued danger of committing blunders, you alone, by refraining from excess of action and by deterring your over-zealous friends from too much speaking, will be constantly bettering your condition. Your best policy for the present, seems to be that which was graphically called by one of America's greatest statesmen, "a masterly inactivity;" nor do I see any reason why you should depart from such policy, even in word — why, as some imperiously demand, you should condescend so much as to declare, for example, your *intention* in regard to the elections of 1852. The oath of a man and the word of a prince, if originally of any value, gain no strength by repetition, and an honorable mind shrinks equally from exacting or conceding such a sacrifice. But there is such a thing as the voluntary surrender of a pledge, and, other means failing, even a written Constitution, which neither time has hallowed nor custom rendered dear, may, I hold, be honorably nullified by the votes of a free people, when a host of malignant Shylocks are on the watch, railing for the forfeit of their bond. With faith on your side without works, the French people, who once made you their first magistrate for your name's sake, will make you so again, gladly rendering back your plighted word, because they feel you to be a State necessity, and instinctively know that in a violent strife of parties the man who can most surely ward off present calamity is their best refuge. This proposition may be a problem in the eyes of those who, with M. Guizot, regard a tomorrow's Monarchy as the only and omnipotent panacea — "the be-all and the end-all here;" but leave the masses to themselves, and in due time they will work it out. The masses are proud of the work of their own hands, and as such are you regarded by them. They often delight in its overthrow, it is true, but they like not that others should do the business for them, much less that another object of worship should be set up in place of their own. Had you frankly thrown yourself upon them from the beginning, eschewing all ultraism, you might at this moment have safely set every party threat at defiance; and even as it is, no Bourbon can be a stumbling-block in your way, for none among the people associate with that time-honored, but also time-dishonored name, the idea of such a just measure of liberty as leaves no room for licentiousness, nor of that equality before the law which pays no respect to persons, nor of that Christian fraternity which, grafted on the most amiable sentiments of our feeble nature, cannot be trampled out of existence by brute force, nor be driven from among men by stupid exaggeration. Neither can any of the sons of Orleans come between you and the people's favor, for their father's faults wrought a void in the national affection, which not all their own peculiar virtues will for a long time be able to fill. Nor can statesman, general, or politician, now known to us, stand any chance beside you, for so limited is the popular information, especially in rural districts, respecting the most distinguished among them, that to their names, if entered for the Presidental course, must be annexed a running commentary explanatory of who and what they are; while to that of Bonaparte need nothing be added — not even what the unprompted heart of France supplied in 1848 — Nephew of the Emperor, hereditary enemy of Kings and destroyer of Republics!

Most prophetically was it said, a few days since, by the journal in which I hope this letter will have the honor of appearing, "that to retain the Government, the (French) nation must sacrifice the Constitution, or to retain the Constitution it must sacrifice the Government;" and, if we substitute for the word "Government," the name of Prince Louis Napoleon, there can be but little doubt, it appears to me, which of these alternatives will happen, supposing that you discreetly leave to others the initiative of what your oath of office forbids you to attempt. Only show the world, by your obedience to law and respect for a majority of the nation, that you love your country better than yourself, and through dread of their common enemy — the Red Republic — all men of order, irrespective of party considerations, will eventually range themselves on your side, and by some means or other, shaping the Constitution to their ends, will, though perhaps at the very last moment, supplicate you to stand up once more a barrier against misrule.

If I deemed this people as fit for the government they in form affect, as I trust they will be, some scores of years hence, there would be the strongest reasons in my mind for deprecating your re-election; but, believing you to be one of the many instruments in the hand of Providence for conducting them through their long revolutionary struggle, I heartily pray for your success. Not that I think you can save France, but that by means of you, France will for a time save herself. What she wants of you is a breathing-turn which will afford space for her to look about and decide on the *immediate* future — to settle, at least for a season, and by a sensible majority of the people, whether, when another hour of agony shall arrive — as arrive it will — her choice must lie only between the bloody sword of a successful soldier and the blood-colored flag of a triumphant demagogue.

But, for yourself, abstain, I entreat you, from every act of violence, however strong be the temptation and however subtle the arguments of those around you. Twice have you undertaken, and, as I believe, with honest heart, the salvation of France in your own way; and twice have you signally failed. Beware — even if superstition be no part of your Imperial inheritance — of a third essay; for *third* failures are proverbially fatal.

Thus much, Sir — if a Frenchman and permitted so to do — would I, with that observance always due to the Chief of a State, say to his Excellency the President; and thus much, too, should I be rejoiced to have him hear from any lips, not only for his own and his country's sake, but likewise for the sake of others, who, strangers like myself, have here concentrated for the time being all the dearest interests of life.

Paris, April 29, 1851.

LETTER XXIX.

* If there is one good quality which a Frenchman lacks, it is patience. He will try all things in turn, but will hold fast to none of them long enough to satisfy all parties concerned of the extent of defects to be remedied. A man proverbially wise recommended in his time the correction of an erring child, but he never said, "Slay him!" The Anglo-Saxon race have been in the habit of amending their political offspring, but the Gallic humor, on the contrary, delights in an entirely new creation; and the worst of this peculiar temperament is, that in any new political experiment, however gross and palpable may be its faults, no two parties are ever agreed as to the time and means of curing them. I can easily understand, when a knot is choking one, why he should cut it, but when there is time for untying it I do not perceive the wisdom of haste and violence, in spite of law and in defiance of prejudice.

* The following remarks upon the state of parties in France are from the pen of our occasional correspondent, "A States-Man," whose opinions as those of an intelligent American residing in Paris are deserving of attention.— *Times*.

Different sets of men here, whose political creeds are pretty much alike, have been lately trying, with more or less mutual good faith, to effect what is called a *fusion;* by which, the metaphor being dropped, is meant another restoration of monarchy and at a single blow. They have had a fair field, and no impediments of muncipal law have been thrown in the way of their treasonable projects, for treasonable those projects certainly are which, in the face of a legally appointed Republic, undisguisedly aim at the discomfiture of a President and the induction of a King.

But with all their pains they have made no sensible progress, because, among other reasons, they differ, it seems, about the division of the expected spoil. Partisans of the elder branch of Royalty claim the first fruits of success as theirs by right of birth, while those of the younger shoot, unmindful that the same popular breath which made them what they were did also unmake them, would fain take their seats, too, above the salt at the table of good things in prospect, despising the crumbs that may chance to fall beneath it. Both, however, reckon without their host — the people, who are not so ready to be *fusioné*, I suspect, as it is believed. For the like mental process has been going on in France since three-score years and more which prevailed in the United States during their transition from a colonial to an independent existence. So long as these owned allegiance to the British crown, England — the "old country," as they termed their fatherland, — was fondly regarded by them as their home, and her King was honored by them as their King; but at the present day, whoever should seek to rekindle in the American heart that superstitious reverence for a crowned head without which monarchy is "not half made up" would be universally treated as an imposter or an idiot. So in France the sentiment of loyalty to a Sovereign because he is a Sovereign, which in former days flourished as vigorously here as in England, where it makes part and parcel of every man's nature, is wholly extinguished, except among a few incurable Legitimist dreamers and their Quixotic disciples. And yet, because this sentiment once survived in England the fall of a single anointed head, it is weakly fancied by these isolated few that in their country also it has outlived not only the wholesale butchery of royal and noble personages, but even the degradation and defilement of everything pertaining to the kingly office and the highest rank.

But, supposing the heir of the Bourbons at the Tuileries — an event quite the reverse of impossible — what would be his condition? To say nothing of more material obstacles at his very advent, under what flag could he meet the greetings of his countrymen? Would he, with the fatal consistency of others of the same race, who learn not and forget not, dare to raise the colorless banner of his ancestors, and prove faithful to the antecedents of his house, or would he envelope his restored rights in those tri-colored folds of his hereditary enemies under which they made the conqueror's tour of Europe? And those rights, the divinity of which is his weakness and his strength, how could he persuade the present race of Frenchmen that they are more than human? His task would be that of a giant, his tools those of a dwarf. Even Napoleon, with all his victorious wreaths new planted on his youthful brow, with a whole continent trembling beneath his blows, and with an army in his right hand compact and irresistible as a Theban phalanx, — even he was sorely perplexed to bring order out of disorder, to assign his proper place to every man, while he himself set things by the rule, and kept them so. And how long did he endure? What chance then of maintaining his position, much less of doing good, under circumstances not dissimilar to those in which that man of iron mould and will was placed, has a quiet gentleman, between thirty and forty years of age, nurtured by tender hands, full of book-learning, if you will, but wholly uninstructed by the world's rough teaching, — what earthly chance, I ask, has he of restoring to troubled France the repose she needs, or to humbled Royalty the dignity it wants?

No, the time of Henry V. is not yet, and a King, therefore, being for the present out of the question, the popular choice at the next presidential election must necessarily fall upon the actual occupant of the Elysée, or it will decide nothing more than what names are to be submitted for preference to the Assembly's wisdom; because, barring a miracle, no candidate *eligible by law*, either from the ranks of order or disorder, can possibly unite in his person a sufficient number of votes to secure his election at the polls. If the people declare by a large majority that they will have Prince Louis Bonaparte to preside over them for another term, all except the Socialists will array themselves by his side, and there will be nothing worse than an *émeute* to crush; but under all other conceivable circumstances a civil war is highly probable, if, forsooth, there be civil virtue enough in the total absence of political training to supply such a sharp remedy for grievances, whether real or imaginary, but both equally inconsistent with the country's internal peace.

If I were as unfortunate in the possession of power as is the French President, and in the love of it as he is reputed to be, I would on the appointed day and hour resign my commission according to my oath, and take a station, which no one could deny me, among the citizens of the Republic. Then, if those citizens saw fit to choose me by an important majority to be again their chief, I would accept office, considering the Constitution, *pro hâc vice*, as nullified, unless previously revised, and respectfully await the action of the legislative body, knowing beforehand that, in dread of a Red Republic, it would never venture to put a veto upon my second elevation to power. But were my majority inconsiderable, or were my name only one of several for which the greatest number of votes had been cast, in both events, regardless of every individual concern, I would retire with unsoiled dignity to private life, refusing to owe aught to a meagre plurality either in or out of the National Assembly, being but too sure that the time was not far distant when all, save the declared enemies of the public good, would clamor for the return of him whose mission in the cause of order had been as yet but half accomplished.

Paris, June 3, 1851.

LETTER XXX.

When the late ex-King, Louis Philippe, came to the French throne he had an opportunity, such as rarely offers, to benefit not only his own country but the whole European Continent. In respect to foreign Powers, he had only to maintain a firm, independent and national bearing, and the popular force which carried him to his high place would have made Legitimist arrogance quail before, instead of affecting to despise, him; and in the domestic relations of the State, had he gradually and discreetly extended the right of suffrage, had he set his face against Parliamentary bribery, had he extended a parental regard to the amelioration of the condition of the laboring classes, and economically administered the finances of France and his own, he would have become the best beloved and most powerful Sovereign ever known to Frenchmen. But no, he would have none of these things.

The friendship of foreign potentates he preferred to the affections of his own people, a working majority in the Chamber to a majority in the hearts of the governed, and a paltry alliance with a member of a reigning family in a second-rate kingdom to the good will of the only country on this side of the Atlantic which in the hour of trouble could and would faithfully have stood him in stead. And so he fell, and has passed away, but the evil he did lives after him, and will not thus pass away, but is now preying upon the vitals of France.

When President Bonaparte came to assume a power so idly lost, he too, like his predecessor, had a glorious part to enact in behalf of Frenchmen and the race of man. Two ways lay before him : one, harnessing himself to the old-fashioned ricketty machine here called government, to pull and haul it, like any other political hack, through the dirtiest official ruts, trimming his course to suit every party by turns except the right one, and satisfying none; the other, to throw himself frankly, as with six millions of votes at his back he might have safely done, into the hands of those who lifted him from exile to a palace, loyally espousing, without regard to party, their common cause, whereby he would most have profited his own. And which has he preferred, light or darkness? The example of a banished Sovereign — was it lost upon him or not? And the trust he reposed in irresponsible friends — has it proved more worthy than that unfailing source of all national strength — a people's love?

Yet much may be said in extenuation of any errors he has committed. Many of the ablest men in France, to their lasting reproach, have held themselves aloof in the hour of need. The National Assembly, too, has set itself in array against him in season and out of season, and the sorriest feature in the history of the last few days is the scornful derision with which that body received the message of the Chief Magistrate of the land. A wise man, however mighty and void of generosity, never scoffs at a foe till he feels his neck beneath his heel; but a foolish congregation, history teaches us, often humbles itself before a single inflexible will which once it reviled. One would think, from their bearing on Tuesday last, that the majorlty of the Representatives hoped by their mocking laughter to drive the President to some act of folly, or at least to let him know that henceforth peace is at an end between him and them. But let them look to it, for if I scan aright the shadows of events, the Presidential crisis will be decided without, and not within, the Assembly. Let them, as their political aspirations all reach beyond the present year — let them look well to the consequences of their untimely and contemptuous mirth, or the bitter sneer of to-day may breed the bloody deed of tomorrow.

If baited beyond measure, the President may possibly turn to bay, and sin unpardonably against the State. But, barring such an act, which increase of years and experience renders highly improbable, I am convinced that no supposable folly on his part can effectually balk his hopes of a re-election at the expiration of his present term of office. I admit that wise and clever men — men, too, of no lowly condition in political life, differ from me widely, but then their opinions are not those of impartial spectators, and it seems to me that they do not properly appreciate the advantages which an inevitable change in the electoral law will bring to the President. Previously to the prorogation of the Assembly a modification of that law, as touching municipal elections alone, but to be extended hereafter to all other elections, was the subject of serious discussion; and the calculation is that its effect will be to restore the elective franchise to 2,000,000 or 3,000,000 of electors so improvidently excluded from the polls by the hasty and intemperate legislation of last year. Now, whenever a bill restoring to so many Frenchmen their rights shall have received the sanction of the people's Representatives, three-fourths of the votes thus recovered will be cast for him in whose name order has hitherto been preserved, and to him will blindly be attributed all the honor, however small may be his due. They will be cast for him, because they will come from men whose vocations require tranquillity. Respectable journeymen, honest peasant laborers, and farmers of small patches, whose way of life renders a fixed residence of three years and the proof of it equally impossible, will naturally cling to one under whom they have enjoyed a respite from trouble, rather than take to another whom they know nothing about.

Then, in considering the chances of M. Bonaparte, who is there to oppose him on the Presidential field? Two candidates alone can be put forward without risking a ridiculous failure. One of these must be the representative of Monarchists, and of united Monarchies — of Legitimists, Orleanists, and Fusionists; the other of Socialists, or, under whatever name they may go, of all enemies to the present establishments of society. The former of the supposed candidates, according to present appearances, will be General Changarnier, a man artificially reserved but naturally talkative and boastful. Under ordinary circumstances self-possessed and taciturn by calculation, it is feared by his best friends that, when standing face to face with bright hopes and a brilliant future, habit will break down before nature and that the tones of the barrack room will pervade the hall of debate. Hence it is that, no perfect confidence being placed in his wisdom, no enthusiasm can be felt or communicated by those who regard him as a convenient instrument for unseating the President. And hence it is, too, that, for fear of his using himself up, his name will be kept back till the latest possible moment. The other candidate — a Red man, either M. Rollin or M. Carnot, but probably the former, the latter not being sufficiently notorious — will, if heartily supported by his party, prove a perfect godsend to M. Bonaparte; for then, rather than risk an evil that may crush them, or trust their last venture to an African general whose character is an enigma, all other parties will eagerly fall back on the man they now denounce.

Say what they may, the partisans of the obnoxious law of May 31st know, for its authors and advocates have repeatedly declared as much, that it was a political blow at the *Mountain*, to show not only what could be, but what should be done. They know, too, that those who made it were not less astonished than other men, to find about 3,000,000 excluded from the privilege of voting, instead of 600,000 or 800,000, the sum total of the floating population on which they had counted; and they ought to know that the continuance of this law in its pristine absurdity, will be a weapon in the hands of their enemies which time cannot wear out nor force destroy. Whatever may have been the President's motives for attempting in such a sweeping manner what the Assembly had already begun, the measure wears every appearance of having been dictated by an unworthy desire to supplant that body in the affections of the common people. Let that, however, be as it may, if his object, a re-election, be in any way advanced by the untoward step he has taken, his will be the regret at having employed such questionable means, while the country will be the gainer by it. At least, I think so. For who so well as he can occupy the Presidential chair while Monarchy in France continues impossible and Republicanism impracticable? Who so well as he can fulfil the requisitions of the present times? He is a prince, and a prince his countrymen will have to rule over them. He is not a soldier, and of military dominion they had enough in his uncle's time. He is by necessity the antipodes of legitimacy, which has left hardly a fibre in the soil, and of Orleanism, which never took root in it. He will not cast in his lot with the Reds, for he knows this country cannot be governed by its *queue*. In a word, if he would serve himself, he must faithfully serve, till its mission be accomplished, the nondescript Government here, which any other President would be likely to displace for something infinitely worse.

That he will remain, as he now is, ineligible, is pronounced to be a certainty; but as opposed to three or four millions of votes, and universal apprehension, which will prevail some months hence, of what use will be a written Constitution, except in the hands of some miscreants who would light a civil war with it? The rest is a matter between him and his own conscience, of which I am not a little distrustful; for a man who, after the shining example given by him at Boulogne to persons of Lopez's stamp, could have the temerity, at the hazard of offending the people of a friendly "sister Republic," to mix himself up with anything pertaining to the Cuban invasion, cannot be over-burdened with scrupulousness. If it be true that Lord Palmerston is in league with him, and that French and English ships of war are to haunt the Gulf of Mexico, visiting and searching American vessels, his Lordship may be indulging nothing more than his customary passion for intermeddling, and the President a sudden weakness for his "friendly relations with Spain." But should anything serious come of it, I can tell these two gentlemen that the "energetic Yankees," as you love to call us, the English cotton spinners and the French silk weavers, will give them both a lesson for meditation in retirement which will last them to the end of their lives.

Everybody in America, of common understanding and honest principles, condemned the expedition to Cuba from first to last. Even the invaders themselves now are loudest in the execration of it. The wisdom, therefore, of non-interference in any way whatever on the part of England or France, is "as plain as way to parish church."

Paris, November 9, 1851.

LETTER XXXI.

Man, as you know, is a credulous being, and one race of men is said to be pre-eminently gullible.

A few months since the cry of a French invasion startled nine-tenths of the inhabitants of the British Isles from their propriety, and made the halls of council ring with a diversity of opinions, some of which were far more amusing than instructive. A crafty and well-feigned indifference, however, on one side of the Channel, and a Militia Bill on the other, restored confidence where it had been shaken, and tranquillity where it had been disturbed. So that now to whisper a doubt of Gallic faith, or Bonapartean honor, would be accounted by more than one of your contemporaries a crime against the peace of Europe. Yet, truth to tell, causes remain unchanged, motives unaltered, ideas fixed; and it is only the means of working mischief, more dynastic than French, that do not rest the same, but, on the contrary, go on day by day increasing in compactness, vigor and virulence.

That the Prince President of France is unscrupulously ambitious is evident from his uniform disregard of every ordinance which has ever stood in the way of his boundless desires. Neither the life, nor the liberty, nor the property of his fellow man has he "set at a pin's fee," whenever an object, right in his eyes, was to be accomplished. And yet this man the French accept as their master — nay! the ministers of religion profanely hail him as the "Saviour of France!"

I have been told by one who was the friend of Louis Napoleon's youth, that the Prince's heart was ever set, with a sort of superstitious faith, upon the untenable eminence he now occupies. To a man who has thus succeeded in the face of every probability nothing must appear impossible — not even the achievement of what is called greatness, in the world's loose talk. — But, till now, he has done nothing and gained nothing which could satisfy an ambition even less craving than his. The ascent from the condition of a penniless wanderer to an estate that, for present power, Louis XIV. himself might almost have envied, has been so easy, when once begun, that it has served to whet, not glut, the passion which aspires to yet a loftier height. To mount, however, an imperial throne, making his stepping-stones a crew of abject senators, with mendacious petitions in their servile hands, is not the exaltation, I fancy, which causes him a moment's uneasy calculation. This he might have done yesterday amid a deafening chorus of hallelujahs. He may do it tomorrow, and all France — all living France, at least, will shout, "Amen!" No, it is something less patent and palpable to the common eye which stirs *his* soul, and fires him with a determination to out-Napoleon Napoleon himself, by some astounding act beyond the borders of his own country, that shall make the sacrifice of her liberties pale before it.

The Emperor, great, perhaps, as mere mortal, lacking virtue, can ever hope to be, with continental Europe at his feet, would have been universally triumphant, had not England, Proteus-like, met him at every turn. But England's soil he was allowed neither to touch nor to tread. He saw it, and perished.

Now, even if the Prince President, by force of a military genius hitherto unsuspected but by himself, could, as did his uncle before him, push emperors from their stools, and crowd his antechambers with uncrowned kings, he would accomplish nothing more than had already proved of no avail to secure a permanence of fortune. But if, in addition to all this, he could put a bit in the mouth of the Island Queen, and make her merchant princes, were it but for a season, tributary to his wants, — if he could illuminate his conquest, however transiently, by the light of her capital in flames, and his triumphant progress, hurried though it might be, from port to port by bonfires of her floating bulwarks, — then, indeed, would he have outstripped his prototype, and then would he, as he thinks, have fulfilled his mission by wiping out the stain upon his country's honor, inflicted by that great and just man who never, except in death, caused an English tear to fall.

That such a vision is no stranger to his waking dreams there are reasons for believing, as was shown some months ago both in and out of Parliament. Since then, in one of the few unguarded moments ever known to him, he was heard to exclaim, "The catastrophe of Waterloo shall be avenged!" For this my authority is good, — so good, in fact, that, were the reporter of his master's word to be publicly announced as such, better had it been for that man if a millstone about his neck had kept him forever in the distant province where he was born to nobler work than that in which he is now engaged. I do not deny that an attempt at such vengeance may seem improbable to your readers, — as improbable even as the attacks on Strasburg and Boulogne, had they been foretold, — almost as improbable, it may be, as a few years since would have been the prediction of a vault from a hired lodging to an imperial palace. But none of them will deem it impossible, if they have a correct notion of the national temper in France to back a daring deed, and of the equilibrium necessary here to be preserved between the demand and supply of glory, or if they have ever witnessed the ill-concealed writhings of a Frenchman whenever the name of Waterloo is pronounced.

Though the time for making the experiment will be adroitly chosen, I have no fear for the ultimate results. Nevertheless, it behoves all men to be upon their guard as to the possible future; and no Administration should be permitted an hour's relaxation while a Bonaparte possesses a tittle of power in France.

You need not be told how easy it is to make occasions when a course is once decided on. But my present object is to direct your attention especially to a particular means, conducting inevitably to war, which is available at all times to France, which may be employed when England is in trouble, and will certainly be seized upon when she is least prepared. Between the French possessions in Africa and the Empire of Morocco lies a strip of territory some thirty leagues in breadth, that in several respects bears a strong resemblance to the undefined borderland connecting England and Scotland in the good old times of rugging and riving. Upon this ground of a disputed ownership the French can, whenever it suits them, find cause of quarrel for the purpose of over-turning a semi-barbarous throne, which they have long coveted and are resolved to have. But England could not and would not remain an indifferent spectator of such proceedings. She will not suffer her important commerce with Morocco to be sacrificed with impunity.

War, therefore, projected and provided for by France, but unforeseen by England, would surely follow. Is it not, then, worth your while, as far as in you lies, to prevent the country from being lulled into a false security by the fallacious cry of " Peace, peace," when there is no peace, but only, in fact, a hollow truce?

Paris, Sept. 27, 1852.

LETTER XXXII.

The Island of Cuba will sooner or later become a component part of the United States of America; when and how, no one can now tell, though the moment and manner of the transformation are of serious import to all parties concerned. It will be changed from what it is to what it ought to be — from comparative weakness to positive strength — from partial cultivation to complete productiveness, and, in a word from Creole existence to American life. Whenever this change shall arrive, it will not be in obedience to mere accidents of war or diplomacy, though these may, indeed, hasten or retard it, but to an invariable law that reigned paramount long before the boasted name of Anglo-Saxon was invented, and has ever since been the moving cause in subjugating the hosts of India, in annihilating the tribes of North America, and will continue to be, as it is now, the rule of action, in rooting out the remnants of a degenerate race from the southern portion of that hemisphere. This law, embodied in the "Parable of the Talents," and as true in our day as it was eighteen centuries ago, teaches, by examples without number, that a rich but neglected soil, like other treasures intrusted to unprofitable servants, shall be taken away and be given to others less faithless than themselves. Cuba might be made to bring forth a hundredfold, and it does not produce sixty; and even of this sixtyfold no inconsiderable part is wasted, in contravention of another divine precept, that "the workman is worthy of his hire," and ought not to be even partially defrauded of the fruits of his toil. The Treasury of Spain opens and shuts periodically, as the "Queen of the Antilles" pours into it a tribute which is wholly unrequited. For what requital is it in return for enormous annual shipments of specie, or its equivalent, to have a foreign garrison to pay, feed, and clothe, a foreign fleet to support, and a foreign governor, who left his home with scarcely a coin in his pocket, to pamper on island produce till he has amassed a fortune worthy of a royal prince? Cuba, therefore, must fall, but only to rise again, regenerated by the ordeal through which she has to pass, and prepared, by the agency of new hands, to repay the fullest usury for gifts of nature which nowhere are surpassed.

It is a singular fact, the truth of which can be established by papers in the French State offices, and by authentic copies of the same in Downing-street, that shortly after the revolution of July there was a proposition made by the Spanish Government to transfer Cuba to France for a term of years, at a fixed rent; but that the English Foreign Secretary, having been apprised of the matter, put an end to the negotiation before it had reached maturity. Now, if Spain would have recourse to a similar expedient with regard to America, or, still better, if she could be induced to sell her property in that island outright, she would thereby be saved from adding another total loss to the heavy miscarriages already sustained by her in that quarter of the world. Interest, backed by the good sense of to-day, cries loudly to her on one side; but false pride, nursed by the bad temper of the past, cries more loudly on the other, and the wrong course she will inevitably follow; for experience is as often lost upon nations as upon individuals, and, till now, no Administration in Spain has exhibited a striking exception to this general rule.

But I do not esteem as a whit more wise those persons whose object is, *per fas et nefas*, a sudden and violent revolution in the relations of Cuba. They forget that when fruit is ripe it will fall of itself, and that while it is green none but blockheads or schoolboys will shake the tree, for fear of having their own crowns broken. Many of those who, in anticipation of the work of time, invaded that forbidden isle, expiated, as is well known, their folly and crime beneath the arm of the executioner. Admitting the strict justice of the sentence passed upon them, no one possessed of common feeling could refrain from yielding unstinted pity for their unhappy fate. But if, with that fate, and the Christian clemency of Spanish Royalty that followed it, yet fresh in the memory of all men, others more wicked, because better informed, than they, will seek to imitate their example in life, I, for one, care not if in death too they furnish a faithful parallel; and you may be sure that 999 of every 1,000 persons in the United States are of my way of thinking, because not a thousandth portion of the American community, it may be safely asserted, are so idle and unprincipled — nay, so stupid, as wantonly to turn their hands to robbery and murder, at the risk of involving their country in war, and of encircling their own necks with a halter.

The transition, come when it may, from a subject to an independent condition, from subordination to a distant Power to confederation with one adjacent, will doubtless occasion some temporary inconvenience to the inhabitants of Cuba; but to the whole commercial world it will, when completed, be of immediate service, by the development of new powers of production and of increased capacities of consumption in that island.

So little, however, are my sympathies enlisted on the side of marauders on a friendly soil, so persuaded am I that America has already more territory than is of use to her, except for the exclusion of strangers, so loathsome in my eyes is he who would set man at odds with his neighbor, and arm nation against nation, and, at the same time, so apprehensive am I of right and might being confounded in a contest between youth on the increase and age on the wane, that if the tempting "bit of ground" could be peacefully floated off some dark night beyond the reach of Yankee cupidity, I, for my part, would cheerfully bid it God speed, as, loosening its deep-sea moorings, it slipped noiselessly from its rocky bed.

If I were an absolute Abolitionist, with the ease of conscience peculiar to wronghead-ed-ness, I would do my utmost to wrench the "Queen of the Antilles" from the Queen of Spain, on the score of the frequent importation of slaves from Africa, which is countenanced, if not encouraged, by officers of the highest rank upon that island, in the service of the Crown. Nothing of the sort, it is needless to say, could happen there after the United States' laws had begun to operate, although, as on the Continent, the property of the white man in his slave, would, of course, be protected, and faithfully protected too, I should hope, if for no other reason, for the sake of the poor negro himself, notwithstanding "Uncle Tom," his "cabin," and the good dame Stowe to boot. I should hope so, because many years must elapse before our sombre-shaded brethren, do what we may, can be fitted for a better state than that they now occupy, and many more, I fear, must be added to these, if writers like the unfair author of the *Cabin* will persist, in spite of sense and honesty, in besmirching the character of the master, in order to contrast its simulated inky hue with the fantastic colors attributed by them to the slave; for, widening by such means the distance between the two, they weaken the arm of the only agent, the owner, through whom emancipation, if ever it is to be, can be accomplished, and thus run counter to their own professed schemes of benevolence.

Slave proprietors in America are, in my opinion, a sadly wronged set of people, and, above all, whenever an English pen or tongue is directed against them. It cannot be too often repeated that their fathers, notwithstanding prayers and remonstrances still on record, had sour grapes in the shape of countless cargoes of black flesh forced upon them by your fathers, and now, that their teeth are set on edge, they are coolly told to go to the Abolitionist practitioner for relief.

Though offences are easily forgiven and forgotten by the backslider himself, and still more easily by the heir to profits of successful crime, it ought ever to be remembered, while a single slave-stain soils the western shores of the Atlantic, that the harbors of Great Britain for a long time swarmed with shipping, owned and employed by Englishmen, for the transportation of human merchandise from the African coast to the markets of America.

If I were a slave owner, making the present French ruler my exemplar, I would no more think of giving emancipation to negroes than he does of conferring freedom on Frenchmen; and, indeed, judging from present appearances, I sometimes begin to doubt whether the latter are more worthy of the realities of liberty than the former. Like him, in all temporal concerns at least, I would make my subjects see with my eyes and hear with my ears; for neither pen, ink, nor paper, plain or printed, any more than plague, pestilence, and famine, if I could exclude them, should enter my domains while Abolitionists and their pernicious doctrines were abroad. On "Uncle Tom's" godmother, then, and her allies, who do evil on the mad chance of extracting a fanciful good from it, would rest the responsibility of leaving the negro in his bliss of ignorance, since to inflict wisdom upon him prematurely, as they are trying to do, must involve him and his master in one common ruin.

Paris, Nov. 10th, 1852.

LETTER XXXIII.

The leading article in your number of December 1st, on negro slavery in the United States, merits the thanks of every American who has feeling enough to appreciate the delicacy of treatment which the subject demanded, and sufficient sense to comprehend the consummate skill and admirable instinct with which it was handled. It ought to be studied by all abolitionist intermeddlers, for it teaches how close akin to evil is zeal without knowledge and enthusiasm without discretion. In a most limited space you have said so much so well, that nothing remains to be added but a few remarks which were suggested to me by the perusal of two extraordinary documents that have lately laid claim to public attention.

In one of these — the "address" prepared by the Earl of Shaftesbury for the "women of England," to be presented by them to their Trans-atlantic "sisters" — its author unequivocally assumes for his own countrymen a share in the pretended guilt of the American slave-owner, on the ground of their forefathers' agency in a traffic which, be it always remembered, the United States' Government was the first to denounce and punish as a crime against the law of nations. The unwelcome burden so manfully, though painfully, placed upon English shoulders by the noble earl, Lord Carlisle, in the other document alluded to, reluctantly fastens there, with, however, the somewhat undignified reservation, "that the onward course of the present century, which has witnessed in England the successive abolitions of the slave trade and of slavery, and in the United States the enactment of the Fugitive Slave Law, is daily tending to diminish the appositeness of this plea of complicity." These words, together with the acknowledgment of the said complicity, are to be found in an essay prefixed to the London edition of Mrs. Stowe's exaggerated, and therefore mischievous, portraiture of life in the Southern States. This prefatory piece of supererogation, allow it to be said in passing, strikes me as being equally feeble and illogical, and so thoroughly revolutionary in character as to be wholly unworthy of the wisdom supposed to be innate, in certain cases, by right of birth. It is feeble, because its tenor throughout is "letting I dare not wait upon I would." It is illogical, because, while with his pen its author goads the anti-slavery party in America to open defiance of laws, he naïvely prescribes, "Let the only weapon of warfare in this high quarrel, be the concurring conscience of mankind." And it is revolutionary, because its tendency is to subvert all rule, by the encouragement it gives to rebellion against constituted authority, and by the commendation it bestows upon "those who, let the law of the land be for the moment what it may, make it the business of their lives to harbor the fugitive slave;" that is, to set at nought the commands of the very men whom they themselves have chosen to be their governors and guides. Once allow this product of *inherited* wisdom to be orthodox, and might will become right. The Anti-renter in New York, the Nullifier in South Carolina, the smuggler everywhere, and all bad men, taking Lord Carlisle's preface as their text-book, will scoff at the sword of justice, which now protects her tribunals, high and low, from the inroads of individual judgment and the onslaughts of fanaticism.

But such testimony as is borne by the two noble volunteers to acts committed by Englishmen so long ago, with its accompanying admission of a responsibility which survives the lapse of time, is of a certain value, not only for its freshness, but on account of the exalted character and station enjoyed by those gentlemen; yet, if it were wanting, the facts of the case are of easy proof, and to the moral sense of every man the heirship to the odious accountability must be as clear as, in the nature of things, it will remain unchangeable. The confession, however, coming from a source so elevated and irreproachable in most respects, answers the excellent purpose of enabling Americans, without any compromise of dignity, to enter court, not as defendants by themselves, but as co-penitents in an action whose commencement was a crime, whose continuance is a plague, and whose end, if precipitated, may be desolation to the master, and must be destruction to the slave. For it would be less cruel to turn your stall-fed beast out to graze upon a macadamised high-road, than to force his liberty upon the untutored negro; and as to instructing him beyond what is necessary to his well-being hereafter, it would be the height of folly to attempt such a thing, so long as half-crazed or reckless adventurers, in a cause which they cannot or will not understand, are ever ready to ply him with publications that are calculated to set in motion the worst passions of a sadly neglected race. Within an hour I have heard a Southern planter, of no ordinary rank in America, and of still higher in Europe, exclaim, " Gladly would I surrender all my slaves without a penny in exchange for them (and hundreds of proprietors are anxious to do the same) to any one who is able and willing to give a sufficient guarantee that, with their newly acquired freedom, they shall have the means of a comfortable existence." Why, a freed negro, wanting such means for immediate use, is but a slave without a master — the most pitiable of mortals — as was proved in your own colonies, where the black man, on the day of his liberation, gained little else than the privilege of supporting his aged parents and helpless children, when he himself had hardly the energy and capacity to provide his own daily sustenance.

Some few of your readers may, perhaps, not be aware of the fact that the General Government at Washington has no more control over State slavery than any man living has over the new French Emperor. The Governments, consequently, of those States wherein slavery exists are the chief mediums through which is to be effected, if the thing be practicable, any fundamental change or partial modification in their domestic concerns. But, besides men in office, who are the first to be consulted, there are, of course, many others high in authority for their personal worth, all of whom ought to be directly addressed by volunteer reformers, if, indeed, notoriety be not the sole object of these persons, and if, in their Christian esteem, "the subject of slavery constitutes," as Lord Carlisle opines, "the most difficult and solemn problem that now engages the attention of mankind."

And this brings me to the point which I had in view when commencing this letter. The two noblemen to whose productions I have referred, with their coadjutors, male and female, do not, in my opinion, go to work the right way to insure success. They should take the bull by the horns if they would avoid being tossed. Instead of sitting quietly at home in their easy chairs, inditing prefaces and addresses, and publishing them by the press or word of mouth, they should gird up their loins, like the Apostles, who toiled while they preached, or like the Crusaders, who fought while they exhorted, and with their own hands should they set about the reformation which they appear to have so much at heart, remembering that words no less than faith, without works, are dead. What I say is intended in all seriousness, not for Lord Carlisle's "concurring conscience of mankind"—a sounding nonentity, but for his own individual conscience, and for the conscience of every one who shapes his course as it is pricked out for him by that abolitionist pioneer on the chart of imaginary duty. I wish to see those who profess to believe that the slave-owner can be converted and that slavery can be ameliorated, put their arguments to the test of actual experiment. Their literary progenies, brought forth at a distance of 3,000 or 4,000 miles, cost them nothing but pen, ink and paper, with now and then a little "windy suspiration of forced breath;" they avail nothing but to provoke, and they prove nothing but an excess of ill-employed time. They may come from the heart, but no one will care whether they do or not, unless some personal sacrifice be at the back of them; and poor is the chance of their reaching the heart through the cold channel of a public meeting, where each individual on his or her person bears a cotton tribute to slave labor, or through the passionless column of a newspaper, most of whose component parts have been moistened with the sweat of a "human chattel."

What I want these gentlemen to do, with or without their fair accomplices, is, straightway, even now in mid-winter, to take the first steamer for America, to go in companies of twenties, sixties and hundreds, to the scenes of their lucubrations, and there to examine for themselves and counsel what are the best measures to be adopted. The Southern planter, I can assure you from my own experience, is remarkable for his hospitality; and the English gentlemen, to say nothing of English ladies, with their purposes honestly set forth, as they necessarily would be, could not fail to meet with a most honorable reception under his roof. Then they would see with their own eyes, and not with the eyes of a romancer, what things are true and what are false, and then, too, by propounding, face to face, such arguments as seemed good to them at a distance, they might, perchance, bring about, at least, a partial purgation of the Anglo-American plague-spot, which now so sorely afflicts them.

To quit a comfortable fireside on an errand of this sort, I admit, would not be the most agreeable undertaking in the month of December; but when the disciple to do the work of his Lord, threw down his net, his only means of livelihood, did he consult his personal comfort? Or, when the anointed king forsook crown and country, wife and children, to redeem the sepulchre of that same Lord, did he expect to find a bed of roses in the East?

Some, if not all, of these sentimental champions of their dark-colored brethren will, I fear, suddenly discover that they have "married a wife" or a husband, as the case may be, or "bought a piece of land, or a yoke of oxen," and will, therefore, "pray to be excused" from doing what has been proposed by me in no spirit of levity. But if so, and if they refuse to do their great Master's business, such as they deem it to be, except by "mint of phrases and sweet words," then I too will crave for indulgence when I recommend to them a becoming silence for the future, as the surest means of preventing the aggravation of an evil, which the best friend and most powerful advocate of the negro ever known in America* was forced to acknowledge had been greatly increased by rash and ignorant interference.

Paris, December 23, 1853.

* Dr. Channing on "Slavery in the United States."

LETTER XXXIV.

Newspapers being intended for public instruction, and not for private uses, I desire to obtrude nothing of a personal nature upon you, except, should your indulgence allow me, to declare that I am not an "infidel," as your correspondent, "An American," very facetiously affects to believe, but, on the contrary, that I am ready, whenever a man can be found who thinks more highly of the Christian religion than I do myself, straightway to forego my own opinions and take his. This I say, not for the satisfaction or edification of my fellow-countryman, to whom I owe scant courtesy, but in order that these few words, if through your kindness they ever see the light, may not be deprived by undeserved aspersion of the little weight which possibly pertains to them of right.

Even if it be true, as your correspondent avers, while I unequivocally deny, that "the laws of every slave State in America forbids you, under pains and penalties, to teach a slave to read," there is, so far as they concern volunteer foreign instruction, no lack of wisdom or justice in such laws. The masters are themselves Christians, and, self-preservation being dictated both by divine and human authority, they are probably the best judges of the degree of knowledge that can be bestowed upon the slave, consistently with the welfare of the whole community. I speak from good information when I affirm that instruction, and religious instruction, too is not withheld from the blacks, and that if the doors were once indiscriminately opened to teachers of all sorts, there would not be a white man in the Southern States who could sleep in safety without a "revolver" within his reach.

"An American" next runs a muck at slavery itself, as though that institution, as he calls it, were esteemed a greater evil by him than by you or me. But even he, in all his self-plenitude, prudently shrinks from indicating "what means should be employed to do away with the difficulty," instead of boldly proclaiming, with Friend Sturge and his three good men and true, that "Now's the day, and now's the hour," or like Lord Shaftesbury, who, having nothing at risk, graciously grants a six-and-thirty months' grace for the complete emancipation of negroes by the million! The noble Earl might, in his mercy to master as well as to slave, have conceded a margin somewhat broader, I think, without damage to character on either side.

I am not a preacher of the Word, as "An American" seems to be, but I am sufficiently versed in the Scriptures to tell him, when he audaciously puts slave-holding and stealing in the same category, that while there is no stronger reference in the Bible to the former act, or habit, than " Slaves, obey in all things your masters," which lends at least a negative countenance to the "institution," there is a very distinct injunction against the latter, with which we are all tolerably familiar from our infancy. I can easily conceive of a child's being justified in disobedience to a father who orders him to violate a written commandment of God, but it surpasses my intelligence to trace any similitude between such disobedience and the insolent defiance of a law, which, after long and anxious deliberation, was framed by the wisest and best men in America, acting under the responsibility of an oath that required them to consult the general good.

It should be remembered by your one-idea-ed correspondent that there are other "neighbors" in the world to be "loved as ourselves" besides the fugitive slave, that there are other interests to be respected which are not less valuable than his, and that, if we "do unto others as we would have them do unto us," the white owner ought to be admitted to some small participation in our universal benevolence.

6*

"An American" would have done much better had he left alone "the men of New England and of New England descent, who cannot obey the Fugitive Law," because they not only do obey it, but will be compelled to obey it. I happen to know that part of the country as well as, I suspect, if not better than, he, for I am no more a Southerner than I am "an infidel," and, though my affections and prejudices are naturally with those of my more immediate kin, truth constrains me to dissent from the immodest assertion that the people of New England "have ever been, and are now, the most conscientious men on that (the American) continent." The port of Boston swarmed with slave-ships, — so much for the "have ever been;" and, as for the "are now"—— but the Great Napoleon's maxim about the domestic ablution of articles in a certain condition I am not disposed to neglect. *Verbum sat sapienti*, but "the way of a fool is right in his own eyes," even if a rod be upheld before him.

Paris, Dec. 27, 1853.

LETTER XXXV.

Russia, by might or assumed right, has for some time exercised a protectorate over a portion of the Sultan's subjects; and, as a guarantee of the continuance of this pretended right, she has seized upon certain countries which do not belong to her. Whether iniquity or impudence more abounds in this transaction it is hard to say, but is it any worse than what England (by your own accounts) has been guilty of in India, France in Algeria, Austria and Prussia in Poland, or the United States in the territory of the aborigines of America? Not a whit. Whence comes, then, the clamor against the Czar which is continually dinned in our ears? "A love of fair play" is answered on one side, and "hatred of oppression" on the other. Now, this is sheer nonsense, not to add hypocrisy. It comes from fear — rank, though not unreasonable, fear — of the great Northern Power which threatens to deluge all Europe. More evil arises from self-deception than from any lie that can be palmed upon us by others, and concealment of the truth often leads to more error than positive falsehood. From active fraud in others we are able to defend ourselves, but from lurking mischief in our own bosoms there is no protection. Europe has eyes, but she sees not; she has ears, but she will not hear. The first Emperor Napoleon declared that in fifty years she would become either republican or Cossack. Republicanism has been tried, and has failed, and now the other alternative "looms in the distance." All turns upon the present, and upon what the present shall bring forth. If the Emperor of Russia be not beaten out of the position he occupies, if he retain but a single outpost, he will in the long run rest master of the field. His policy is not of to-day nor of yesterday, nor is it his alone or his brother's before him, but it is emphatically Russian, and Russian it will be, till the words of Napoleon be fulfilled, unless united Europe take the bull by the horns, and, instead of being tossed, toss him. If Turkey were alone concerned, if she alone were materially interested in her manly resistance, not an arm would be lifted in her behalf, not a word would be said about "fair play", or of "oppression," for not a single Power could come into court with clean hands. But common danger breeds common feeling, and Heaven grant that its product may be also common sense; for, if common action in the right direction do not follow, woe be to Europe!

So well as I can comprehend the heterogeneous mass of facts and fictions, assertions and contradictions, which add weight without strength to most of the journals of Europe, it seems to me that the main, if not only hope of preserving the general peace rests on the chance of coaxing the Czar to become a party to a joint protectorate, to be extended over all the Christian subjects of the Sultan, in place of that singlehanded one which he has heretofore exercised in his own solitary self-sufficiency. Now, this protectorate, which implies either weakness or wickedness in the sovereign against whom it may at will be employed, and which therefore cannot be of his own seeking, is consistent or inconsistent with the law of nations; it is right, or it is wrong. If right, why have other Powers meddled with it, and with its legitimate consequences, the occupation of the Principalities, the slaughter of thousands and the expenditure of millions? But, if wrong, under what pretext do these said Powers wish to share it? The answer is plain. They dare not, and this is the only reason under the sun why they cannot, strip Russia of it, and they slyly hope to weaken its effects by becoming participators in the disreputable and cunningly devised scheme. I doubt their success. Truth and plain dealing, in the pursuit of an honorable object, will carry a man or a nation through a world of trouble, but no sort of dealing will sanctify the subversion, by division, of the Sultan's authority. Neither Russia, nor England, nor France have any more right to interfere with the Christian population of Turkey, than the United States have to come between the Crown of Spain and a host of Yankee Cuban proprietors who are clamorous for protection, or rather for annexation, in which protection is always sure to end. Is not the Sultan as independent a sovereign as Queen Victoria or the Emperor Napoleon? and is he not as free to defy foreign interference as President Pierce? And what would the Queen of England, or the Emperor of France, or the President of the United States say to any earthly potentate who dared to put himself between the ruler and the ruled?

Their answers, if any were vouchsafed, would be, I guess, not sweet, but short. Believe me, Turkey is not yet weak enough to be put into leading-strings.

If that portion of her population which is not infidel be oppressed, of which there has lately been no proof, let it continue to suffer till suffering bring forth strength, rather than call in third parties, who will infallibly finish matters by finding sovereign and subject both in the wrong. It will cost the "Four Powers" or the "Two Powers," who are the only working parties, — for Austria and Prussia feel that in case of a European war they would be between the Devil and the Deep Sea, and therefore will have none of it, — it will cost England and France much less to banish all foreign machinations from Turkish territory at once, and to push back the Czar into his proper place, than it will to construct, and year after year maintain, the many-headed protectorate on which some men's dreams are running. Such a protectorate would be worthless without a continuous unanimity among the protectors, on which no one could count, and an ever-ready instrument of mischief to a mischievous majority with a wily Russian at its head, who would extract from numbers a moral force which, unsupported, he could never look to have.

War is the concentration of every crime, and they are worthy of all praise who, regardless of babbling fools, labor in the interests of peace. But, much as I fear the one and love the other, were I so unfortunate as to occupy Lord Aberdeen's place, rather than share in any unrighteous protectorate over Turkish subjects, or allow Russia to be their sole protector, I would let loose every dog of war that could be unmuzzled. To do this, if the Czar *will* have his own way, and to rectify the "balance of power," if, indeed, that famous piece of mechanism have other than an ideal existence, such an opportunity as the present may not occur again for many a day. The universal cry which I have within a few weeks heard resounding through the "States," the united cry of Europe, is, that Russia would fain bestride the old world like a Colossus. Public opinion, from whose omnipotent tribunal there is no appeal in these latter days, has condemned her. This, then, is the moment for striking a heavy blow, which will prevent far heavier blows hereafter — a blow which shall force the bloated giantess of the North to disgorge the fruits of her unholy rapine, to render back to Poland, Sweden, Persia and Turkey what once belonged to them. Powerful coadjutors would be found by you in those countries. A common hatred is a stronger bond of alliance than a common love. The one is a natural growth, the other is but a graft. Millions, while hailing you as their saviour, would by your moral aid alone effect their own salvation. Every honest man's head and heart are against the Czar Nicholas, and in the hour of need every hand, too, will be raised against him. He must yield, not in word only, but in deed. Material guarantees, such as he demanded, must in his turn be given by him, or else how will the account stand between Turkey and her sworn allies? He has mocked at treaties, and it is vain, therefore, to bind him with parchment alone, for whenever it suited his views he would fling the worthless sheepskin in the faces of those whom he had shorn. Like the repudiators of Spain and America, who are a cause of reproach to their countrymen, he is either above or below law; like them, he loves another man's goods better than his own fame; and, like them, too, he should be scourged, all gentler means failing, till he comply with the requisitions of honor and honesty, and learn to be content with his own.

Paris, December 22, 1853.

LETTER XXXVI.

The ingenious but startling conclusions at which you lately arrived, when commenting in no unfriendly spirit upon the Message of the United States' President, have led me to inquire, in your own words, whether, "if the Freesoilers insist on the promptings of their consciences, in opposition to the legal claims of the slaveholders, either the Union must be dissolved, or the Southern States subjugated by force to the opinion of the Northern;" and it is consolatory to remark that your argument, though perfect as far as it goes, does not embrace all the facts in the case. Premising that the subjugation of one portion of the States to another is in itself a virtual dissolution of the Union, I would observe that the American Constitution is a written instrument, held in such high veneration that it has never yet failed to baffle the hand of violence and the subtle tongue, although the perishable material on which it was recorded, already shows the marks of age; that out of the Constitution comes a law, as vital of necessity as its origin, which not only sanctions the institution of slavery, but guarantees it even against the action of the general Government itself; and that this law, as you truly say, the South has on its side. Now, law in the States, without ignoring Lynch law, I venture to assert is as potent as in England, and, too, that it is better hedged about by that "divinity" which is stronger than an "army with banners" than in any other part of the world. Where law, then, is so much reverenced that constable-ship is nearly a sinecure, and where a particular law is clearly "all on one side," there is no great danger, I apprehend, of Southerners wantonly forfeiting their vantage ground, or of Northerners stupidly nullifying an entire legislation under which their ungrateful soil has become far richer than the gold-fields of California.

To this first fact — respect for law and legal authority, inherited by Americans from an English ancestry — must be joined another, which is, that it is not in the power of Abolitionists or Freesoilers to uproot or even loosen slavery at the expense of the Union; for these two sets of people, though in general outline resembling each other, like rats and mice, have neither the same habits, nor will they go in the same tracks. Separately they are weak, and conjointly they can make no progress, for there are but two things in common to them — a love of notoriety savoring of loaves and fishes, and a rickety stalking horse called, "Emancipation," which stands between them and their dupes.

Then, as a third fact, the inhabitants of the non-slaveholding States are generally so busy about their own immediate concerns that slavery, with its attendants and consequences, very seldom enters their thoughts as a subject worthy of discussion. They are satisfied that the present arrangement in regard to it, which was made by the best and wisest men ever known to America, with Washington at their head, must be better than any that can be devised by certain self-constituted negro patrons, who, fortuneless for the most part in their previous careers, are but too happy to turn their hands to any job which will lift them from starving insignificance. They believe, and with reason, that the black man in the Southern States is infinitely better off, materially speaking, than any radical change can make him; that morally and physically he is vastly inferior to the white man, whom he was born to serve; and that, as to his spiritual welfare, it would be greatly advanced if his volunteer champions, both the well-meaning and the mischievous, would refrain from that worse than useless interference which of late years has compelled the slave-owner to enact laws for the security of life and property at the expense of the intellectual improvement of the slave. And, further, they are convinced — with truth on their side, I think, — that the extinction of slavery in the United States is an absolute impossibility so long as the present Constitution, the laws proceeding from it, and the people living under it, remain unchanged. Until the fifteen slave-holding States cede to the general Government the management of their domestic concerns, no important alteration can be effected in the condition of the negro, except certain ameliorations which are sure to follow the cessation of obtrusive intervention; and that these States will ever unite in such a self-sacrificing measure is not for a moment to be supposed.

But, even if the Government at Washington had the unlimited control of the matter, what could be done? Could instant emancipation be granted? As well might you yourselves let loose your beasts of burden and draught cattle to pasture on the fertile fields of England, while you took on your own shoulders the harness and the yoke. Or would gradual emancipation be preferred? Gradual emancipation and gradual amputation I reckon in the same category.

After much reflection, I am happy to differ from those who are of opinion that the institution of slavery will ever prove the occasion or the means of riving asunder the American Union. I can never be persuaded that the undefined and equivocal rights of three millions, or of three times three millions of blacks, who have in every way gained by the transplantation of their ancestors, will upset the definite interests of twenty-five millions of whites, which in twenty-five years will become the interests of fifty millions. No; it is not slavery that will undo the great work of Washington when its day of doom shall arrive, but it will be that against which he in his solemn, his all but inspired, farewell address cautioned his fellow-countrymen. He told them to beware of mixing themselves up with the affairs of others, and by implication he bid them be content with their own; for it is perfectly obvious that neither he nor his great and good coadjutors ever anticipated such a national calamity as the passion of annexation. It must be admitted, however, that the acquisition of the province of Louisiana fifteen years subsequently to the adoption of the Constitution, out of which three States were formed, although mere territory was not the immediate object in view, was a wise and even necessary measure, because without it the mouths of the great rivers of the West which empty into the Gulf of Mexico, would, in the hand of strangers, have been perpetual issues of evil. Florida was attached to the United States under nearly similar circumstances; but as for Texas, the annexation of that country, called for by no political necessity, was a blunder, the inevitable result of which was war, and the end of which we have yet to see.

And yet, notwithstanding this greediness of territory, which will receive its due reward only when the mongrel population of Mexico become voters, there is one principle of duration, perhaps of permanent safety, in the United States' Union, which M. de Tocqueville in his *Democracy* most forcibly describes, when contrasting it with the antagonistic principle that prevails in the Russian Empire. Twenty-five years ago this profound thinker, whose spirit borders on the prophetic, thus wrote:—"The one (the American) employs liberty as his principal means; the other (the Russian) makes use of servitude. Their points of departure are different, their roads are not the same; nevertheless, each of them seems called by the hidden design of Providence to hold some day or other the destinies of one-half of the world in his hands."

Now, liberty is a strong staff, and the popular principle, which lives in other lands besides America, is the best staff with which to beat back Russia into her due proportions. It is the "peoples," not the sovereigns, that can dwarf her, for beyond a certain point she is invulnerable to attacks from the West. But let the several countries which she has subdued and degraded, once feel sure of being loyally backed by England and France in the struggle to recover their rights, and the Czar's sixty millions would soon dwindle to one-half, greatly to the advantage of your Indian Empire.

Paris, December 31, 1853.

LETTER XXXVII.

Since the commencement of the war with Russia there has now and then appeared in the English papers an expression of surprise, real or affected, that the Americans, in their sympathies, are not on your side. It has been attempted to be shown how, by every calculation of self-interest, they ought to set their faces against the Czar, and pray for blessings on his enemies. They have been repeatedly told how poor and limited is their commerce with the barbarians of the North, and how rich and boundless is their intercourse with those who are "fighting the battles of liberty and civilization." On the one hand, motives the most mercenary are presented to a people who, if greedy of gain, are lavish of expense; and, on the other, the most jesuitical warnings are uttered against the contagion of a despotic Government, when the English themselves are in closest contact with another Government which is not a whit less despotic either in theory or in practice.

Without stopping to decide whether Americans are more benevolently inclined to Russia than to those who, in spite of negative protestations, are evidently straining every nerve to humiliate her, it is not difficult to comprehend why such a disposition should be not uncommon throughout the States. If I mistake not, there exists a strong and general conviction among disinterested persons that the present frightful struggle between Christian nations in arms is a disgrace to the nineteenth century; that the object of it is as unattainable and unwise as it is indefensible; that no contingent or prospective danger to Europe or to India was sufficiently menacing to justify in the sight of God the slaughter of His chief handi-work on earth at the rate of 200,000 souls a year, or in the sight of man the destruction of his hard earnings, so as to outstrip the almost miraculous productiveness of the present day; and that when Russia consents, as she has done, to the demands of the allies concerning the Sultan's Greek subjects, the protectorate of the Principalities, and the navigation of the Danube, to require her, in the plenitude of her strength and the height of her pride, to assist in tying her own hands, is an indignity to which none would submit, save a fool who is more than one-half coward. Is it to be wondered at then, if, among other impartial observers, some Americans be found who, seeing Russia banned as an annexionist by the allies, call upon these, as another set of self-righteous accusers were once exhorted, to " cast the first stone?"

If American sympathies do indeed lean towards him against whom, single-handed as he fights, are banded the hosts of the West, some good reasons may perhaps be suggested for what is in your esteem an unnatural state of feeling. While English diplomatists and consuls have been unwearied in their efforts to circumvent and destroy American influence on American territory, the Russian Government has not only always maintained amicable relations with that of the United States, but it has never attempted to thwart American agents in the performance of their duties. Nor has a Russian Minister for Foreign Affairs at any time ever formally and deliberately enunciated, as did Lord Clarendon, an intention to undertake the supervision of matters on the other side of the Atlantic. It was not Russian, but English, accredited agents who, aided by French officials, have within a few years succeeded in baffling the United States' Government in designs which, if accomplished, would have benefited the commerce of all nations. The Sandwich Islands, St. Domingo and the State of Ecuador on the Pacific, bear witness to their mischievous and clever machinations. England, likewise, through her representative, tried to force upon the Central American Government of Guatemala a Belgian colonization treaty, execrated and repudiated by that Government, she herself being under bonds to the United States not to settle any of her own subjects in that quarter of the world.

Then, again, the English Press, not to be slack in offending those whom it is bound by duty and interest to conciliate, never lets slip an opportunity for abusing and ridiculing the Americans, not even when to do so it is necessary to confound a few outlawed men, aliens for the most part, with the whole nation. Whether it be the atrocious seizure of a harmless trading ship by Cuban underlings, or the untoward arrest of a plenipotentiary, the occasion is pounced upon with a rabidness which shows how venomous is the intent that lies behind. I know your reply will be, as it has been, that you are in the habit of roughly handling your own Government and governors, not excepting even Royalty itself, when by chance a "truant disposition" untimeously appears, and that therefore you are quite at liberty to speak your mind about others. But there is a wide difference between one who is at liberty to answer and one who has no organ of communication.

Some people have fancied that there is another good cause for loving you less and the Russians more. They believe that, before now, had not you and the French Emperor had Russia on your hands, Spain, like Turkey, would have become the stalking horse of the two first maritime Powers of Europe for the prosecution of a Crimean expedition in the Western Hemisphere. Whatever credit may have been due to this surmise matters very little at present, with your impossible task before you, since it is pretty clear that no contrivance and no application of physical force can permanently deprive Russia of a predominance in the Black Sea, for which she is indebted to nature and to circumstances that are independent of the durable control of her enemies. Austria, you may be sure, will never draw a sword to destroy it, her own constitution and conditions of existence being too dependent on Russian influences to encourage her in an act so bold. From the beginning, not through wantonness, but weakness, she has been playing fast and loose with the two allies of the West, whose diplomatic agents, however, to do them justice, knowing the ticklish and dangerous nature of the party, adroitly humored her, as one does a nervous horse, who may do as he is bid, or free himself of the harness at a jump. Whatever may be the cause, there is no denying that Austria has never gone heartily with you, and at your utmost need, rely upon it, she will be found wanting. If Russia were not sure of this, do you imagine that she would dare to reject your conditions of peace? — that she would be mad enough to resist a world in arms, such as would be Austria, England, France, and Turkey, united in head, hand and heart?

Allow me to repeat, in the only journal whose universal currency tempts one to address it, that if there be any hostile sentiment in America towards the allies, apart from the justice or injustice of their cause, it is in a great measure owing to the intrigues of foreign agents and to the calumnies of a foreign Press. In the course of time the latter bane may furnish its own appropriate antidote; but it seems as if no teachings of experience could ever convince the rulers of mankind that in national as in individual concerns unauthorized meddling is always presumptuous, and may be dangerous.

History in many instances confirms my words, and, to go no further back than three score years and ten, what have the inhabitants of Great Britain gained by quixotically, and always in a thankless cause, launching themselves upon the broad sea of battle, murder and sudden death, but a crushing debt, which it dizzies the brain to reckon, and a continental unpopularity, which fifty alliances can never extinguish?

Be persuaded, then, in time that all foreign interference is an ill-paid trade, that the sooner it is abandoned in the East the better it will be for you, and that the less it is practised in the West the more prosperous will be your condition.*

Paris, May 9, 1855.

---

* We adverted cursorily on a former occasion to a letter which appeared in our columns from an able correspondent, well known to our readers under the signature, not inapplicable to him in either sense, of a "STATES-MAN." The object of our correspondent is not what we should hoped it would have been, — to clear the free men of America from the stigma implied in the charge that the sympathies of America are not on our side. To the great mass of men, who judge matters on their first aspect, and have neither leisure nor inclination to sound the depths of political questions, there is something shocking and even revolting, in the admission that, though policy may keep the United States neutral in the present contest, and interest may plead as loudly in favor of Russia as of England and France, the feelings and sympathies of America, the conscience and heart of the nation, which are not under the control of interest nor subject to considerations of State policy, side with the Powers of the East in their present deadly struggle with the Powers of the West.—*Times.*

LETTER XXXVIII.

When Oxenstiern, the Chancellor of Sweden, whom Cromwell called "the wise man of the Continent," was about to send his son on a visit to foreign Courts, he said to him, "Go and see by what fools the world is governed;" and, if the dead could speak, might not we in our day hear the self-same lips exclaiming, "Go and see by what consummate folly the world is set and kept on fire?"

According to English authority, the rulers of three great nations, superficially regarding the current of events and neglecting the tide of the times, have allowed their countries to "drift into a war," which, in spite of attempts to "make the worse appear the better reason," many wise and experienced men think might have been warded off indefinitely, without detriment to freedom or to civilization, but which now, though man may continue it, Heaven or accident alone can ever bring to a close. While thus repeating what others say, I admit that an American, whatever may be his sympathies, has no excuse for meddling in the gigantic tragedy of the age, except so far as the rights of his country may be concerned.

But the neutral rights of his country, by English confession, have been violated, and that, too, with pre-meditation, on American soil; and though there is no proof as yet that this violation carried with it an intent to slight or offend the American Government or people, a summary vindication of public law became necessary. In attempting this there was no delay, and if the flagrant error committed had been frankly acknowledged, with suitable apology and atonement — of which we have heard much, but know nothing — even the semblance of a quarrel would never have appeared. But no!

the occasion to serve some crooked purpose of their own was too tempting for such men as Oxenstiern described; hence the sharp practice so lately witnessed, which has set a deal of bitter blood in motion, provoked unseemly language and revived unwelcome reminiscences.

While some assert that the American Attorney-General wrote certain letters on speculation for a rise in the political market, — letters, by-the-by, from one officer of the Government to another, and therefore beyond the precincts of every foreign tribunal, — others suggest that the English Prime Minister sent his ships across the Atlantic to operate on the nerves of the corn-holders for a fall, — a menace, whatever may have been the motive, directed against the most sensitive portion of the American coast, which imperatively demands, under existing circumstances, the amplest satisfaction. For it is now generally conceded, I believe, that the United States cannot be dragooned, as Greece was in the Don Pacifico squabble, and surely no sane man seriously apprehends the invasion of Ireland or of Cuba by the American Government itself, or by any body of misguided men, whom, if my recollection of a certain Boulogne expedition fail not, that Government is quite as able and willing as the English to circumvent.

Notwithstanding, however, the "consummate folly" recently exhibited in high quarters, it is not probable that the late disreputable bickerings will produce any worse mischief than what you yourself have already indicated as the disastrous consequence, at some future day, of habitually playing with edged tools by the present generation. And yet, should our blustering and blundering official "gothamists" succeed in embroiling two nations which are under every possible bond to keep the peace towards each other, truth to tell, there would not be much more cause for wonder than there is in the contest which, every day we live, is turning the riches of man to nought, and sending the owner of them unhouselled to his last account.

Every legitimate cause of dissention between England and the United States having been some time ago removed, those Powers, if forced into a fight by snarling and bullying politicians, must, to be logical, continue to fight on till, wearied and disgusted at their own unnatural conduct, they are ready to cry, like children, in each others' faces, unless, perchance, they should sagely resolve to prosecute the matter in Kilkenny fashion to the latter end. The demoralizing effects on both sides alike of such a warfare would be deplorable indeed; but in a political point of view, if the experiment was not of too long duration, America would, perhaps, be benefited, for that country seems to need a little rough experience from without, now and then, to inculcate on her too happy children the "value of the Union," and to weld anew the State-links, which are apt to lose somewhat of their tenacity in the atmosphere of a long uninterrupted peace.

And, even materially speaking, it is not so clear that the more youthful of the parties would be the greater sufferer. The American commercial marine would probably be damaged, as it was in the war of 1812, to the extent of about 25 per cent., portions of the seaboard might be plundered or laid waste, and the blood of millions might, a second time, be made to boil over the flames of a desecrated capitol. But, to more than balance such wholesale devastation, which, however, could be easily remedied, though not forgotten, how would England fare, and what would be her expiation? For every American dollar destroyed she would forfeit, directly or indirectly, the fifth of a pound sterling; and, whether her colonial possessions remained untouched or not by hostile foot, what would be her condition at home, even if safe from foreign aggression, with everything stagnant, save the unbridled passions of thousands of workmen without work? Why, unless she could grow corn in her streets, and rake up cotton from the seashore, her parks, her halls, nay, her very firesides would be invaded by a host of the naked, whom no tricks of office could cover, and of the starving, whom no honeyed words of Statecraft could send empty away.

Paris, Nov. 21, 1855.

LETTER XXXIX.

Notwithstanding the fallen estate of man, there must be an innate virtue in human nature which redeems it from the calamitous effects of misgovernment, or long ago the world would have become one universal scene of discord, if not of dissolution. Notwithstanding that the normal condition of our species, ever since Cain beat out his brother's brains, has been one of war, yet, thanks to the Christian religion, to the civilizing influences of commerce, to the better instruction of communities, and, by consequence, to the increased pressure of public opinion upon public action, wars have become less frequent and of less duration. Few and scant, however, are the obligations which any nation in our day is under to its Ministers — its head servants — for a peaceful present or for the prospect of a prosperous future. Every improvement in respect to these must be imputed in large proportion to private individual excellence, and very seldom to official worth. Theoretically, the best and wisest men rule over us, but practically they seem the reverse of good and wise when tested by results, and whenever the ends which crown their works are compared with the ends which crown the works of others, who serve directly neither Prince, nor President, nor any earthly Power Supreme.

A man of much experience in the highways of the world once exclaimed, "Political honesty is a monstrous anomaly!" And I am somewhat inclined to believe that he was not far wrong — that political professions of faith and political practice may fairly be put upon a par with dicers' oaths and lovers' deeds. Had common honesty and discretion, for example, been the rule of action among the magnates of the earth during the last two years and upwards, would France and Russia have ventured on the dangerous game they did, their only stake the right of entry to a church? Would England have dealt so loosely in menace that at length her wares were held to be base metal? Would France have dwelt so long in doubtful action that the Czar was completely duped? Supposing that honesty and frankness had pervaded the councils of nations — supposing that Austria had declared her intent never to aid any one but by much talking, that Prussia had announced her determination to take heed to herself alone, that Sardinia had shown her resolve to throw herself into the fight as she has done, and that Sweden had proclaimed her decision never to fling her sword into the Russian scale, would Nicholas have ever dared what he did dare? Would not the world now be richer by a million of souls or more, with time enough to square their dread accounts, and by millions on millions of money, which can never be redeemed, though it may be replaced? If private enterprises were subordinate to the same clumsy and "crooked wisdom" which turns awry the current of public events, where would have been our railways and canals, our telegraphs and our steamships? If the clerks of a great commercial establishment, from the clerk confidential to the embryo copyist, had taken for examples the Ministerial servants of Queen Victoria or of the United States, what would have been their fate? Certificates of indifferent honesty, by a stretch of criminal compassion, might possibly have been accorded to the discharged delinquents, but a profound silence, I apprehend, would have been kept as to their active sense of duty and as to their performance of that duty.

Owing to a negligent, dilatory and slipshod manner of doing business, two subjects of dissension, which any clear-headed man of honor could have settled in the course of twenty-four hours, have thrown into violent commotion two nations which, in the words of one of your foremost writers, "are bound together more than two nations ever were by a similarity of interests." The late Minister of the United States to England, I am told on good authority, was assured from the moment of his arrival in that country of the ardent desire of the English Government to be well quit of Central America and of everything pertaining to it, provided that the riddance could be effected without any sacrifice of honor. And what was there to prevent your shaking off such an unprofitable encumbrance, I should like to know, without stopping to question the wisdom of ever having assumed it? The only answer which I have as yet received, that it would not do for you to be clamored and bullied out of your asserted rights, is far from being satisfactory. When we behold an empty-handed individual, in cotton frock, boldly asserting his real or supposed rights in front of a steel-clad gentleman, revolver in hand, that man we may "write down ass," if we will, or christen him fool, but coward or bully — companions close akin — never, while our vernacular shall remain in joint.

In spite of incessant and indecent charges against the American character in the European Press, both of recent and ancient date, I much doubt if Americans are more possessed of the spirit of bullyism than other men. With their handful of ships opposed to your navy, "such as ocean never bore before," and with their apology for an army to set in array against an English force, "such as no Englishmen ever yet commanded," I put it to your common sense and good judgment whether it is likely that my countrymen ever entertained the wild and silly notion of brow-beating yours. It is ungenerous, nay, it is useless, the attempt to shift the weightier mass of blame from English to American shoulders. The "letting out of waters" began on this side of the ocean, when you sent to Washington a negotiator of treaties who had proved himself at Madrid, as I heard his fellow-diplomatist call him, "*Le moins intelligent de tous les hommes d'ésprit.*" But it must be owned, on the other hand, that his American collaborator in that bungling job, the Bulwer-Clayton treaty, gains nothing by comparison with him. Then, much mischief was caused by Lord Clarendon's inadvertent speech about the English and French superintendence of American affairs, the ill effects of which he tried every means but the right one to remedy. Instead of simply telling his fellow-lords that a wrong construction had been put upon his words, (a declaration which would have been hailed by every American with delight and unbounded credence), his Lordship, it seems, contented himself with writing a note to General Webb, having a talk with Mr. Buchanan, and indicting a despatch to Mr. Crampton. And now, after the lapse of many months, by a rare chance, the parties who are most interested begin to see a little daylight where, indeed, there ought never to have been the slightest obscurity. Was there ever a more slovenly procedure? Quite as carelessly was the abitration proposition managed. Her Majesty's Secretary for Foreign Affairs spoke about it to the American Minister in London, wrote about it to to her representative in Washington, then discoursed about it and of its rejection and renewal, and now the whole turns out to be a great mistake and mystification. Time has been lost, ill feelings have been aroused, unfounded complaints have been uttered, and the work must be commenced anew. Is it for such trifling that men in office are paid and pampered? Afterwards comes the enlistment affair — " a ridiculous cause of quarrel," you may say, but for that very reason the more dangerous, and the more quickly to be disposed of in peaceful fashion. If England and America are doomed to fight, (for the comfort of the chronicler, now and ever, if from no higher motive), let it be for something tangible, definable, and of real importance — something which one side insists upon having, and which the other persists in refusing. In such a fight the parties would have at least the satisfaction of knowing which of them carried the point in dispute. But, even in this matter of enlistment, it was not the Americans who lifted the "first stone." Your sapient rulers " relied on American advice and information," they say, when the only advice and information they needed were to be met with in law books common to everybody. Your special pleading in their behalf is a deal too fine. They would not for the world " hire or retain" on American soil, contrary to written law, a single man to serve Queen Victoria; but they would "make generally known" their willingness to receive such service. And pray where is the mighty difference in the eye of morality and of honor, aye, and even of law itself, if the question could be fairly tested, between impudently "hiring and retaining" by high inducements my neighbor's servants or dependents to quit his roof for mine, and the "making it generally known" to them that if they will sneakingly give me the preference a warm reception shall await them? Then, the enlisting agents must needs "make generally known" their mission on every wall and from every house-top. Indeed, so openly and successfully did they perform their parts, that even the "Blue

Noses" of Nova Scotia, whom that veracious historian, Mr. Samuel Slick, never accused of "smartness," mocked at the sharpsighted Yankees for having been outwitted by provincials.

But, as it turned out, those who were acting as enrollers, directly or indirectly, for the English Government, had blundered from the beginning: "like master, like man." Their manœuvres might possibly have been winked at, had they not been forced upon the attention of the public; and much bickering would have thus been spared. At one time the stoppage of proceedings by authority of English Ministers, and an apology, with promise of forbearance for the future, seemed about to set all things right, when an untoward discovery came to show how difficult it is to repair a first false step. The English Minister at Washington is now charged with being a complice in the "ridiculous affair." Incredible as is the accusation, still more incredible is it that without incontrovertible proof such an accusation should have been brought against a gentleman of Mr. Crampton's acknowledged virtues by those who have always held him in the highest esteem.

And here, in the 1857th year of the Lord-of Peace, are seen two great nations, who have not in their common blood a single drop of bitterness the one towards the other, nor in their common concerns a single cause for shedding blood, in a state of uncertainty whether they may not wake some morning to find themselves defacing God's image in the person of a kinsman, and destroying by wholesale the witty inventions of man, such as none but a being once little lower than the angels could have devised. And all this because of the littleness of our great men! Interminable scribblers! they have proved themselves the veriest know-nothings and do-nothings under the sun. In America, as in England, the square and the round holes are most unartistically filled; and, impatient at seeing the material interests of nations banded about, I sometimes fancy, forgetful for the moment of interests infinitely higher, that if a Cromwell or a Napoleon could come to judgment now and then, the right men might fall into the right places, and that the world would swing more easily on its hinges than it does just at this moment in your country or in mine.

Paris, March 26, 1856.

LETTER XL.

Some persons believe, and many fear, that war between Great Britain and the United States will be the upshot of the wily expedients, flat contradictions, and sharp practice which, growing out of the Bulwer-Clayton treaty and the recruiting scheme, have lately kept the reflecting, moral, industrious, and really responsible portions of two great communities in a state of wonderment bordering upon terror. Sharing neither the belief nor the fear of such persons, it would seem to me a very idle task to address myself to the subject of their apprehensions, were it not that in the history of human folly all things are possible — even that apprehensions the best founded may degenerate by their very intensity into indifference, thereby encouraging the self-willed audacity or presumptuous malignity of agents, especially those most highly placed, when left to themselves, to indulge in the wildest freaks of statecraft. For this reason, methinks, it behoves us, the people, Englishmen and Americans, to bestir ourselves now, and so to use whatever influence each one may have, as to make the will of our public servants subordinate and subservient to our wills, giving these gentlemen to understand, either by public meetings or other constitutional means, that we will have neither wars nor the rumors of wars to torment us, except for reasons good and sufficient in our own eyes. It is the height of absurdity to hope that such pettifogging politics as have abounded of late in Anglo-American relations can by any possibility be consistent with a permanent well-being between two countries holding an equally high rank. I pretend not to parcel out the blame as it should rest on this side or on that. The well where truth has been sunk is too deep for my penetration. Neither do I assert that in every matter of difference the Americans can fairly cast the "first stone;" nor do I deny that they have as much glass to be broken at home as other nations have. Of special pleading we have already had more than enough, and no pleadings, by whatever arguments backed, can make void the one fact that the "recruitment difficulty," with all its untoward fruits, is of English root and growth. Most emphatically may it be declared that this "first step" was not like other proverbial first steps, the only one involving a heavy cost; and the less worthy of consideration will they be regarded who took it, when it is remembered how logically and eloquently the "English Press," *The Times*, condemned it, and how fervently the best men in Parliament resisted it, never yielding till the last moment, and then against their better judgment, to the ignoble threat of Ministers to resign office if not allowed to be delivered of their foreign bantling.

But, though England did make a false move, that was no reason for ungenerously keeping her in a false position. If, as you have often asserted, and doubtless believe, an apology for the violation of the American recruitment laws was ever roundly made, free from all peddling self-justification and accusatory remonstrance, and accompanied by a promise of forbearance hereafter, comprised in the recognition of a great principle — the only thing worth weighing in the balance of a great nation — then that apology ought to have been frankly and loyally accepted. But was such an apology ever made? I doubt it; for, had it been nobly given, it would have been generously received, because the Americans are not a mean-spirited people, nor are their rulers insensible to public opinion, notwithstanding the monstrous productions of English pens, which have almost convinced the European world that we are a set of piratical freebooters, and indeed "little better than one of the damned."

While the phantom apology was bandied about, the "complicity" of the English Minister in Washington surged above the troubled surface of politics to add vexation to the strife. Whether Mr. Crampton was guilty or not guilty of the charge brought against him, is not worthy of a guess. He affirmed upon his honor, and his Government endorsed his affirmation, that he was innocent, and thereupon, had a suitable apology existed, the leaves which bore witness to this pitiful passage in the history of two kindred nations should have been torn from the record. But the quarrel had been aggravated, and some persons, not ill-inclined to the representative of England, fancied, from what they knew of him, that he might have been unwittingly blameworthy even while thinking himself safe on the windy side of honesty. The truth, in my opinion, is, that Mr. Crampton was not up to his work, and that second or third-rate men are not fit to represent the English nation in the capital of the United States. The States can no more have little affairs to manage than England can have "little wars" to wage. Americans, the foremost of the first, personate their country at the Court of St. James's, and pray on what principle do you send a dwarf to do a giant's work in an atmosphere where none but the strongest can thrive? Genius, talent — nay, even knavery itself, if coupled with intelligence, can be accurately gauged and can be turned to some account, but dullness or stupidity, like a bog or quagmire, is susceptible of no measure, and defies all calculation.

Paris, June 7, 1856.

LETTERS

TO THE

"NEW YORK COURIER AND ENQUIRER."

LETTER I.

* As the present is an interesting moment to all who are concerned in the affairs of Europe, it may be that your numerous readers would like to receive, from one on this side of the water, an account of the impressions made upon his mind by certain events, which have lately taken the lead of all others in attracting public attention. I allude, of course, to the "Spanish marriages," as they are called, and I make use of the unpretending word *impressions*, because the whole affair is so thickly clothed with well devised and authentic statements and counter-statements, in form and substance perfectly incompatible with each other, that anything like a precise knowledge of facts in the case, defying contradictions, it would be equally foolhardy and absurd to assume. As it appears to me then that you may possibly welcome my letter,

---

* We take great pleasure in laying before our readers the following letter from an American resident in Paris, who has heretofore done his country very essential service by able, well timed and effective replies, through the *London Times*, to the virulent denunciations of the British Press.—*Courier and Enquirer.*

not for any merit in its execution, but for the rarity of its matter, just as you might the description of a bull-fight, or of any other buffoonry, I will send it for publication.

According to an act of renunciation passed in 1712, by the Duke of Orleans for himself and descendants, and the declaration of Philip V. of Spain, made in the same year; according to a treaty between Austria and Spain, signed in 1725; and in accordance with the Spanish Constitution adopted in 1845, wherein reference is made to the treaty of Utrecht, it seems, or at least we are told, that not only was provision made against the crowns of France and Spain falling upon the same head, but also against the latter of these baubles ever resting upon the brow of any son of Orleans. That this was, and continues to be, the general interpretation of the instruments above cited, is evident from the angry remonstrances lately made on all sides to the French King's marriage of his son to the Infanta of Spain; and that it *was* the interpretation hitherto apprehended, if not actually put upon them, by Louis Philippe himself, is likewise evident from the secrecy and precipitancy with which his matrimonial schemes have been conducted. The marriages of the Spanish Queen to her cousin, and of her sister to the Duke of Montpensier, are now what are here described as *facts accomplished*, and that which preceded them, whether infamous or outrageous in regard to the person of the youthful Sovereign, as the *London Times* asserts, or tricky and fraudulent in regard to every step in the proceedings, as all the world believes, will furnish materials for history, if history be so fortunate as ever to lay her hands upon the facts. The *Times*, and I need not tell you it is by far the best *published* authority in Europe, without entering upon details, more than intimates that most unmanly violence, and at the defenceless hour of midnight, was excercised towards the occupant of the Spanish throne;

in which, from enquiries made in different quarters likely to be well informed, I am inclined to think it is *not* mistaken. What this violence was, will perhaps never be known more accurately than it is now; but that a dissolute mother, whose life has been a libel on her sex, and a crafty kinsman, whose age and experience should have taught him better things, conspired to bring about a consummation eagerly coveted by both, through means not unlike those which Lot's daughters employed, is openly proclaimed and not discredited.

Moreover, it is believed that M. Guizot and his iron-willed but fair-of-speech master, have over-reached and out-witted the English cabinet, have played falsely, and by slight of hand and *an odd trick,* have won the game. But let them both look to it, for if Lord Palmerston and his compeers be judged aright, when it is least expected, another Syrian stab will let out the superfluous humors of this fast-and-loose couple, or another Tahiti *coup de main* will draggle them through the mud again.

But to present the facts of the case according to their supposed truth: Louis Philippe and his first Minister, or rather head clerk, entered with the English Ministry into an agreement respecting the Spanish marriages, which they have since seen fit to violate. It is true they assert the contrary, but as yet their words are not credited; for instead of denying the compact, they have recourse to excuses, and instead of justifying their own conduct, they vainly attempt to criminate that of others. England is charged by them with having actively favored a Coburg Prince, contrary to her pledged word, thereby liberating France from her engagements; and when a home-thrust, in the shape of a protest, was made by the English Minister, the French King's reply, as I had it from one of the diplomatic corps, (neither an Englishman nor an American), amounted almost word for word, to this: " That he had a perfect right to marry his son to any princess in Europe, and by consequence to a Spanish one; but that if a question ever rose as to the right of the Duke of Montpensier's children to the Spanish throne, he should stand by, an idle spectator, leaving it to be decided wholly by the Spanish people themselves."

The upshot of the matter is, that the French King, though he loved the English alliance much, loved Spanish gold more; and having found he could go without English crutches, he flattered himself that English support could be altogether dispensed with. But I for one believe him to be mistaken in this. Hitherto he has been able to marry his children only to petty German or foreign princes and princesses, poorer, with one exception, in every thing, save blood, than most private gentleman possessed of what is usually considered a fortune; and he was too happy to ally himself with one of the great houses of Europe, not to mention that the dazzling dowry in view — the unrighteous fruits of plunder — was to him, whose darling vice is what Byron calls the "good, old gentlemanly one," a temptation stronger than *his* flesh and blood could withstand.

And what is to come of all this? Very like before long a civil war, or something as bad, may be again raging in Spain, and that beautiful, but degraded, country may become once more the battle field for those, who always were and always will be antagonists, notwithstanding the incessant billing and cooing that have been going on of late years. If they do not come to actual blows themselves, they will strike not the less fiercely with the arms of others. At all events the *entente cordiale* is ended, and all sincere men must be glad to see that heart-sickening and hypocritical farce finished. It was never a feeling more than skin-deep, and always reminded me of a ferocious tiger whipped into good behavior, and a surly mastiff coaxed into decency; because it is no secret that an Englishman despises a Frenchman, just in proportion as he is hated in return.

Now all this should be no subject of mourning to us Americans, for the more snarling and growling there is, the less disposed will either side be to impertinent meddling in our affairs, and for the future there need be no fear that any party will be anxious to put its hand between the wood and the bark, as was attempted to be done during our negotiations for Texas.

Paris, Oct. 17, 1846.

LETTER II.

It appears to me that the more honest a man is, the more likely he is to be taken in by a designing knave — that is, the first time, but not the second, unless to his honesty be united a most inordinate share of silliness. Now the English, as every body knows, have lately been shamelessly duped by the French King at Madrid, — so shamelessly, indeed, that the sense of humiliation was lost sight of for a moment in their anger at having been over-reached. And yet no one, whose opinion is of value, thinks the less worthily of them on that account. But if, after such mortifying experience, they be deluded again by that mockery, called an *entente cordiale*, into once more embarking their fortunes in the same boat with the Royal *Escamoteur*, what but their own simplicity will they have to thank for every consequence, however disastrous, should they spring a leak, which his keen wit alone foresaw, perhaps contrived, and solely provided against? Still, incredible as you may think it, such a result is not at all impossible, if we are to judge from the dulcet notes which are now daily exchanged across the Channel.

At first the English Press could find no abuse sharp enough to inflict upon the perpetrators of the "Spanish fraud." Neither Louis Philippe, nor his Ministry, nor his Ambassador, the immediate agent in the transaction, escaped the execrations which, it was evident, some, if not all of them, deserved. Upon the Unanointed himself, for, as you are aware, the French King has never ventured upon a coronation, the English Secretary for Foreign Affairs was heard by one of my friends to bestow an epithet peculiar to our vernacular, richly merited, but rather too strong for repetition in a public journal. The British Queen, filled with grief at a slight cast upon the pretensions of her kinsman of Coburg blood, and with indignation as at a personal affront, like Rachel, "refused to be comforted," and, as I have learned within an hour from a gentleman just returned to Paris from the royal presence, still "cries aloud and spares not." In a word, one universal shout of reprobation was wafted from Dover to Calais, to be clamorously echoed and responded to here, when all at once the fate of Cracow, in very natural sequence to the folly at Madrid, was sounded in the ears of Europe, and the scene changed. France and England, seeing at a glance that the very first moment of dissension between them had been seized upon by a Power, equally watchful and unscrupulous, as an occasion long desired for annihilating the last remnant of Polish independence, hastened to lower the high tone hitherto assumed towards each other, and to put on at least a show of decency and moderation. But in so doing, more than one of the principal organs of public opinion did not hesitate to declare their conviction that Louis Philippe not only well knew for months what were the intentions of the Northern Powers, but acquiesced in them for the purpose of advancing his own family interests and of securing to himself a quiet life. And they might have added that not only for months, but for years, has he been accessory to an enormous crime against the rights of man. For as long ago as 1833, a secret treaty was entered into by Russia, Prussia and Austria to the effect that, "on a concurrence of certain circumstances," Cracow, in spite of the most solemn compacts, should be devoted to political destruction. And this concurrence of circumstances depended, as we have since seen, only on a fitting occasion offering itself, after the oppressed had been goaded into rebellion, and after the worm had been trampled upon till even the worm turned upon its tormentors in the madness of despair. Do you ask how I know all this? It is by means of a gentleman once high in the confidence of the Russian Emperor, and now in Paris, as well as through another who himself was the digester of the infamous contract — a contract communicated directly to Louis Philippe, but by him dishonestly concealed from his ministry. For you must know that he is his own foreign secretary, and holds, most unconstitutionally, a correspondence, apart from the ministerial one, with his representatives at different courts. Do you wonder why his king-craftiness, which every coffee-house frequenter talks of, is not brought home to him with overwhelming proofs? It is because he is too astute to leave any traces in his dark paths that can be sworn to; and because, greedy as he is of gold, he is lavishness itself whenever written documents, which might come to light in condemnation of him, are to be had for money.

Here is an instance of his extreme caution. In 1840, when the affairs of the East wore so portentous an aspect that an English gentleman of almost the highest diplomatic rank, on the authority of one of the French Ministry, told me that "war was inevitable," although messages were incessantly exchanged between the King and his Ambassador in London, not one of them was ever committed to paper, but every word was communicated verbally through the Count de Montheron.

Louis Philippe has been called by his parasites the Napoleon of peace; and certainly, were it not for his paltry cunning, he might be justly styled the cleverest man in all Europe. But let him take heed, lest, lacking art to conceal his artifice, like that great and bad ruler, he become his own destroyer. For here there are, as it were, two nations — *France superficielle* and *France réelle;* and it is on the former, composed of office-holders, speculators and overgrown bankers, that his popularity rests; while from the latter, which comprises men of honor, of substance and of true nobility, he has nothing to hope. And why should he look for any thing at their hands, when he cannot command their respect? And how can he command their respect, or the respect of any one, capable as he has shown himself to be of every meanness, small and great, of hypocritically embracing at one time, with tears in his eyes, the members of a Cabinet anxious to give up office, but before his preparations were ready, and then chuckling over the dexterous cheat, by which he had cajoled them into withdrawing their resignations; and at another, of intriguing against a friendly government on the other side of the Atlantic, notwithstanding a voluntary and formal promise to remain neutral? But if we are forced to mourn over the degradation of powers such as fall to the lot of few men, and if we must grieve that the pages of history are to be devoted to a name like his, it is some consolation to reflect that one layer at least, which shall envelope it for immortality, will be furnished from the records of royal infamy, whereon the ink is hardly dry. And yet, perhaps, at the present moment he is a blessing to the civilized world, if not to France itself; for though he certainly does drag his country through the mire every now and then, still he is the advocate of peace, however unworthy be his motives, and peace he will have, cost what it may.

Paris, Dec. 7, 1846.

LETTER III.

It is hardly possible for a citizen of the "States" fully to appreciate the advantages which attach themselves to him as an inhabitant of the New World among the denizens of the Old, till he has passed some time in foreign countries; nor, until he has dwelt among strangers in a strange land, can he properly estimate the blessings which belong to him in his own. If in manners and appearance he is unexceptionable, and if his letters of introduction have been written by persons that had a right to give them, and are addressed to those who can present him to the society, however distinguished, in which he desires to move, no obstacle opposes itself to the accomplishment of his wishes. Whether he be a manufacturer from New England, a merchant from New York, a lawyer from Pennsylvania, or a planter from a Southern or a Western State, saloons, the most difficult of access to one who is native-born, are instantly thrown open to him, and even an approach to Royalty itself is rendered easy and agreeable. That this should happen upon the Continent is not so much to be wondered at, when every circumstance is taken into consideration; but that in England, aristocratic England, where castes are as distinctly marked, and with reason too, as in many portions of the East, and where, for the most part, each man knows and keeps through life the place allotted to him at his birth,— that in such a country a plain American gentleman, with suitable credentials and wherewithal to support them, can enter at once into the highest society and all its enjoyments, to which a mere London merchant, however rich and respectable, or a Westminster practitioner, however eminent, would never dream of aspiring, seems to me a flattering privilege accorded to the untitled countrymen of Washington, which they should not, as is frequently the case, unduly estimate, or sadly misuse.

Not that I would have them think more meanly of themselves than they ought, (of which, by the by, there is little danger,) nor, that they should lower in their own persons by obsequiousness and sycophancy the unadorned dignity of every well-bred man, who is conscious of right, but that they are bound to attribute to their country's form of government, which recognises no privilege of birth, and to its institutions, which respect the individual, rather than to any personal merit, most, if not all, of their success. I am a Republican by birth and conviction; I am too a lover of the people and one of them; it is also my sure belief and daily prayer that some years hence that insult to common sense, an absolute sovereignty, will be unknown in Europe. Nevertheless, I would have mankind levelled up rather than down, even in the courtesies of life, and it grieves me to see imputed to Democracy that frequent absence of modesty and regard to the rights of others, which, through bravado or sheer obtrusiveness, characterizes some of our countrymen abroad.

Then, within the limits of that land so dear to all of us, and not less dear to those who are temporary exiles from it, what blissful security is felt in place of that unquiet rest, which here attends what is called a general state of peace. Look, for example, now at the different nations of Europe, and observe the rotten condition they are in. See too, what menacing aspects they assume towards each other, notwithstanding treaties, modern and time-worn, stare them in the face, and the dearest interests of humanity call upon them to forbear. England and France are in a worse position with regard to each other than they were, because of the broken *entente cordiale*, whose reality, except between the two governments, never existed. England, like one sick of the palsy, feels helpless Ireland hanging at her side, while that wretched country, equally incapable of self-regeneration and of receiving from others the principles of a new existence, returns upon its hereditary tormentor a portion of its many woes. An harvest of dragons' teeth is the daily retribution from a sister-Isle to her, who, envied and therefore disliked throughout the Continent, has not a single ally on whose fidelity she can rely. True, she claims Portugal as an ancient friend, and lately has lent her moral aid, if nothing more, to sustain in the person of its Sovereign, those very principles which she opposed when the outcast, Don Miguel, was their representative; but the friendship is all on one side. France, isolated by her hardhearted and selfish King, struggles for supremacy in Spain with a high hand, but her hand, like every other raised in that unhappy region, lacks the power of doing or of receiving good. Austria, a thing of shreds and patches, to be torn to pieces at the first general convulsion, cringing and tyrannizing by turns, is an object of hate to all and of love to none.

The rest of Germany, rumbling with discontent, is slowly but surely preparing for a fearful contest between popular right and royal might, which must take place, unless regal Justice, descending from her high perch, listen to the oppressed many, ere it be too late to ward off from the protected few their well-deserved doom. Parts of Switzerland have long been at daggers'-drawing with each other. All Italy is but an ill-assorted pack of cards, to be dealt at will by the first bold adventurer, whose skill knows neither fear nor dread whenever the war-cry of nations is raised. While Russia, the incubus of Europe, the feared and the loathed of all, lies, like a beast of prey beyond the reach of the huntsman, prepared for every wile and for every violence.

It is really heart-sickening for one who loves his fellow man, to see creatures, formed after the image of their Maker, misgoverned and depressed by kings and ministers, by knaves and fools;— to hear the people's abasement pleaded as an excuse for sinking them still lower, by defrauding them of every chance of self-elevation; and to know that their rights are withheld under the pretext, that perchance the first exercise of them may be in the wrong direction. Why, in the country where I now am, in France, a kingdom which affects to be the foremost in the world, there are but 200,000 electors out of thirty-two millions of inhabitants, and a majority of the Deputies, miscalled Representatives of the people, are paid servants of the crown, hired to do its bidding at all times and on all occasions. And the worst of all is, that for this evil there seems to be no remedy; the opponents of the government themselves agreeing with it, that Frenchmen are not sufficiently enlightened to choose their own legislators. It was only a few days since that I asked a Carlist nobleman, of high attainments and great intelligence, why the right of suffrage was not more extended here, and his reply was, "You know how I detest Louis Philippe, his ministry and all that belongs to them; and yet in this matter I think that they are blameless, for on my conscience I believe my countrymen to be wholly unfit for such an experiment." "Then why," was my answer, "do you not provide a remedy for the evil by gradually creating electors, who will be constrained by pride and interest to qualify themselves for the performance of their duty, when it is for want of such a remedy that wrongs are tolerated, which, if perpetrated in England or in one of the

United States, would rouse the whole community to arms, unless speedily atoned for or repaired?"

It cannot be denied that the affairs of Europe look gloomy and threatening, and yet I do not see how war can immediately come out of them ; for, to say nothing of the spirit of submission which has fallen upon every cabinet save that of Russia, the rich capitalists and bankers, who alone can provide the means for carrying it on, will be most backward in doing so, involved as they are in thousands of commercial speculations, the results of a long peace. And then, owing to the enormous investments lately made in railroads, and to the immense importation of breadstuffs within the last six months, — into France alone two-fold greater than was ever known during an equal period, — specie has become so scarce that, to give you one instance of many, there now remains in the National Bank in Paris not one third of two hundred and eighty millions, which were a little while ago within its vaults.

When I think of all these things, and call to mind the boundless elements of happiness within our reach at home, I cannot help cursing in my heart that passion for legislation, which will not leave man alone to work out his own prosperity, and that impious defiance of God's eternal law and the good man's humble prayer, which has already wasted on Mexican ground, and is now, while I write, pouring out like worthless water, the heart's blood of many of the best and bravest amongst us.

Paris, Jan. 2, 1847.

LETTER IV.

Of two speeches, anxiously looked for by some persons and curiously by all, only one has as yet been delivered. The King of the French has spoken. The Queen of England has in her turn to speak. His Majesty's, therefore, is alone before us, and it requires not a second perusal to convince any one how "fearfully and wonderfully" it is made. But to its author belongs the fear which its words imply, and to its readers the wonderment which, on dangerous occasions, words adroitly put together always inspire. Still, Hope is its burden from beginning to end. If scarcity, portending famine pervade the land, and if an exhausted National Bank, menacing thousands with ruin, fill the commercial community with alarm, a reliance upon the Chambers seems to sustain the Royal speaker, though it cannot disguise his timorous anticipations. While protesting against an "infraction of treaties," which he must have foreseen would be the inevitable consequence of "the marriage of his beloved son with his beloved niece," he has the hardihood to declare that, "his relations with all Foreign Powers afford him the firmest confidence that the peace of the world is insured."

With my letter, you will receive a copy of the Diplomatic Papers on the Spanish marriages, just laid upon the tables of the Chambers by M. Guizot, in which may be seen how easy it is to arrive at a disastrous result by pursuing in an unworthy manner an unworthy end. Stripped of all its trickish gloss, the story of the corresponding diplomatists, Lord Palmerston and M. Guizot, is a very plain one. Louis Philippe, long ago seeing he could not effect the marriage of his son with the Queen of Spain, resolved to content himself with the Infanta, her sister, and heir presumptive to her throne ; soothing his paternal solicitude with the reflection that a dowry would be forthcoming, which a Spanish Princess of the olden time might have been proud to offer. To accomplish his object with the consent of England, an all-important consideration in his eyes, he agreed to wait till Isabella became the mother of children, provided that their father were of no other than the blood of Philip V. But then, in spite of his agreement, and as if in despite of England, he very coolly proceeded to carry out his scheme immediately, not because England had proved faithless to her engagements, but because, forsooth, she had not been as active as he would have had her in opposing certain intrigues in favor of a Coburg Prince, more nearly related, by the by, to his own family, than to that of the British Sovereign.

You may say, that all this is a very small matter. True! So was the passing of the Rubicon a small matter in itself. But the face of Europe is not the less changed on account of it, by the withdrawal of that moral force, however imaginary, which stood between the oppressor and the oppressed, so long as England and France in outward show remained upon a friendly footing with each other. And war, so far from being an impossibility, is regarded by many as a highly probable, and not very distant, solution of present difficulties.

Wars, like whirlwinds, are doubtless curses for the time being, but a general war in Europe at this moment, in the same manner as those eccentric commotions in the atmosphere, with much temporary evil, might be productive of great permanent good. Let one arise, and Russia's systematic encroachments must be met in the first instance by Germany. And to do this successfully, resistance must come from a contented and united people. But to render the Germans either one or the other, concessions must be made to them by their rulers, which have long been sought for in vain: The King of Prussia, who, it is said, loves too well the cup that "cheereth god and man," will be compelled to grant the Constitution to his subjects, which for years has been promised, and for which they are fully prepared: The Emperor of Austria, born almost an idiot, will be obliged to relax his unholy grasp from provinces which do not belong to him: And it is not impossible, however improbable, that a liberal Confederation may be constructed in Italy, which shall forever exclude from that land of perverted blessings the contaminating touch of foreign hands.

Paris, January 15, 1847.

LETTER V.

The French have an amiable custom of *tutoying* their intimate friends, that is, of making use, in familiar intercourse, of the second person in the singular instead of the plural number. Their children, too, in sweet and artless simplicity do the same. But whenever I hear a sudden *theeing* and *thouing* commenced by two "robustious periwig-pated fellows," who till lately have been at swords' points, or at best on terms of indifference, the suspicion invariably seizes me that before long they will make a visit early in the morning to the *Bois de Boulogne*,* there to refrigerate their untimely tenderness by a recurrence to those first principles of force which were antecedent to all human law.

England and France have, during the last few years, presented a somewhat parallel case to the one supposed. Bitter enemies almost since their recorded histories began, but fast friends never, their precocious love, like every unnatural

* Rendezvous of duellists.

product, has prematurely perished in the using of it. Yet, though the ill-will be not wanting, there is no present apprehension of their proceeding beyond angry words, since, between the will and the power, fortunately for the world's peace, there is as wide a difference as between a surplus and a deficient revenue, or, between a well-fed and a starving population.

A few days subsequently to my last letter, the British Queen's speech was pronounced before her assembled Parliament. I do not say that it was made by her, because, as you are aware, she has no more to do in the construction of it than has the throne upon which she sits; and therefore, I presume, one cannot be charged with irreverence if he venture to criticise it. Its themes, you will perceive, are the misery of her Irish subjects, the Madrid fraud, and the Cracow crime. To remedy in some degree the first, the ports are to be opened, which, had it been done when Sir Robert Peel proposed it on his individual responsibility, would have saved a world of suffering and a mass of human life; then, the navigation-laws are to be suspended, — an excellent measure without doubt, but one that nine months ago would have brought forth nine-fold more good than it will now; and lastly, a substitute, in certain establishments,* will be allowed to replace that enormous portion of man's food which has hitherto been turned into poison that destroys him.

With regard to the second subject of the Royal Discourse — the Montpensier marriage, a solemn announcement is made, that "a correspondence exists," — a statement which, however pertinent, could hardly have taken any one by surprise, seeing that everybody had had for days an opportunity of reading the said correspondence from beginning to end a

---

* Distilleries.

dozen times. Nor would the world have been lost in amazement, had it been also told, that this same correspondence originated, according to the Speaker's own knowledge, in gross prevarication, that it abounded in pitiful, personal altercation, unworthy to appear in State Papers, and that for special pleading it would do no discredit to an Old Bailey lawyer.

Against "the Extinction of the Free State of Cracow"— the third matter treated of, it is declared that a "Protest has been made,"— a thing of far less value than the parchment upon which it was engrossed, for who ever heard of a protest, which is a contemptible avowal of excess of will and want of power, six months after its utterance?

In thus briefly reviewing the words of Royalty spoken on the other side of the channel, as has been already done by me in respect to those lately delivered upon this, my object is to show your readers that, when considered in relation to that much traduced document, an American President's Message, they gain nothing by the comparison.

I am most unwilling to minister to a foolish national vanity, but, as partly suggested by what has just been said, I will add, what has often occurred to me, that the obloquy, so freely cast upon us and ours by strangers, seems to take its rise, not in a desire to correct our errors, but in envy of our unexampled prosperity, and not in contempt, but in distrust, of our increasing strength, which is seen to be independent of foreign influences. Let us take heed to ourselves, therefore, and ever bear in mind that, if there be mischief in store for us, it can be provoked into life, even according to such tacit admission of unfriends, only by our own wantonness or wickedness.

As England with its eight hundred millions sterling of debt, and France with its annual seventy-five millions of francs, deficit, know that a war between them is impracticable, and that their mutual security depends in a great measure upon the united front which can be presented by them to the world, they are now engaged in a small game of coquetry, and trying by indirect means to solder the slivered *entente cordiale*, to which the ministerial journals on both sides, properly instructed of course, lend their hearty, though covert, aid. And this endeavor to preserve peace, whatever be the motive and whatever the sacrifice of dignity, must gladden the hearts of the wise and good; for there can be no reasonable doubt that, even in the actual state of the Christian world, imperfectly civilized and still less christianized as it is, not a single interest can be found, whose vindication requires the shedding of one drop of human blood. Nevertheless, the citizens of the New World have no slight reason for self-gratulation that their interests are not wrapt up with those of the Old, for never did the affairs of the latter wear a gloomier aspect, except when war, with its insatiate cry, was raging through the land. It is no exaggeration, though it may be self-repetition on my part, to say that there is not a State on this side of the Atlantic which is, either internally or externally, in a safe and satisfactory condition at the present moment. Russia, a nation of bondsmen ruled with an iron rod, has, like the first murderer, her hand against every one and every one's hand against her. For even the wretched tools in her late deeds of darkness, flimsy Austria and factious Prussia, tremble with hate as well as fear before her, because in an hour of need, and *their* turns will come, they can look in no quarter for effectual succor, so long as they insanely combat the righteous demands of their subjects, whose intense though noiseless enthusiasm reminds one of the melted lava at the crater's edge, waiting but for the fitting moment to boil over with death-dealing fury. England, on the one hand, can claim feeble Portugal alone for an ally, which, after the exhaustion of its puny strength in civil broils, will be worse than a dead weight on her shoulders; and France, on the other, has only a hireling hand-maiden in distracted Spain, that in any emergency will prove, as has always been the case, a curse instead of a blessing to her. And all this too while the people of both countries are daily going from bad to worse, morally and physically, as must ever happen, when food-riots are the employment of honest men and the pastime of rogues.

Paris, Feb. 15, 1847.

LETTER VI.

Time seems in Europe to be "out of joint." Months fly by, and the gloomy reality they leave behind looks bright in comparison with the dark prospect which the coming months reveal. Every day increases the perplexity of yesterday; every event makes "confusion worse confounded;" and the anxious enquiry on all sides is, when and how this painful uncertainty is like to end.

Since the departure of the last mail to America, a Royal decree has been promulgated at Berlin which must powerfully and permanently affect, in all their relations, the inhabitants of Prussia. Thirty-two years ago their King, FREDERICK WILLIAM III., promised them a constitutional representation, in recompense for their heroic and successful efforts to repel the French invasion. This promise, never forgotten, though few only of those to whom the pledge was originally given are probably now alive to witness its redemption, has at length been partially fulfilled by his successor, the reigning Sovereign. True, the flood-gates of civil rights have not been thrown widely open, but an additional sluice, as it were, has been raised which can never be shut again; for the Germans are proverbially as tenacious in holding fast to what they have secured, as they are patient in waiting for that which has been once guaranteed to them. And if the boon now bestowed is in appearance but a poor apology for a Constitution, still it points the way to better things which are yet in store.

It would be unjust, however, to suppose that this popular concession is a solitary leap from absolutism to liberalism; for within less than the last half century, such has been the progress towards freedom in Prussia, that the legalized voters there more than doubly outnumber those in France. The first forward step ever taken was to abolish the local jurisdiction and prerogatives of the Seigniors, and, by consequence, to elevate serfs to the condition of freemen: The second, to create municipal corporations, wherein citizens of even moderate means enjoy the right of suffrage: The third, to provide for the maintenance of religion and popular instruction: And the fourth, to organize a militia, which, in an hour of dire extremity, sent the foreign tyrant vanquished to his home, and will not prove less effective, should the unhappy occasion offer, against domestic tyranny. But all this in nowise detracts from the high credit due to those Councillors of the Crown, who dared, at the present critical moment, to act as they have done, in defiance of Russian opposition, Austrian remonstrance, and, strange as it may sound, French repugnance. For it was while the three Northern Courts were in joint deliberation, at the suggestion of England, upon the course to be pursued by them in respect to the Montpensier controversy, that the attempt was made by these bold men to liberalize still further the institutions of their country whose sympathy and aid they openly, though not officially, announced could be surely counted upon by their former ally of Saxon blood, in any difficulty which might arise out of the Spanish marriages.

But what has been done by Prussia, like every thing else now taking place, seems only to complicate still more the actual state of affairs; because, notwithstanding she is alienated to a certain extent from her late coadjutors in crime, any approximation to the self-styled champion of liberal institutions upon the Continent of Europe is not thereby rendered more easy. And constitutional France herself must, in her turn, if she would avoid complete isolation, take an unnatural refuge in the arms of those very enemies to liberty, whose outrageous conduct towards Italy, Switzerland and Poland, she has been professedly deprecating for years. But it is doubtful whether she will be allowed to do even this, for these Powers have merely tolerated her revolutionary King, and the Sovereign, to whom the Duchess of Montpensier is presumptive heiress, has never been recognized by them as the rightful occupant of the Spanish throne. And if not admitted to the fellowship of overbearing Russia and tyrannic Austria, in what direction can she look for support? If she is in the ascendant at Madrid, she is not so in Spain: In Italy she is not beloved, — in Turkey she is distrusted, — in Holland she is hated and throughout Germany she is feared.

There is nothing which more strongly marks the troublous state of the present times than the raising of troops and money, or the attempt to do so, in every quarter. France has just voted between four and five millions of francs to the increase of her effective force in the interior, and every soldier absent on the usual six months' furlough is ordered to return to his post. Anarchical Spain would do as much and more, were it not that her law of recruitment, owing to Carlist influence, is successfully resisted, and that, while even rickety

Austria can effect a loan of forty millions of florins, she cannot lay her hand upon a single dollar which belongs to her, the national revenues having been pledged for years, to repay the enormous sums that her worthless rulers have wasted in their reckless course of folly and crime. Certain of the Swiss Cantons are making military preparations, which are so far beyond their means that they must be the work of some foreign hand: In Portugal, where the tottering Queen could not keep her place a single day but for English support, the pillage of banks, in the name of a junta, and forced contributions, have superseded, amid civil broils, the necessity of regular supplies: And into Poland regiment follows regiment in such quick succession that they already number one hundred thousand men, in whose presence a groaning population yields without submission to the law of the sword?

But of far more pressing import than either of the facts I have mentioned, is the daily increasing scarcity of food throughout all Europe. Famine sits by the hearth of the million, and laughs at every attempt to dislodge her. In parts of Scotland, as well as in Ireland, to such fearful extremities are men reduced, that the dead are left for the dying to bury. And even in several Departments of France, a country better provided for than most others, the farmer hardly dare carry his grain to market for fear of leaving his life there with his merchandize; because the empty hand of the peasant, with wife and children looking to it for bread, sets at defiance the official sword, which frequently drops from the dead hand of him who was compelled to draw it in a loathsome cause.

And whence comes all this? Is it from the failure of a harvest, or the destruction of a crop? No! These may be the occasion, but they are not the cause of the evil. The cause lies deeper. It lies in the perverse contravention of that great law of the Almighty — the base and groundwork of the economy of nations as well as of individuals — the first free-trade principle ever enunciated, which teaches us to "love our neighbor as ourselves and to do unto others as we would have that they should do unto us." In blind and impious defiance of this holy precept, nations have refused to receive, in fair exchange for their own products, the gifts of nature at the hands of strangers; and, through greediness of gain, which they vainly imagined must be in exact proportion to the loss of others, they have succeeded in entailing a curse upon their several soils. But had the rule of action, which the All-wise Lawgiver first promulgated, been duly observed, if only since the commencement of the present century, the cry of famishing wretches would never have been heard, as it now is, in one part of the globe, when there is food enough and to spare in others. Want would have dogged the steps of idleness alone, and industry would have asked no paid advocate to uphold its inalienable right to a fair proportion in the fruits of the earth.

Paris, March 15, 1847.

LETTER VII.

There has lately been a national Fast in England, specially ordained, in the words of the Royal proclamation, " to avert the heavy judgments of the Almighty;" as though that great and good Being would punish the poor Irish for the sins of their tormentors; or, as if these last, by a self-inflicted penance of twenty-four hours, could expiate the iniquities they have been perpetrating towards a dependent country ever since the scandalous *annexation* of it was accomplished.

Men are ready enough to cry out, " It is the hand of God ! " whenever a calamity, national or individual, befals them ; but they are not so hasty to acknowledge a diabolical agency when the work of their own hands is evil. So the English people, impiously laying at the door of Providence the awful accumulation of woe beneath which Ireland is literally writhing, seem to forget that it is their own misrule, and not heaven's wrath, which is depopulating one of heaven's fairest regions. They fancy that their consciences are void of offence towards their starving fellow-subjects, because the failure, of a certain crop, to which millions looked for subsistence, could not be imputed to them ; but whose fault was it that a whole nation's welfare turned upon the healthy state of a single root ? Posterity will regard with contemptuous horror the besotted bigotry whi h, till within a few years, robbed the Irish Roman Catholic of his dues ; legalizing a deputed tyranny, the worst sort of oppression, in his land ; and fitting him, like the over-driven bullock, to stumble and fall at the very first obstacle.

Yet, how much is there to admire in the English character, although till recently the English government has been the most arrogant and overbearing on the face of the earth, and although Englishmen themselves have shown how practicable it is to live and flourish in the enjoyment of an inordinate self-esteem, and in sovereign indifference to the opinions of others. Napoleon, as is well known, called them a nation of shop-keepers ; but, commercial as may be their habits, the narrow, peddling spirit which animates the rulers of the people whom he governed, cannot be laid to their charge. After recognizing the justice of a claim, the House of Commons would have paid, and not have attempted to elude, it, as was done in the case of the twenty-five millions of francs, extorted from the Chamher of Deputies by General Jackson's rude but well directed measures. And in corroboration of my remark, observe with what high and politic motives the payment of the interest on the Russian-Dutch loan is continued, in compliance with the spirit, and in defiance of the letter, of the bond. *May certain defaulting members of a kindred community soon follow so bright an example, and, without being more generous, learn to be more just.*

The present embarrassed condition of France in respect to food, is chiefly attributable to the remissness of ministers who, although seasonably and repeatedly warned of the coming dearth by one of their own officers, the very person on whose authority I write, wilfully closed their ears to the threatened danger, for fear of exciting a premature alarm, and of thereby damaging their prospects at the elections then close at hand. Even the government journal now admits that " there has been an extreme want of foresight," and the truth of its words is confirmed by daily accounts of food-riots in many of the Departments, with all their fatal consequences. Frequent convictions before the tribunals follow of course; but, paradoxical as it may appear, the wonder is, that they are not either more or less frequent. For above all piaise, is the virtue which can refrain from violence when wife and children are crying for bread, and stern must be the heart that can punish the miserable peasant whom distress has driven to desperation. Much, however, as other parts of the kingdom may suffer, Paris is always secure from want, for the *good* King Louis Philippe knows full well that on its contentment hangs the fate of his august dynasty.

Spain is sinking deeper into the mire every day. Her debt is nearly equal to the half of England's enormous burden, and by giving preference to domestic over foreign creditors she has been guilty of as flagrant an act of repudiation as was ever committed in America. Her ministers, in contempt of justice and decency, have within a few weeks driven from the Senate a distinguished individual, whose only crime was a refusal to assume the command in a distant province, where all the world knew that a prison was in readiness for his reception. And her Queen, disgusted at a first interview with an imbecile partner, neither is, nor is like, legitimately to be, in a way to prevent the Montpensier issue, now soon expected, from mounting the throne.

Portugal would be without a sovereign tomorrow, were it not that England lends a moral, but at the same time a most immoral, aid to support a cause which should be left to perish in its own infamous weakness.

But, notwithstanding these and other dark pictures, which regard to truth compels one to draw, all things are constantly working together for the gradual emancipation of man from the rule of hereditary power, and nothing, I am convinced, as you may one day be, will more effectually contribute to such a happy consummation than the opening of every port in Europe and America to manly competition and unshackled intercourse.

Paris, April 1, 1847.

LETTER VIII.

I have entered Paris hundreds of times, and in all sorts of humors, but, whether sad or cheerful, my sadness has always vanished at the Barrier, like a package of contraband goods, conscious of no right of entry, and my cheerfulness has always changed into the thoughtless gaiety of youth, whenever I found myself amid the busy, merry-making crowd, which seemed possessed of an eternal vivacity. Yet the other day, after a twelvemonth's absence, on returning to this city, whose continuous flow of joy, if not of happiness, real or superficial, knows no ebb; within whose walls—and this can be said of no other place—life is more than tolerable, nay, often proves a blessing, even without the solace of a single friend; and upon whose brilliant boulevards, Elysian Fields and terraced gardens, is always met a sovereign remedy for the restless heart or the unquiet spirit—I found that either Paris or I had undergone a very sensible alteration since we parted. My coachman, uninstructed by me, took a direction that led close to the spot where nature's beautiful works had been made tributaries to the urgent necessities of a patriotic cause, which, in the stern destruction of its course, painfully demonstrated the odious and selfish blindness of a wilful government, ending, by necessity, in irreparable mischief,—the spot where once waved many an aged tree, for whose grateful shade the high or humble pedestrian, upon a summer's day, though less than the hard-tasked laborer, released awhile to take his mid-day meal and rest, could not feel otherwise than truly thankful. The living ornaments of this queenly city, which tedious time alone, but not even Parisian art, can replace, were hewn down in a single night, leaving the shops they sheltered as bare and mean as was poor Gervase Skinner's homely front beneath his shaven poll, when at length he was allowed to escape from his persecutors, and from the madhouse where they had confined him. During a half-hour's drive through the most public thoroughfares, and at a fashionable hour, not one handsome equipage, not one smiling face, nor a single attempt at pastime was it my fortune to encounter. Now, as Paris without its sparkling boulevards, its boulevards without their arborous array, and this round world wanting one of its essential elements, were things of which I had not begun to dream, I certainly did not, "in my heart of heart," bless King Louis

Philippe, whom I knew to be the responsible author of the graceless metamorphosis which my eyes beheld.

Some fourteen years ago, no wall, I remember, was sacred from the profanation of an attempted resemblance, in manner most unseemly, to the Royal Personage who inhabited the Tuileries. Since then, however, till the 22d of last February, fines and imprisonments, aided by armed sentinels, have superseded the use of the whitewasher's brush. But at the present moment caricatures of falling, fallen and flying majesty, are as plenty as the squares in the shop windows; nor is one word of pity heard on any side in behalf of the fugitive Monarch. Party he had none deserving the name, friends but a few, personal adherents not many. Charles X. when he abandoned his throne of *divine right*, went off, at least, like a gentleman, as he really was, in his own carriage, and followed by a gallant train of devoted cavaliers; but Louis Philippe, who escaped like the wicked man, "flying when no one pursueth," fell lower than from a throne justly forfeited to those that gave it—*he fell from his reputation*, and found himself in a hired cab, a foreign steamer, and in a strange land, whose Queen he had deceived, and whose government he had defied. The affrighted prince and his family might have departed with unsullied personal dignity: Thousands of Frenchmen were at hand to save them from every harm: All were too glad to be rid of him and of his.

Seventeen years since there was not a man in the wide world who had, in the multifarious cast of characters, such a grand and godlike one to enact as the "King of the Barricades." For nearly half a century now Europe has been in the course of active change. Individual man has been asserting, and not always unsuccessfully, his inalienable, but for long unceded, rights, which of course could be done only at the expense of sovereigns. Constitutions have been demanded, and constitutions have been granted; but rarely till the iron hand of the people made itself heard at the gate of the palace. The republican principle, rooted and reared in America on being transplanted thither, has in its returning fruitfulness so quietly and universally pervaded every country here, that to suppose an absolute monarch will exist in Europe many years hence, is a stretch of fancy far beyond my comprehension. England, however, the most liberal and democratic power on this side of the Atlantic—France I do not take into account for the moment, as she is yet but one remove from anarchy—will be the last to cut away her monarchic and aristocratic appendages, for the obvious reason that Englishmen, having more practical good sense than most people, yield reasonably to the popular cry, as was the case in Emancipation and Reform, and thus will they stave off the day of regeneration till all classes are gradually fitted for its enjoyment. Why did not Louis Philippe act in like manner? He might have been THE MAN of his day; and it was not for lack of perspicacity that he was not. For when he came to the throne, he must have seen that it was not a mere popular breath which had whistled his predecessor down the wind to perch him in his place, but a deep-drawn inspiration not to be trifled with. He knew perfectly well what was the moving cause that carried him from his Chateau of Neuilly to the palace of the Tuileries; he knew that the voice of the people—a great, generous and daring people—called to him in a tone of deepest distress, to lead them forth from the thick darkness which his cousin-kings had suffered to accumulate upon their land—to instruct them in self-government by judiciously enlarging the right of suffrage, and in economy, by setting them a pure example—to rescue, by the spread of education, one-half of their offspring from the grossness of ignorance, and, in a word, to tell confiding millions how best to live for the advancement of their own happiness and thereby of their country's glory.

But in the face of such knowledge what did this transient idol of a deluded nation do, and what did he not do? He strove to gag the Press by incarcerating its editors, and by robbing them in fines of thousands upon thousands of francs. He turned his ministers off if they proved too honest and unpliant, or ruthlessly dismissed them after they had filed their hands past cleansing, working at his abominations. He gave neither bread, nor the means of earning it, to a willing and long-suffering people, but squandered millions of money in fortifications cunningly devised to out-thunder the wail of the starving. He trenched fearfully upon State revenues, he heavily mortgaged his own property, and he unblushingly bought majorities in both Chambers. He practically declared what Louis XIV. said—"I am the State," and yet, just retribution! he too, like the dethroned monarch of old, who gathered his food with the beasts of the field, learned at last, by woful experience, that power abused is power lost; and that, stripped of the phantom gewgaws of royalty, even a king is nothing but a "bare forked animal," differing nought, save in virtue or in vice, from his fellow-men, whom he has either served or betrayed.

Paris, May 3, 1848.

LETTER IX.

The late French Revolution seems to be regarded too generally as through a falsely magnifying lens, and by some persons it is wrongly speculated upon as an isolated fact. Whereas it is, in truth, only one of the signs of the times. A physician would be ridiculed who mistook a blotch on the face of a patient, sick of a fever, for the disease itself. The geologist would be scoffed at who taught his disciples that the temporary outbreak of a flame on the mountain's side was the beginning and the end of a volcano, whose crater was visible at the top, ready at any moment to belch forth torrents of fire. So he who looks upon the last eruption in France as anything more or less than a manifest revelation and outpouring of the spirit that has long been agitating and regenerating Europe, is either stupidly blind or has wilfully shut his eyes against the truth.

The worm will writhe when it is trod upon. Men will cry out when they are hurt. All nature is imbued with the spirit of resistance against oppression. Is it a wonder then, that mankind, after being ridden over for centuries, has in these latter days turned thought and word into action, and, like a mettlesome horse, his full strength attained, has, in contempt of imbecile, timorous and dishonest masters, become restive under whip and spur?

Looking no further back than can a man of middle age, compare the state in which Europe was forty or fifty years ago, marking its gradations to its present condition, and say if the revolutionary spirit, now palpably embodied, is a thing of yesterday. Take England for an example, and, recollecting what she once was, and what has been her onward democratic march, think on what she is. She was a hot-bed of sinecures, aristocratic pretensions, monopolies and kindred impositions; her people were not more fairly represented than the French under Louis Philippe; boroughs, rightly christened *rotten*, were bought and sold as openly as cattle in the market. Parliamentary influence and church patronage were acknowledged articles of traffic, and princely fortunes were often swamped or wrecked past redemption by systematic bribery of the worst possible description. Then too that in this iniquitous whole no part might be wanting in conformity, a considerable portion of the community, who saw fit to worship their Maker otherwise than according to the canons of the established Church, were under an infamous ban of incapacity. But at length the spirit of man was stirred, and the voice of a multitude, that no one could number, was heard pronouncing the words, Emancipation! Reform! The protected *Few* made a stand once and again, like that of the grim monster himself, against the unprotected *Many*, but it was of no avail. In one instance the monarch yielded, though only when told by his ministry, while surrendering their trusts, that his sole alternatives were " Concession or Hanover;" and in the other the nobles bowed in acquiescence, but not until assured beyond question that their House was in danger of falling upon their own heads.

England, then, has for a long time been in the course of bloodless revolution, not yet finished. Abuses have shrunk, though not disappeared, under the touch of a reformed Parliament. Roman Catholic, and Dissenter, and soon, too, will the Jew, exercise the rights and enjoy the privileges which pertain to society; and everybody is at liberty to purchase what he wants in the cheapest market he can find. Such *was* and such *is* England. But other Powers of Europe, either wanting the sense to see, or the wisdom to acknowledge, the gigantic spirit of the age, through obtuseness or folly, refused to go with the times, and have consequently been carried away by them. Now and then, it is true, grudging concessions are made, but rarely, if ever, before the "toe of the peasant galled the kibe of the noble," and never, even then, did the inutility of half measures fail to appear. The consequence of all which is, that the advocates of regal dominion and those of self-government, are in general array against each other, and have more than once lately brought their difference in opinion to bloody conclusions. All the world is aware that such has eminently been the case in the country and on the spot where I now write, and the keenest capacities are sorely taxed to form even a plausible opinion upon the term which affairs are most likely next to take, though a legitimate republic and healthful liberty, as immediate results, are beyond hope.

I was delighted at the Revolution of February, because France under the late dynasty was far on the high road to bankruptcy and complete demoralization, so that her "last state" cannot possibly be "worse than her first." Still, I am by no means so sanguine as some persons profess to be in the success of the present experiment, for, in the first place, a Frenchman's idea of a republic, according to our notions, is not only vague but almost negative, the utmost stretch of his fancy reaching no further than to an absence of royalty and to universal fraternization, which is a phrase beyond the comprehension of practical men. Then, it is almost certain that there will be but one *Chamber*, which, unless things have changed their names, will constitute what is called an oligarchy. Moreover, the first step taken by the sovereign people, though a good step, has been badly taken. Mirabeau truly said that an assembly of more than one hundred men is a mob. What then can reasonably be hoped or expected in the way of constitution manufacturing from a mob of nine hundred men, more than one half of whom are provincial physicians or lawyers, skilled, it may be in the human constitution, or in the constitutions of courts, and the rest a miscellaneous collection of gentlemen, who, in the few coming months, through sheer ignorance of state affairs, will probably do more mischief than they ever did good in so many years of their existence? The opening days of the National Assembly would have done discredit to the early meetings of a college spouting club, and though M. de Lamartine has made a brilliant display of eloquence, the wretched condition of France, French finances, and above all of Parisian operatives, is no more relieved by it than the horrors of burning Rome were by Nero's exquisite fiddling.

Paris, May 11, 1848.

LETTER X.

In a letter signed a "STATES'-MAN," published in the *London Times* of the 10th inst., I spoke of the likelihood of the Representatives in the French National Assembly being driven out, some time or other, from their Chamber by the hand of violence; and five days later, that is, on the 15th, my prediction was accomplished. It is not my intention to trouble you with details of that day's history, all of which will be found in public journals or private letters, carried out by the next steamer, but in this short note I would take a cursory view of things and persons as they have been and now are.

Immediately after the famous 16th of April, when the Provisional Goverment was surprised and besieged in the Hotel de Ville by a rabble of twenty thousand men, M. de Lamartine, the foremast man of the day was guilty, it is thought, of a grave political error. When found by General Changarnier on that occasion he was very pale and evidently disheatened, though of a courageous nature. "Why do you not call out the National Guard," said the General, "and defend yourselves, instead of suffering these ruffians to coop you up here?"

"Apply to M. Ledru Rollin, for it is his business," replied the Minister of Foreign Affairs.

M. Rollin, who was one of those at whose instigation the insurrectionary movement had been got up, though he has since seen fit to change his tactics, gave the required order for beating the *rappel*, but not until he had been badgered into doing so by the rough arguments of the unceremonious soldier. The consequence of which was, that the National Guard turned out in great force, and danger for the time was averted. Then, at a moment so propitious for exposing delusion and unmasking treason, if he on whom all eyes were fixed in hope, and who almost alone was above suspicion, if he had stood boldly forth the champion of a practicable Republic, untrammelled by the idle fancies of the socialist and the optimist, and if he had proved himself the unscrupulous contemner of ultra democracy, brutal clubism and utopian communism; if he had denounced as dangerous the authors of these phantasmas, instead of timorously hugging them to his heart and refusing to abandon them; if, in short, he had been true to the occasion and to himself, the pitiful and disgraceful scenes which last Monday witnessed would never have occurred.

And, indeed, pitiful and disgraceful they truly were, for what could be more so than the sight of a faithful citizen-guard betrayed by its leader, a self-styled republican, of noble family and of ignoble heart*—an august Assembly—the choice of thirty-two millions of freemen—rudely hustled from their hall by the excited dregs of the populace—the President ignominiously expelled, and the peace of society on the point of perishing in civil broil? But in justice I should say, in passing, that this is only one side of the picture. The other is honorable in the highest degree to French character, nay, even glorious in its beauty. France was without even a nominal government. It had vanished. Traitors were at the

*General Courtois.

Hotel de Ville. They called themselves supreme. And truly for a while the balance quivered between rule and misrule, between peace and war. Then it was that the *générale* echoed through the streets of Paris—more than a hundred thousand citizen-soldiers, completely armed, rushed to the rescue—the Chamber of the Assembly was cleared, and its members were re-conducted to their places—the legitimate Executive was re-constituted—the rebel chiefs—some of them the very culprits Lamartine had cherished—were cast into prison, and men once more breathed freely. All this was the work of three short hours, and in this little space were taken and retaken, by main force, two of the most important buildings in the city, and that too, wonderful to relate, without the loss of a single life! A parallel case I do not remember in history.

M. de Lamartine's most unpardonable and unstatesman-like offence, if not crime, was committed in the earliest days of the National Assembly. With his overwhelming majority of votes, and his admitted preëminence, it was the almost universal hope that he would place himself at the head of the moderate party—itself stronger by far than all others together, and thus secure the tranquillity, peace and order so all essential to France, and so ready a means of making her the richest and happiest nation of Europe. But what did he do? Too tender of his newly-fledged popularity, he weakly joined in the false cry, "There are no parties!"—as though parties and politics were not inseparable; and to his timid, or at least, mistaken course, in refusing bravely to lead whither the good were eager to follow, is to be imputed a large portion of the trouble which has since ensued, and more than one black shade in the dark futurity which mocks the eye of man.

The truth is, that the present Executive of France is a mosaic, incongruous and therefore inefficient,—its Assembly an unwieldy machine, and what is worse, if worse can be, its Treasury a nearly empty coffer, which a few months may drain to its last sou. Then, commerce of every sort being all but stopped, how are the extraordinary expenses to be met? such as, for example, about one hundred thousand francs a day to workmen who are too idle or unskilful to earn a living; twenty-two thousand five hundred to Representatives who do nothing but wrangle, save when by their carelessness in appointing officers of high trust, or stupidity in issuing orders, they suffer themselves to be thrust into the street; and about the same amount to some sixteen hundred of the *gamins* of Paris, who for the safety of the state must be kept out of mischief, and allowed to play soldier, at the expense of the honest *bourgeoisie*, who think themselves quite equal in their military capacity to the preservation of order, if, indeed, order can be preserved by any body.

Every one is asking, but no one can tell, how the Government is going to raise money. If it is to be by taxing the capitalists, or men of independent fortunes, their property, invested for the most part in public funds of some sort or other, and in railways, has diminished one-half in value, and pays, when it does pay, in paper, which a few months hence may possibly be only a remove or two above the ancient *assignats* in point of respectability. If owners of lands are to be squeezed, very many of them have already mortgaged their estates, and, if these hard times continue, they, together with all they possess, will soon be past redemption. If the mortgagees are to suffer, they have long ago dispossessed themselves of their cash to the mortgagers. And if bankers are to be fleeced, they hold nothing but protested bills, and, for the time being, valueless notes of hand. What, then, is to be done in order that this land, absolutely teeming with blessings, shall be saved from the evil which improvidence, extravagance and rapacity have been heaping up against her? M. de Lamartine, with his surpassing eloquence, will perhaps answer the question, always provided he make no third blunder, but I am persuaded nobody else can.

Paris, May 25, 1848.

LETTER XI.

On Monday, May 22d, the United States' Minister, resident at Paris, presented to the members of the Executive Government an address, " tendering, in the name and behalf of the American people, the congratulations of Congress to the people of France upon the *success* of their recent efforts to *consolidate* the principles of liberty in a republican form of government."

The measure was well-intended doubtless, it was harmless too, but at the same time it was amusing in the highest degree; for it reminded one of a certain homely saying, the purport of which is, the folly of untimeously counting the progeny of the feathery tenants of a barn-yard before incubation has done its perfect work. The Americans themselves are too shrewd by far to cry out before they are well clear of the wood, but, it would seem, that they are not so very unwilling to instigate others to such inopportune self-glorification. That like encouragement was needed here, however, no one will believe who witnessed last Sunday's fête, the object of which, whether real or pretended, as yet remains in complete obscurity. Some persons say it was made in honor of the nine hundred Representatives; some say that it was to do reverence to the Republic in its swaddling clothes; and others that between two and three hundred thousand dollars were wasted for the sake of rejoicing the hearts of the Parisians, — as though rejoicing were becoming in a city where one hundred and fifteen thousand of its inhabitants are registered paupers, and all the rest are, without exaggeration, if things do not change for the better, on the high road to ruin.

You can hardly be aware of the deep and general distress which has fallen on this people. Most persons of fortune had invested great portions of their wealth in the *Rentes*, or National Securities, and railways guaranteed by government; many of them were owners of real estate; while everybody, if the proud title of *propriétaire* were not to be aspired to, was too happy to see his or her name inscribed, even for a small amount, upon the *Grand Livre*, or enrolled among the universal carriers who had superseded the owners of mail-coaches and *diligences*. But at present railways pay nothing, houses are equally unprofitable, and in less than six months, it is universally believed and said, that public securities will be in no better plight. Men who had invested large capitals in extensive manufactories, have been obliged to discharge most of their workmen, and they, as well as the smaller dealers, whenever you enter their halls of sale, almost beg you to purchase their merchandise at your own price. A wholesale manufacturer of gilt bronzes, for example, whom I have known for years to be a liberal, careful and honest trader, told me a day or two since that he had been obliged to discharge five hundred workmen, that he had lost an immense sum of money at his banker's, where he was obliged to keep it for daily purposes, that he would be forced to work with his own hands, and that, in a word, he was ruined.

In all fevers, whether political or otherwise, as there is a beginning so must there be a duration and an end. But the duration and the end, it is needless to say, greatly depend upon the treatment to which the patient is subjected.

If *one* powerful and skilful hand be made responsible for the issue, all may go well; but if a multiplicity of councillors be relied on, there may be safety, but not to the unhappy sufferer. Now, it so happens that France has many among her children who are faithful, and able to handle her tenderly and judiciously in her present sad extremity; but the heartless quacks, who revel in her distemper for their own base purposes, are fool-hardy and unscrupulous, crying in the ears of the moderate and timid party — an immense majority, by the by, — that there is danger of "reaction," by which means the arm of the strong and good is robbed of half its strength. The National Assembly is like the deck of a man-of-war going into action with a double complement of men — each man in his neighbor's way. The five members of the Executive Government do not work well together. Lamartine, who, if it had been in him, might have become the Washington of his country, loses, by the actions of those connected with him and his own inaction, more popularity in twenty-four hours, than even his surpassing eloquence can restore in as many days. Ledru Rollin, his stumbling-block and millstone, is, to use no stronger term, held in general dis-esteem; and as for their three colleagues, all to be said of them is, that they need only the gripe of a determined and powerful master on their shoulders to make them do good service to their country.

Absence of royalty is here called a Republic; but what are names if realities are wanting? One great essential in republicanism is, not to interfere with private rights, but to leave every man to manage his concerns according to his own will, as long as he encroach not on the legal privileges of others. But what sort of a Republic is that which gulps, as is now threatened, a dozen railways at once — private property, all of them, in a certain sense — and pays, as the price of its gormandizing, in a depreciated currency, which, being thus inordinately swelled in bulk and thrown suddenly into the market, must necessarily suffer a still greater depreciation.

A general European war is not thought to be near, but European peace is still further off. Unity is wanting in Italy; weakness and distraction reign in Austria; rank treason slaps England in the face; Poland, according to M. de Lamartine, is no better off in regard to her sympathisers than was the rich man in hell when told that there was an impassable gulph between him and those who might have cooled his parched tongue; Russia is biding her time; and all Germany is a hodge-podge. Certainly, if there be "a special providence in the fall of a sparrow," never was there a more auspicious moment for bettering man's condition, in so far as the characters of reigning princes bear upon it. The Emperor of Russia looks on from afar and smiles; the King of Prussia hugs the wine cup too closely; the Emperor of Austria is the reverse of wise; the King of Naples is grossness itself; the Queen of Spain is — is — a woman, and therefore of her I will say no more than that both she and her royal cousin of Portugal are curses instead of blessings to their afflicted countries. But still I doubt not that the spirit of true liberty, now at last awake, will in its own good time extract from this incongruous medley of ingredients a feast of good things which will rejoice the heart and gladden the eyes of every man who loves his fellow-man as he ought.

Paris, May 25, 1848.

LETTER XII.

During the last week there has been a comparative calm here, an unwholesome calm, not the tranquility of health. National Guards, and troops of the line have been called out, but a mere display of force was sufficient to overcome the turbulent workmen who threatened the peace of the city, not without some show of reason on their side.

When the first Revolution took place in France, the people had something to fight for and against. They had the common rights of humanity to recover, and a grinding nobility to crush. When the revolution of 1830, exchanged a sovereign *Log* for a sovereign *Stork*, they had still something worth striking a blow for, which was to rid themselves of a preposterous fiction, that of king-ship by divine right. But when the Revolution of 1848, in its success, surprised its inventors as much as its victims, they had no one great political object in view, after having un-made the work of royalty which their own hands had fashioned. They had tried their skill at king-making, and the attempt was a failure; not knowing, therefore, which way to turn, and imagining that a republic consisted simply in an absence of monarchy, they shouted *vive la République!* Hitherto they had fought and bled and got nothing for their pains, save a *bourgeoisie* that looked down on them, while they themselves, thanks to Louis Philippe's selfish and cruel policy, were left by thousands without employment, and consequently without bread. It behoved then the men whom the 24th of February put in power, to take some immediate and effectual steps for supplying the wants of these sufferers, who were willing to work, but were by necessity idle. National workshops were consequently established, and it was weakly imagined that a remedy for an evil, which all acknowledged, was thus provided; whereas the remedy has proved, by its injudicious application, worse, if anything, than the disease itself. A young and inexperienced man was placed at the head of these shops, one Emile Thomas, who has within a few days been spirited away to Bordeaux, in the care of two police agents, by order of government, which, rather than do openly and boldly what it conceived to be right, was willing to expose its own weakness, at the same time that it grossly violated private rights. This person had been guilty of disobedience, and he or those about him had permitted abuses in the administration entrusted to their hands, which you will see set forth in the speech of the Minister himself during last Saturday's debate in the Assembly. Instead of encouraging good workmen to remain with good masters, and giving useful employment to able laborers; instead of selecting the most worthy among the indigent, and sending the lazy and dissolute away; thirty sous a day were offered to every vagabond in France. Whereupon, paupers, within and without Paris, hastened to claim the reward of idleness, for no useful work was done in these resorts — offenders against the laws, convicted and unconvicted, came in for their shares — cheats, under different names, received the charity, over and over again in the course of the same twenty-four hours, and, in a word, every worthless fellow, who had had a falling out with work, rushed to the plunder of the State; so that the number to be supported by the public for doing nothing having swelled to one hundred and fifteen thousand, the cost to the country since the 1st of March, has been about a million of francs a month! It was thought proper to effect a reform in this socialist experiment, and, an *émeute* being feared, the military, as I have said, were paraded in great force.

The owners of many of the principal railways have published most powerful and conclusive remonstrances against the contemplated appropriation of their property by the State. On the other hand, the arguments advanced by Ministers in favor of their infamous project are paltry and discreditable. But one consideration, which, it is feared, will outweigh in the minds of the latter a thousand remonstrances, is that the perpetration of their proposed folly will " put money in their pockets," to obtain which they are even now almost at their wits' end. In the month of June, it is thought, that the dividends on public securities, amonnting to thirty millions of francs, will be punctually paid, as the bank has promised to provide the necessary funds, but I have met with no man who is bold enough to believe that the one hundred and fifty millions due in September will be forthcoming, unless the men at present in power be displaced for their betters, and things take a more favorable turn.

The Committee on the Constitution, it is said, will in about a fortnight have finished their work, which the National Assembly will then take into its consideration. And when I tell you that there is to be but one Chamber and a sort of Council, which will have all the vices and none of the virtues of a Senate, you must fear with me that the present attempt at a popular government is in great danger of being a great failure.

Paris, June 1, 1848.

LETTER XIII.

Montesquieu somewhere says, " that a republic, which has always a tendency to produce many men of mediocrity, if its administrators are fortunate, will be happily administered, and wisely, if they are wise." Here, however, at the present moment, although mediocrity abounds, men distinguished either for their good fortune or their wisdom, have not, as yet, shown themselves; but, on the contrary, distraction in council and weakness in execution, are the attributes of those who rule over the land.

I have before mentioned the violation of individual liberty in the person of a man named Thomas, whom the Government, not daring to arrest on account of his popularity among the workmen of Paris, sent in vile durance to Bordeaux, under the pretext that his services were required there in a mission which, on its being offered to him, he scornfully rejected. Since that high-handed measure, which was the effect of weakness and fear, another and more striking example of timidity and want of strength has been exhibited in the National Assembly, both by it and by the Executive powers.

The *Procureur Général* and the *Procureur* of the Republic, the first law officers under the Minister of Justice, demanded that Louis Blanc, formerly a member of the Provisional Government, and now one of the Representatives of the people, should be delivered over to take his trial among those indicted for the famous attack of the 15th of May. The Ministers consented that leave to prosecute the supposed traitor, or, at least, accomplice of traitors, should be asked of the Assembly, and then coolly and treacherously left their *employés*, in the lurch, when the time had come for voting.

The Assembly, too, did not behave itself less shamefully, for, after having twice decided, by a majority of nine to seven, in favor of the proposition in the usual manner, that is, by rising and sitting, when called upon to vote by ballot, it shrunk from its convictions, and gave a majority in the negative. The consequence of which was, that the two *Procureurs* threw up their commissions in disgust, the Minister of Justice, who had played a pitiful part, according to the testimony of these gentlemen, was obliged to resign, and the Administration itself came within an ace of being dissolved.

M. de Circourt, a gentlemen well known in America, upon whose institutions he has written often and well, — a person, too, of distinguished merit, both in politics and literature, — was lately appointed Minister to Washington, but because of a cabal got up against him, the government was frightened into offering him the gross insult of putting another man in his place.

The mischievousness too of the powers that be, keeps pace with their feebleness, for the project of robbing the proprietors of railways, or "appropriating," as it is called, their property to the State, is still entertained. Indeed, a considerable majority, in an Assembly of more than eight hundred, lately gave priority of discussion to this outrageous measure over another of real importance, whose object was to consolidate the floating debt of treasury bonds and the funds of the savings banks.

Still there are persons who believe, or affect to believe, that all things are working well, but rest assured of one fact, that until those now in power are changed for better men, there can be no reasonable expectation of any improvement in France.

Paris, June 8, 1848.

LETTER XIV.

By means of your regular correspondents and the public journals, you will receive, at the same time with this note, details of four days' civil war, waged within the French capital since the departure of the mail from this place for the steamer of the 24th; and, if they take you less by surprise than did those of the three days' struggle in February, they will, I am persuaded, excite you to increased wonder, not unmixed with horror and disgust. You will read, perhaps without believing, accounts of Frenchmen in the middle of the nineteenth century, butchering Frenchmen by thousands— of their shooting, hanging, beating to death, *and even mutilating, while yet alive, prisoners and bearers of flags of truce.* You may, I say, read all this without credence, and yet your incredulity will be misplaced.

The impressions made upon my mind by the scenes and actors in the false and fantastic drama which this country has lately presented, have, as you well know, been, in certain respects, of the most gloomy cast.

When the curtain fell on Louis Philippe and his few followers, they all evanished like a phantom troop. It rose, and the Provisional Government appeared. This improvised piece of patchwork told the authors of its high estate — its creators — the dregs of an immoral and infested city — how good, and great, and virtuous, and glorious they were. It fawned upon and flattered a brute body which it feared. It proffered unearned bread to the needy, whether they were so by their own faults or otherwise — mock labor to the unemployed, and a support to everybody. It promised more than even its almost unbounded power could execute, and executed less than even the commonest honesty would have promised.

But the hour of its dissolution arrived, when the National Assembly — a multitudinous and incongruous collection of unschooled polemics, unskilled politicians, and uninstructed statesmen — came dragging into existence with its nine hundred members, puffed up with impossible or impracticable conceits. True, there were not wanting to this assemblage many good men, wise and brave, such as have never failed France in her hour of need; but what was its first grand achievement? An Executive abortion — an epitomised edition of the Provisional Government — whose childish vaunt has been — " Lo, the wondrous and bloodless works of our hands! The evil day is, thanks to us, yet afar off! Have patient trust in our strength, and still greater things shall ye see." But procrastination is not prevention. This shrunken Executive abstract of its Provisional prototype, after having, either in stubborn obtuseness or fiendish malice, laid, or tried to lay, its profane hands on all the material interests which society holds sacred, rashly gave to the sworn foes of order, an opportunity to do their devilish work, such as even in their most sanguine moods these enemies of the public peace could have hardly dared to hope. It attempted to disband at a single stroke the National workshops — those monstrous monuments of its own folly, which harbored more than a hundred thousand of violent men, the victims of their own or others' crimes, — impoverished laborers, lazy vagabonds, liberated galley slaves, — and by so doing it has raised the very stones of the street up against it in judgment; it has changed them into one red hue with fratricidal blood; it has converted Paris into an armed camp and a house of mourning; and all France it has covered with shame.

Paris, June 29, 1848.

LETTER XV.

The gigantic movement which has been lately witnessed in Europe, cannot but ameliorate the general condition of man, whatever be the amount of individual suffering that may grow out of it. A great and radical change was needed, and, to what extent, a very slight glance, by way of review, will show.

The Germans, who are a patient, quiet, and, to a certain extent, docile people, however enthusiastic when deeply moved, have been for years almost bursting with discontent. From time to time a political sop has been thrown to them as we throw a bone to a dog when we dare no longer withhold it for fear of his sharp teeth; but though drop by drop will at last fill a bucket, there is such a thing as letting the moment go by beyond which the operation of filling up becomes impracticable. And thus has it happened in Germany.

Part of Northern Italy was under the dominion of Austria, but when was ever a step-mother's rule, and much less that of a self-constituted and self-interested guardian, an adequate substitute for the protection which nature and natural instincts require? Another portion of it was under kingly authority, and what that meant, according to the ancient order of things, no one need be told. Further to the south, the ill or well-being of the population depended rather on the individual character of a sovereign, and the caprice of a man, than on the guarantee which constitution and laws afford. Tuscany was ruled over by a kind-hearted prince, and therefore was not unblest, but, on the other hand Lucca and one or two other little principalities were theoretically, if not practically, under a sway as despotic as that of Russia, and their Governors, like the Centurion of old, could say to this man, go! and he went, and to another, come! and he came, and no one was bold enough to gainsay their authority.

Rome, till the pontificate of Pius IX., was ever a scene of misrule, and Naples had never ceased to be a hot-bed of abuses.

Who, then, shall dare to say that a general regeneration, a thorough cleansing, was not demanded from one end of the Continent to the other; and who will venture to assert, even in the face of all the crimes which have been perpetrated within the last six months, that men would not have been guilty of a yet greater enormity, if they had still sat tranquilly enduring the blasting influence of a curse that grew by what it fed on?

The amount of material misery inflicted on the world by Napoleon, no one can calculate. For, passing by the official returns of killed and wounded and missing in his numerous campaigns, and the names of many places on the maps of Europe and of the East, which have been immortalized, directly or indirectly through his agency, by scenes of fire and carnage, lust and plunder, who can tell how many villages, once happy in their insignificance, were turned into barren spots by the flaming ploughshare of war, and how many thousands of peasants, once rejoicing in plenty and domestic peace, were chased forth houseless and hopeless, to die piecemeal, after having seen their wives and daughters perish beneath the licentiousness of a ribald soldiery? And yet Napoleon sent the world at least one hundred years ahead of what it was before he came. Before it knew him, its eyes were not half open. It regarded kings as gods till it saw them bowing in humble reverence at the nod of a *ci-devant* lieutenant of artillery, and the royal purple as a divine inheritance, till it saw how easily an Emperor of self-creation could shift its gaudy folds from shoulder to shoulder, or trample them under his own boot-heel. The good which Napoleon did to the world lives after him, *and is now bearing fruit,* while the evil, of which he was the author, is overgrown or forgotten.

And so it will be with the present anarchy which pervades men's ideas in Europe — even more, perhaps, than their outward show would indicate, much as that may be. Europe is older by years that it was a few months since. Nations, like individuals, are old or young, according as they are more or less mature of thought. The United States, though a thing of yesterday in the world's history, are centuries in advance of time-worn communities, by whom they are regarded as but little better than a congregation of barbarians. In some respects, it is true, we lack refinement to a great degree — a certain sort of refinement, that is, which the present constitution of our society forbids; but on the score of *civilization,* whenever I hear the want of that brought up against us by strangers, my invariable and unanswerable answer is, "Are we not capable of self-government, that surest test of civilization, and where is the people that can compare with us in this?"

No system, be it natural or artificial, can exist forever in a state of ferment and fever. Affairs in Europe will before long become more calm. A great but unreal calm will succeed. Men tire of continual agitation. A truce is sometimes welcome even to the conqueror. *But the calm will not endure.* The stone of reform which had been rolling tediously along till the beginning of the present year, — to be then flung hither and thither, overturning and destroying, — may, and probably will, be again retarded in its course; but never can it be fully stopped, unless the nature of man changes, till the European, like the American, has assured himself of each several right of which his fathers were robbed before they knew its value or were able to defend it.

Paris, August 10, 1848.

LETTER XVI.

Believing, as I do, that an absence of hereditary royalty and nobility is a blessing to man's estate, wherever mankind is sufficiently enlightened and civilized to dispense with such costly and senseless gewgaws, I cannot look but with a kindly eye on all those who are struggling to rid themselves of that monstrous figment, birth-excellence, which, like the feudal system, having served its turn, must ere long take its place among other antiquated instances of a by-gone time, to be the historian's study, or the romancers amusement, according as their several fancies shall dictate.

It is now about sixty years since the struggle commenced in this country, and France even yet is in a state of transition. Wholly unsuited as is the Frenchman of our day, for any but a very liberal monarchy, still less is he fitted for a republic, lacking, as he does, almost every requisite that goes to constitute a Republican. Brave among the bravest, he wants civil courage, and falters before the threat of a mob-leader, whom he would leap to encounter upon a barricade, though fire and steel opposed him at every point. He enters a popular assembly — a club, perhaps, — clothed with the best reasoning which human wisdom can devise, but he trusts mainly to the sword for securing to them the success they deserve. If in a minority, he will not yield to the majority, because, in his mind, sharp arms are a legitimate substitute for dull arguments. If out of work, or if advancement come slowly, or if self-love be wounded, drowning all patriotism in the dirty puddle of his own petty interests, he tears up society by the roots. Impatient by nature, if the seed he has sown spring not up at once as "flush as May," he treads it under foot in anger, or fretfully plucks it from its place, in a vain search for the cause of his disappointment.

I have lately had submitted to my inspection an official account of the events of February 24th, contained in an *extra* number of the *Moniteur*, struck off for the special use of Government, and, on reading it, I was surprised to see with what facility a few demagogues, backed by a handful of obstreperous students and workmen, set the grandson of Louis Philippe aside. It was these same demagogues, and not the population of Paris, much less the voice of the French people, that nominated the Provisional Government, all of whose acts, by the by, the National Assembly is now daily employed in remedying or reversing; and it was they who, drunk with the fumes of new authority and uninstructed in the ways of State, backed by their rabble followers, heaped disgrace upon France the 15th of May, and during the four days of June covered her with mourning and shame. But then the scene shifted. Their imbecility or iniquity — it matters not which—being too oppressive for longer endurance, when the glare of civil war flashed over half the capital, they dropped from their high places, like pheasants from a perch, on snuffing the brimstone of their destroyers. In the dire extremity of the moment a man, who better knew how to wield the steel than to manage State affairs — a Republican by heritage, by practice and by suffering, and therefore the fitter instrument wherewith to combat pseudo-Republicans, was called upon to undo the mischief which they had done, and the Assembly, filled with distrust of them, one and all, and unconvinced, as well it might be, that a Republic was the one thing needful for France, clung to him in its hour of peril, as children to a protecting guardian, and still clings to him and his fifty thousand men of war beneath or within the walls of Paris, as if in his person they beheld their only saviour and in his camp their only ark of safety.

Paris, August 16, 1848.

LETTER XVII.

One great truth yet to be learned in Europe is, that Government, like the Sabbath, was made for man, and not man for Government. Since recorded history began, few have been the instances in which rulers have ceded to the ruled, except on compulsion, any of those inalienable rights which neither negligence, nor statute nor lapse of time, can ever annihilate. Long and bloody has been the struggle between the usurpers and the champions of those precious prerogatives which, taken collectively, constitute the political existence of the individual. But the day has at length fully dawned when kings, like other mortals, are held accountable for their acts by the people themselves. When their thrones are regarded as a vain pageant, and their authority "by the grace of God" an idle fiction. Whatever good, however, may eventually come out of this crisis in human affairs, incalculable present evil has sprung from it on every side. For, honest and moderate as are nine-tenths of the liberals throughout Europe, the remaining tenth is so extreme in its opinions and so unscrupulous in its actions, that, to say nothing of the disgrace and wrong thereby wrought to the cause and friends of constitutional freedom, it daily increases the many obstacles which stand between it and its legitimate objects.

The assassination of the Arch-Bishop of Paris, of Prince Lichnowsky at Frankfort, of Count Latour at Vienna, of Count Lembourg at Pesth, and of M. de Rossi at Rome, added to the attempted murder of the Duke of Modena, and the senseless and ruffian-like contempt for the Father of Catholic Christendom, are all the handi-work of red republicans and ultra democrats. But these are not the only or the greatest criminals; the greatest are those bad governors who, by folly aud iniquity, have driven such men to courses so ruinous to themselves and to the interests they profess to serve.

The republican cause is unhappily made the scape-goat of all these sins, and many a year must pass before it can be cleansed from their polluting effects. Not even in France is there likely to be found any exception from this lasting contamination — France, which is constant to nothing, where there are no fixed ideas on government, where common sense so little abounds, where the idol of to-day is stigmatized to-morrow, and where the name of an adventurer, surrounded by a halo borrowed from a great man's glory, outweighs in the esteem of the multitude a long life's service. It is the common people who are revolutionists in our century. In the last it was the middle classes. The latter found much to destroy, and tares and wheat were rooted up together. The former, whose griefs are for the most part those inseparable from a highly artificial state of society, make persons and personal policies their watchwords of insurrection, and would fain turn France into a fallow ground, on which Communism and Socialism can carry out their quixotic experiments. In the act of destruction both orders of men have shown themselves adepts by turn, but in re-construction failures most signal have followed the best efforts of both from the innate defects of French character to which I have above alluded.

Everything which presents itself to my view or to my recollection convinces me that the opinion I ventured to give on a former occasion respecting the probability of France's returning for a season to a monarchial form of government was not a hasty opinion. It is strengthened on considering the highly conservative character of the National Assembly, although the product of universal suffrage, operated upon by the inflammatory circulars of the arch-radical, Ledru Rollin. And it is confirmed by the reports of the latest elections, by which it appears that out of seven candidates returned four are Legitimists, two Orleanists, and only one Republican. This would doubtless be a subject of lamentation to every lover of popular liberty and of the human race, were it not that the French people are incapable of self-government at present from their extreme ignorance, were it not that of the thirty-five millions of inhabitants there are sixteen millions who can neither read nor write, and were it not a fact, made plainer and plainer every day, that the Republic of last February was a juggle from the beginning, a premature creation unsuited to the actual state of things, and therefore, in the common interest of all parties, to be got rid of, as soon as it can be, without further bloodshed.

Paris, Dec. 9, 1848.

LETTER XVIII.

France and French Government are often judged with too little indulgence by those who have been brought up under English and American rule, or, to say the least, with a severity not sufficiently tempered by experience. Discontent and inconstancy are laid to the charge of Frenchmen, when the blame should rather be cast on their institutions, and the perversion of them. For many years the internal administration of affairs in this country has been conducted on principles, directly the reverse of what would be considered wise or safe by the constituents of a well-organized representative government, on either side of the Atlantic. And not the least mischievous of these principles is that which has resulted in the *centralization* of all power within the walls of the capital, whereby the Provinces have been kept, as it were, in leading strings, their administrative faculties unemployed, and their self-dependence undeveloped.

In England and the United States, whether in state, county or township, men are accustomed to think and act for themselves, and even when they pin their faith to that of a party, they cannot fail to imbibe some faint notion respecting the mechanism of government, and to acquire some sense of personal responsibility and importance. But not so has it hitherto been in France, where has always been wanting that practical political training, penetrating every quarter, however remote, which alone is calculated to fit a population for the enjoyment and rational exercise of a constitutional freedom. And this has come of the hard necessity of referring every enterprise, for advisement and approbation, to some ministerial department at Paris, previously to its adoption; whence have arisen innumerable instances, in which a tardy consent has found the sinews of the boldest projectors unstrung, or an indefinite delay has brought ruin and its train to all concerned. Whereas in the other two countries mentioned, let some local object of interest call forth the attention of the neighborhood, and whether a church is to be built, a bridge constructed, or a road repaired, it is the inhabitants who commence, conduct and conclude the affair, and it is they alone on whom depend the rapidity and excellence of the execution. If money, in the shape of taxes, is taken from their earnings, they see the product of it in solid masonry, in spanning arches, or in crooked ways made straight and rough places smooth; which is certainly more satisfactory than to feel forever an untiring, relentless and invisible hand, extending from the centre to the furthest extremity of the land, and eternally fumbling in their pockets for every stray penny, which goes, when found, they know not where, evanishing as mysteriously as the fawning smile of a candidate the day after an election.

Now, if throughout the several Departments of France, the people had been long habituated to a local and subsidiary administration of public business; if they themselves had always been permitted to choose their prefects and other subordinate officers, instead of having placed over them individuals who were entirely strangers to the wants and capacities of their communities; if, in a word, they had been systematically taught a sturdy reliance on self, can it be imagined that they would have met the exigencies of 1830 and 1848 in such a spirit of helpless imbecility as they did, and that they would have so passively and subserviently submitted to the frantic and polluted emissions of the capital? They had been so accustomed to grunt and sweat under a weary provincial life, that when these things came, they received them, as a matter of course, much in the same way as a fine lady of a little country town does the last fashions from Paris. But better fortune, it is to be hoped, is in store for those whose unequal lot has hitherto doomed them to pay the tax-gatherer, ask no questions and be still. For unless the unwholesome, unnatural reign of centralization be soon terminated here, and unless the whole country alike be brought to a condition, wherein, as in the human body, each several member shall have a fair chance of performing its proper functions, we need look for little permanent progress, less stability in principles and no greatness,— *except there happen to be in store a military despotism, which will mock at all details.*

During the next two years, affairs will probably go on much as they do now — commerce flourishing, the national debt increasing, parties quarrelling, and hardly two persons thinking alike. *But then, in 1852, before which time the Constitution cannot be legally changed, there will come a fearful moment for the Republic and its institutions.*

Paris, Jan. 9, 1850.

LETTER XIX.

Public Securities here have risen greatly, and are still rising; true it is too that commerce, external and internal, is flourishing, and for the last twelve months has brought in immense profits; but the fact is not less indisputable, that the present state of national affairs is universally regarded as only provisional, and that many well informed persons openly declare their most serious conviction of the approach of another bloody crisis.

The *Rentes* are constantly increasing in market value, because people, weary of keeping their capital unemployed, and unwilling to invest it in houses which are half tenantless, or in lands which are overburdened with taxes, in fear and trembling do as their neighbors do, and trust their all to an inscription in the Great Book. Commerce thrives very much as a once promising youth, stunted by accident, shoots suddenly up to an unnatural tallness, on a partial recovery from a violent fit of illness. And that the present is only a transitory state of being, is manifested by the pertinacity with which the most remarkable individuals of the country, refrain, since the Revolution, from accepting place in the ministry; by the backwardness of commercial men to engage in any except very limited undertakings; and by the general economy which is visible in every household, where circumstances allow it to be practised. But as for the violent issue, about which some persons are so apprehensive, I must avow that, for the present at least, I can discern neither motives nor means sufficiently powerful and practical to produce it.

The Republic, as you know, was a surprise, not only for the nation at large, but not less so for those by whose agency it came into existence. But the Republic was accepted, and, such as it is, it must be endured till the question, *What can be substituted for it?* is more practically resolvable than at the present moment.

When Louis Bonaparte was raised to the Presidency of France by the vote of six millions, he might, it is believed in some quarters entitled to great respect, have secured to himself, almost as easily, a title more sounding in name than that which he bears, and a tenure of office as durable as his own life. When the events of the 29th of December and of the 13th of June arrived, the game, though somewhat more difficult, was, it is thought, still in his hand. But opportunity after opportunity went by, and in no way did he violate, or attempt in manner patent to violate, the Constitution. Why then you may ask, do people mistrust him, and why, while they regard him as a mere stop-gap, do they stand in fear of him? Simply, it may be answered, because of the difficult position in which he is placed. In a little while his term of office will expire, and by the Constitution he is not immediately re-eligible. In order to render him a legitimate candidate for the ensuing Presidency, that instrument must be altered; and in order to alter it, a Convention Assembly must be elected by the people, which by the terms of the instrument itself cannot be done before the spring of 1852. Now, it is a very dubious matter whether the present National Assembly will ever consent to any such Convention being called together, or, should the measure be decided on, whether the object proposed could be attained. For it must be borne in mind that there are other persons besides Bonaparte, without whose co-operation he can do nothing, who would like to be chief magistrate of their country as well as he; and that, should they aid him to a re-election for ten years, which would be tantamount to a life interest, their own fates as subordinates they might forthwith consider as forever sealed. And is it to be supposed that men like Changarnier and Lamoricière, all bursting with ambition, like Thiers and Odillon Barrot, each choke full of aspirations, will be content to sit quietly down beneath the withering shadow of such a one as Bonaparte! Here then is to be perceived no trifling cause of civic commotion; and should the attempt to baffle the Emperor's nephew succeed, he is not, if I read him rightly, much predisposed to "crook the pregnant hinges of the knee," and passively submit. He who in the face of every probability, and in despite of sagest counsel, twice dared to beard the French King with arms in hand, is not very likely to quit a palace in possession, and a throne, it may be, in perspective, to encounter, empty-handed, hungry creditors and remorseless bailiffs. He will first try gentle means, I doubt not, judging from the line of conduct till now pursued by him, but, let these fail, *he is the last man in the world to shrink from using the most sovereign of all arguments, a strong will pointed with sharp steel.* If left to himself, hard as it is to calculate on what the hero of Strasburg and Boulogne may or may not do, the chances are that he will do nothing to compromise his cause, till compelled to it by the progress of events. But, unhappily, there are those about him, selfyclept friends, who would, if they could, prematurely push him on to what might prove his ruin. Not thirty days ago such serious fears were entertained in most high quarters, of some senseless attempt, that, *to my certain knowledge, certain leading individuals, than whom none occupy or deserve to occupy more exalted places in the world's esteem, found it necessary to bind themselves by contract to resist to the utmost all violence on the part of the President and his personal adherents.*

Unwelcome as was the Republic from the first moment of its advent, and unloved as it now is, what chance is there of its duration, may be naturally asked. It must be admitted that Frenchmen, their habits, their prejudices and their antecedents do not accord well with a popular form of government; but it is also undeniable that they are every day becoming less and less fitted for living under a monarchy, unless it be a monarchy only in name. Yet as there must be something or other for them to bear allegiance to, it is clear that for the time being and perhaps for some years to come, Kings must yield precedence to Presidents, because no one Prince has at present power enough to seize the abandoned sceptre, because no one party has individual strength enough to contend against all the rest, and finally, because no one man has faith enough in himself to save the country from the moral paralysis under which it groans, or can sufficiently command the faith of others to make them his agents in the great work of salvation.

France can never again be other than a democratic country, however her chief magistrate may be designated. Her inhabitants have drunk too deeply of the cup of Liberty, have too sensibly enjoyed the delights of voting, and are too keenly alive to their own innate strength, ever long to brook other than the most liberal and popular of governments, however unfitted for it as yet they may be. The present Republic may, and probably will, break down, owing either to the unbridled passions of the ultra-radicals, the unteachable conservatism of the old-fashioned Carlists, the distracted counsels of the self-serving Orleanists, or the suicidal indifference of the weary and half bankrupt *bourgeoisie*. The Reds may make another armed effort to regain the ascendancy, but they will miserably fail, for all parties, however opposed to each other on other points, cannot, in the cause of self-preservation, do otherwise than join heart and hand in the defence of order. The Legitimists and Orleanists may stupidly refuse to be reconciled; the honest Republicans may obstinately shut their eyes to the possibility of a King and a Court; and he who now occupies the State saddle may, with the English Eclipse owner in his first race, believe, if not exclaim, "the winning-post past, and the rest nowhere!" But however long this state of suspense may endure, and however certain it is that nothing stable save a Republic can eventually grow out of all these things, almost equally sure may you be that there will be one more bout at Monarchy here, and that the Duke of Bordeaux, who is wisely waiting till he is wanted, till the national appetite for change is glutted, till fatigue has done its perfect work, and in a word, till the remembrance of olden times and brighter days returns armed with the force of absence, that he alone will turn out to be, what he was proclaimed at his birth, the "Gift of God."

Paris, February 4, 1850.

LETTER XX.

Since the 2d of December, 1851, there have been several narratives published in Paris, which profess to give accurate accounts of the events of that day, and of the circumstances which immediately led to them. In all these narratives facts are distorted, or, if facts were too patent to be turned awry, deeds of a most questionable nature are boldly attributed to the unparalleled wisdom and unequalled courage of their sole author, the Prince Louis Napoleon. In regard to some particulars, however, the authors of these panegyrics preserve, with one accord, a most politic silence. Yet, it seems to me, that such things should not be allowed to pass wholly unrecorded, when one is attempting to measure out equal justice to all parties, as it is my purpose now to do.

These partisan writers say nothing of personal abuse and derisive terms applied by a brutal soldiery to men whose world-wide fame is justly their country's boast, nor of the unholy means, the bribes, the "potations pottle deep" and the base appeals to a gangrened vanity, by which that soldiery was for the occasion brutalized. They make no mention of "bare fists" shaken, and looks of menace cast, by their goaler sentinels at the Representatives of National Sovereignty, impounded, like vagrant cattle, within the bars of a damp court-yard on the Quai d' Orsay for two long hours of a winter's day, nor of the indignities attending their subsequent incarceration. No allusion is made by them to cellular vans — vehicles constructed for the conveyance of the worst criminals and only one degree less hateful than the loathsome hearse, nor of the suffering from cold and hunger endured by those who, already chilled by the wintry hand of age, were transported by such means to their fortress prison.

Nevertheless, these things happened, and the testimony on which I rely in saying so is sure.

It would be lost time to recapitulate the history of the last few years in France to any one who has paid even ordinary attention to the rapid succession of events which have there been exhibited, to the alternate wonder and terror of Europe. To her own children has been conveyed, within a space less than the average of human life, a mournful lesson which blindness itself may read, and to the inhabitants of other lands, blessed with more stable governments, a fearful warning which folly alone will neglect. Equally needless would it be to recount the continual strife — not the least odious feature in that history, which, since December of 1848, was ever on the increase between the President of the Republic and the National Assembly, between the Right and the Left of that Body, and among the several factions into which those two hostile corps were divided. But not the less is it to be lamented by every lover of constitutional freedom that, owing to distrust and discord in their own ranks, the advocates of order allowed their antagonists of the *Mountain*, whom they far outnumbered, to throw the deciding weight of their votes now into this scale and now into that, sometimes on the impulse of caprice, but oftener in obedience to a fixed principle of demolition, from which there was little deviation. Mutual and bitter, however, as was the enmity that reigned among the different portions of the Assembly, the aversion which subsisted in full force between the Chief of the State and his nominal co-equal in power, showed itself most decidedly and uniformly on the part of the former, as facts and dates will fully prove.

In May, 1850, the President, through his Ministry, took an active share in framing and enacting a law, the object of which was an arbitrary restriction of the exercise of universal suffrage, that had solemnly been conceded to the Nation by the Constitution of 1848. This law, which, among other qualifications of an elector, required a residence of three years at least in the same *Commune*, disfranchised by this exaction alone, a vast number of respectable persons, whose way of life compelled them to an occasional change of domicile, according as the demand for labor shifted from place to place. So that, instead of a few hundred thousand vagabonds being excluded from the privilege of voting, which was the intent and expectation of its authors, two or three millions of honest citizens were by its operation deprived of their legal rights. Seeing then that the new law, that of May 31st, as it was termed, on being brought to the test of trial in a few isolated instances, neither fulfilled the end for which it was intended, nor satisfied any but the ultra-conservative classes, the Assembly very wisely resolved to alter it. For which purpose, previously to the adjournment of that body in August, 1851, certain steps were taken in committee towards a change in the principle of municipal elections, which had it answered the exigence of the case, would, by a single legislative act, have been forthwith applied to every other sort of election. During the three months of prorogation the consideration of the measure in question was necessarily suspended, but it would doubtless have been resumed in good season and conducted to a favorable termination, had not the President, hoping to undermine his adversaries' ground and secure to himself the lion's share of popular affection, proclaimed in a message to the Representatives his determination, so far as in him lay, to restore to the people at once and without stint, the universal vote, — the very thing, indeed, of which they had been deprived principally through his agency. The Message itself was in form uncourteous, and in substance far from being acceptable to many members who, in the face of their recorded sentiments of the preceding year, were thus suddenly called upon, as it were, to stultify themselves. Nevertheless, such was the general unwillingness to thwart, or so great was the fear of offending, its author, that he was suffered to carry off all the fruits of victory, through the countenance of a minority, which, by the conversion of two voices alone, would have been turned into a majority.

This seemingly adverse decision appeared to me at the time an exceedingly unfortunate one, because it afforded the defeated party an opportunity, he ardently coveted, to assume the character of victim in behalf of the people, whose favor he was bent on winning at the expense of his parliamentary antagonists. The proposition, as one proceeding from the Head of the State, should, in my opinion, have been entertained with all respect, and at a later day, every ground of quarrel having been in the mean time avoided, any amendments which the subject required might have been easily grafted upon it. Unhappily it was abruptly repudiated, and yet the insignificant majority by which this was done, added to the importance of the minority which, as already said, was acting in a great measure against its own decidedly pronounced convictions, showed how heartily disposed to conciliation was the mass of the Assembly. And that this was in fact the prevailing spirit of that Body manifestly appeared in the immense, though legally insufficient, numbers, which in the month of August had formally declared that the Constitution ought to be amended, for the well-understood purpose of legalizing the re-election of Prince Louis Napoleon, without awaiting the interval prescribed by that instrument. Moreover, soon after the prorogation there were meetings throughout the Departments of the Councils General, composed in part of Representatives, whose opinions doubtless greatly swayed their colleagues, and, with the same object avowedly in view, the nearly unanimous decision of these Councils was that the Constitution stood in need of a fundamental reform.

On the 4th of November, the Assembly came together again in Paris, and the President's insulting communication having been disposed of, as already described, the Quæstors' motion, so called, was brought forward, and in a manner to lead one to suppose that its framers meant it to be a still more practical and defiant response to the Chief Magistrate than that he had just received. In all respects it was ill-conditioned. The time for presenting it, a moment of profound irritation, was badly chosen, its tone was at once weak and menacing, and the management of it from beginning to end was puerile and clumsy. It theoretically demanded what could not practically be conceded, and lost the substance, in grasping at the exaggerated shadow, of a right. Had it become a law, the Assembly, under the loose designation of "the armed force" might have taken every soldier in the country under its own control, and left the President without a sentinel at his door; and "all the authorities," civil as well as military, would have been subject, under certain circumstances, to the orders of a single quæstor, if the terms of the luckless Bill had been literally fulfilled.* It was in reality a provocation to hostilities, and almost a declaration of war against a man who had all the material force on his side, and who took no pains to conceal his readiness and anxiety to use it. And at the same time, under the sorry pretext of regulating the exercise of a power indisputably conferred by the Constitution on the Assembly, it allowed, by its timorous policy, that

---

* Proposition déposée avec demande d'urgence. Art. 1, § 3. A cet effet, il (le Président de l'Assemblée Nationale) a le droit de requérir *la force armée et toutes les autorités* dont il juge le concours nécessaire.

Art. 2. Le Président (de l'Assemblée Nationale) peut déléguer son droit de réquisition aux questeurs, *ou à l'un d'eux.*

very power to be first questioned, then denied, and at last annulled.

Of the existence of this power no one can doubt who has read the French Constitution of 1848, which says: "The National Assembly determines the amount of military force established for its safety, and disposes of the same,"* and still less can any one who has read the recorded events of last November and December deny that a prompt use of such power would have saved, at least for a while, the Body to which it belonged. For if, instead of the Quæstors' proposition, a sufficient number of troops of the *line* had been instantly collected, in accordance with a right so plainly stated, and if a competent general had been appointed to command them, there is every reason to believe that the *Coup d' Etat* of December 2d, would have been prevented. Because, previously to that date there existed no influence with the army in any quarter strong enough to induce one portion of it to make war in cold blood upon their fellows, whether at the beck of an aspiring demagogue or at the instigation of a knot of mercenary intriguers. Besides, it should have been foreseen that the Quæstors' blow, made up as it was of three parts bravado and one part coward, being once fairly dealt, whatever fate befell it, was sure to return with redoubled force upon the authors and abettors of it.

But the affair was soon decided, and consequence quickly followed cause. The *Mountain*, which a few days before, through hatred to the President, had effected a majority of two voices against him, now, stupidly fancying themselves the masters and arbiters of the situation, flew round to his side and defeated the men of order, never suspecting, probably, in

---

* Constitution de la République Francaise, 1848. Art. 32, § 5. L'Assemblée Nationale détermine le lieu de ses séances. Elle fixe l'importance des forces militairs établies pour sa sureté, et elle en disposée.

their senseless animosity, that by so doing they were involving themselves and their adversaries in one common ruin. Many timid persons, also, such as abound in all popularly elected bodies, joined what appeared to be the stronger side, not through affection for it, but in dread of violence and in trembling solicitude for a peaceful solution to a frightful embarrassment. But our present concern is the result of the vote — a majority for the government of more than one hundred, and the inference to be drawn from it — that the predominant wish of the Assembly was to maintain amicable relations with the Chief of the executive power.

A vote, however, in the contrary sense, I am well assured, would only have accelerated the events of December, for two of the four persons who, as it afterwards appeared, were in the full confidence of Louis Napoleon, openly expressed their discontent at a victory, somewhat unexpected, or at least their preparedness for every event. To say no more, that they were annoyed at being balked of an opportunity for immediate action, is the interpretation that has since been put, not without reason, upon words, which at the time were reported to me by witnesses worthy of all credence.

A friend of mine, on entering the Elysée, just after the result of the discussion had been published, having addressed a well-meant compliment to M. de Persigny on his party's success, that gentleman, so far from receiving it as would have done a man guiltless of any covert design, peevishly answered, " So much the worse ! " thereby indicating most emphatically his chagrin at the loss of an occasion to execute some preconcerted scheme. And an intimate of M. de Morny's told me that, having rallied his *Elysian* friend on the morning subsequent to the debate, upon the absence of his name from the list of voters, jocosely attributing it to some excuse frail as the Quæstors' and not less fair, the embryo minister replied, that at the hour indicated he was in the President's cabinet, whither he had driven full speed, because, having seen M. Baze, the quæstor, and General Changarnier in close conference, and being doubtful of consequences, he wished to communicate his apprehensions to the Prince, who was resolved, he knew, in case of defeat, to re-enforce unavailing arguments with a few choice regiments of soldiers. Throughout, too, the whole of the momentous day, horses, saddled and bridled, were in the court of the palace, ready to be mounted at a moment's notice.

All the circumstances which immediately preceded the 2d of December demonstrate that the Assembly, though irritable, illogical, discordant and fitful by turns, was, in its reluctance to provoke a dangerous foe, timorous, credulous, and long-suffering, almost to the point of folly; and that opposed to such impotency was the silent, cold-blooded fatalism of one who scrupled at no violence, and hesitated at no illegality. Even the reception and treatment of the Bill on the responsibility of the President and other officers of State, sent by the Council to the Assembly, evinced the general spirit of forbearance which actuated the Representatives, who, it should be remarked in passing, were legally bound to give that document a hearing. And the committee, to whom it was confided, by modifying its conditions, and deferring the discussion of it, faithfully expressed the desire of their principals to appease rather than to exasperate a rival power.

Yet, in the face of probability, and without a shadow of proof, the mendacious cry of conspiracy was raised, as has often been done before in that country, for the purpose of screening from merited ignominy traitorous projects which admit of no substantial palliation. But men of veracity who, if a conspiracy had existed, must have been either of, or cognizant of, it, on account of their avowed political principles and peculiarly important relations, have informed me that the tale was only a groundless fabrication, invented expressly for the occasion.

Supposing, however, that the design had been seriously entertained to seize and imprison the Chief Magistrate of France, and had even been carried into execution, the evil consequences would have eventually fallen, not on the intended victim, but on the short-sighted inventors of it. For, blunted as is the moral sense of the common people by rioting in revolutions, they never would have looked calmly on while the nephew of the Emperor was gratuitously insulted. Or, if they had, inasmuch as before the 2d of December no offence worthy of punishment could be laid to his charge, had he, with the unerring instinct of a patriot's love, submitted for the moment to the indignity aimed at him, rather than jeopard by civil conflict his own integrity and the public weal, not only would he have won renown purer and more lasting than that of him whose name he wears, but on himself would he have centered the hopes of the intelligent and the virtuous, who now stand aloof, lamenting their country's freedom, but with faith in its resurrection, nor would he have forfeited the more vulgar support of the masses, by whose fickle sufferance at present he lives from day to day. Distraction and discord in the enemy's camp would have opened his prison doors as soon as they had closed upon him, and no competitor could for an instant have barred his way to power.

Indeed, I know not where such a competitor, under the circumstances supposed, was to have been found. Could the Monarchists have agreed on one — they who never were of accord even when fortune seemed to promise a blessing on their union? Could the Republicans have supplied one, broken in hopes and thinned in numbers as they had been?

Could the Socialists and Communists, branded as they were by the rest of the community with a Cain-like mark? Or, setting all party distinctions aside, could the Assembly have suitably responded to the exigencies of the country in her hour of need? The Assembly! The glory of that wondrous medley of wisdom and folly, of prudence and passion, of patriotism and intrigue, had long since departed, its clever but babbling President had worked his appointed mischief, its chiefs had demoralized their followers, and those followers themselves had become little better than a disorganized mob. And was this a body of men, trembling, as it were, upon the verge of dissolution, and morally attenuated almost to imbecility, was this a body likely to compass and imagine treason against a Power already swelled beyond all natural proportions? Or, was there within its limits sufficient unity of will and purpose discreetly to meet the consequences that treason of such a sort, if successful, must have brought in its train? No one, not even among those who once belonged to it, will have the hardihood to answer by an affirmative, but all, whose information is on a level with a moderate share of fairness and intelligence, will agree in this, that of the two Depositories of popular Sovereignty one was ambitious beyond measure, the other weak beyond bounds; and that the former, seeing the people agape in fear and amazement at eternal bickerings above their comprehension, and the military, with outstretched arms, ready in the impatience of ignorance to embrace the first bold comer, yielded to a temptation he had longed for, seized an occasion he had worked for, and, heedless of every engagement, grasped the glittering prize whose brilliancy had lighted him through the darkest passages of an eventful life.

The Prince President's admirers would fain persuade us that the *coup d' état* was a stroke of the highest policy most marvellously executed. But it will be found on examination that his plans admitted of no possible failure, except through the impossible treachery of the few who were his confidents, whose lives and fortunes were dependent upon his own. For in his hands were the garrison of the city and the treasury of the nation, neither officers nor soldiers knew any rallying name save his, and all or nearly all of them were but too ready to close their itching palms upon the lavish largesses he widely flung among the high and low, to quicken, if need were, the desire for vengeance that had rankled in the heart of the military ever since the disgraces inflicted upon them in 1848 by the populace of Paris. The Assembly, moreover, by its own suicidal act was unarmed, and the people by their listlessness were without the means of defence. What great risk, then, did it involve, and what prodigious skill did it require, to seize some scores of men during the helpless hours of rest and darkness, even if among them happened to be found renowned warriors, eminent statesmen and the representatives of some of the most distinguished names in France? Wherein was exhibited the consummate strategy so much vaunted? Was it in surrounding the National Printing Office with an armed guard, while its captive occupants, deprived of their natural slumbers and menaced with instant death on every side in case of attempted evasion,[*] were forced to cover sheet after sheet with the announcement of a portentous treason? Or, was it in the fiery haste with which the proclamations of that treason were posted in every conspicuous spot, where the deluded victims of it might read the news of their enslavement? Or, was it in barring out from their hall of meeting the members of

---

[*] Histoire du 2 Décembre. P. Mayer. pp. 50.51, Les armes furent chargées en silence, les soldats apposés aux portes, aux fenêtres, dans les corridors et les ateliers, et la consigne donnée: Elle était simple: Fusiller tout ce qui tenterait de sortir ou de s'approcher d'une fenêtre.

the Assembly, and driving a portion of them, not figuratively but literally, at the point of the bayonet till more than one of them felt the sharp steel piercing their loins?* Or, finally, was it in the slaughtering a host, which will never be numbered in this world, of individuals, whose only offence was a venial curiosity, or ignorance unwarned by the friendly sentinel, as in the "days of June," an inattention to municipal regulations stuck here and there at distant intervals, or, perchance, a natural insensibility to danger? Why, brute force and ordinary cunning would have sufficed to do all this.

But, unfortunately, to back this sort of force and cunning, experience in conspiracy was not wanting — experience which, gained at Strasburg and Boulogne, and matured within the castle of Ham, greatly diminished whatever risk there was of a third failure. It could not, however, diminish the amount of responsibility, nor the expense at which that responsibility was incurred. I refer not now to the nullification of a recorded pledge, nor to the waste of blood, (accidental perhaps), which the rain-soaked earth long refused to drink. With these things, I, a stranger, have nothing to do. To his own conconscience alone must the President stand or fall, since his countrymen, through weariness of the past and dread of the future, have absolved him by millions of votes — if, indeed, valid absolution can come from hands trembling under menace, direct or indirect.† But there is another and more heinous offence against society, against constitutional liberty,

---

* Three gent'emen were thus wounded. My authority is M. de ——, one of the most honorable and best known men in France, who was of the company.

† The vote given last December for President ought not to be regarded as free. It was one of terror for some, of necessity for others. The choice lay between Louis Napoleon and nothing. Men, willing to purchase tranquillity at every price, preferred him to nothing; while republicans, socialists and communists, watched by the police. voted Yes! with open ballot, under the threat of being sent to join their friends in exile.

against the spirit of the nineteenth century, against humanity itself, and it is this for which the self-constituted master of France is arraigned before the tribunal of public opinion throughout the civilized world, — a tribunal, thank Heaven! that can be neither silenced, nor shackled nor banished by the decree of any despot. This it is, too, for which he will be condemned by the righteous judgment of his own generation, and by the inexorable verdict of a retributive posterity.

In speaking thus I do not ask for myself, nor do I recognise in any foreigner, immunity for intermeddling in French affairs, but I do claim for every man who pretends to the dignity of man, the privilege of protesting whenever and wherever he sees the rights of his race invaded, and the march of liberty impeded, by unruly ambition of every kind.

But granting that Louis Napoleon's apologists are not altogether wrong in attributing to him prodigious shrewdness and cleverness, in extricating himself from a position which they assume to have been peculiarly difficult, still my opinion is, that, setting aside the criminality of the deed, no one deserving the name of statesman could have been guilty of the political blunder he committed on the 2d of December. For seldom has a transitory representative of power had a surer and safer course before him than he had previously to that day. The Assembly, as we have seen, and the upper classes, as is known, being unable to agree on any other candidate or on any definite line of policy, were more than willing to accept him; the *Bourgeoisie*, in exaggerated dread of Socialism, were warmly in his favor; and the work-people, obtusely impassioned for a name, were intent on having none but a Bonaparte to rule over them. All, therefore, that he had to do was quietly to await events and allow others, who had a better right, to make void the Constitution in his behalf, instead of violating it himself. And then, if men of blood and misrule, under the banner of Socialism or of any other dangerous fallacy, had ventured to attack the interests and relations of society, he, as the champion and constitutional defender of order, would have been held harmless by universal consent, whatever consequences might have followed the anticipated outbreak of 1852. But he rashly dared to turn responsibility from its natural channels, and its swelling flood will some day end by choking him. So far from bettering his condition, he has changed it, morally if not materially, for the worse. The intelligent and educated portions of the community are on the alert for an hour of vengeance, when vengeance untempered by mercy will be taken upon the offender. The middle orders, shocked at the contemptuous disregard of law and justice lately displayed in punishment before conviction and confiscation without judgment, will never lift so much as a finger to save him. And the common people finding, as they must before long, that their last state is no better than their first, will, according to their wonted instinct, eagerly throttle the prey which others, more skilful than themselves, shall have brought to a stand.

We sometimes hear of persons who are the slaves of one exaggerated idea, that has been developed to deformity by wilful indulgence. Among such, Prince Louis Napoleon holds no ordinary rank. He is, or effects to be, a fatalist. He fancies, or would fain make others believe, that, like inspired men of old, he has a mission to perform, that to him belongs the accomplishment of the work which his famous relative left unfinished, and that, in short, the salvation of France is to be wrought out solely by his ability to "close the era of revolutions."* And it is, perhaps, his obstinate perseverance in this notion — the offspring of an unstable judg-

* Appel au Peuple Français par le Président, le 2 Décembre, 1851. Cette mission consiste a fermer l'ère des révolutions. * * * *

ment and a distrust of God's Providence, that has been in part the cause of the success which crowned his third and last assault upon legitimate authority. Influenced by it, he heeds not the counsel of the limited number of the wise and prudent who can be induced to approach him, and hearkens only to a herd of sycophants whose delight is in administering to his own propensities.

Accident, too, has curiously contributed, in one instance, at least, to strengthen this absurd idea within a mind predisposed, it may be, by inheritance, to superstition. The instance referred to I am tempted to relate, because my informant, once an intimate in the family of the ex-Queen Hortense, is a foreigner of rank, whose honorable character and independent position forbid the suspicion that he is capable of fabricating an idle tale.

"Is it not strange," said her Majesty to this gentleman one day, "that my son Louis has the presentiment that some time or another he will become," (not Emperor or King of France, but) "the President of a French Republic?"

And who can tell if the promise, thus made to himself by the youthful dreamer, was not in a considerable measure the parent of the position which the man in his maturity now occupies?

That with such remarkable happiness at foretelling events, he has not yet abandoned the habit of divination, is no matter of wonder; and I was not, therefore, surprised at hearing, a short time since, of an oracular declaration of his, made on one of those rare occasions when he opens his mouth, in the following words: — "My life presents four distinct phases. The first comprised the follies of youth, such as the expeditions against Strasburg and Boulogne: they served to make me known. The second was my Presidency. The third is my Dictatorship. The fourth, and last, will be my fall beneath the assassin's blow." And the conviction that, like his grandam, the Empress, he is the child of destiny, that like his affected prototype, the first Napoleon, he has his own familiar star, will, without doubt, eventually lead him to perdition, by persuading him that the suggestions of an ungovernable will are the inspirations of a high intelligence.

Then, besides this fatuity of character in the individual, if we search within the nation he aspires to govern, whether there be aught which by its inherent qualities must militate against his permanence of power, we shall find that the instrument he hugs with such rapture as the means of achieving his utopian schemes, the very instrument by aid of which he cut his way to hollow greatness — the Centralization System, which in its day served well its turn, but which now has become the country's bane, will, like a two-edged sword, its shaft worn out, inevitably destroy the hand that uses it.

Under this system the people have so long been treated like children, that, like children, they feel and acknowledge a dependence on supreme authority which makes them desperately helpless whenever an emergency arises. Hence their inaptitude to withstand any sudden attack, as has been shown by the successful surprises they have undergone in the course of the last twenty-five years, and hence too is it that a liberal constitutional policy is the exception, and an alternation between despotism and anarchy the rule of their existence.

But, besides this moral degeneracy, a certain dangerous habit of mind has sprung from the same source, which has caused the downfall of more than one occupant of a palace, and will, if I mistake not, arrest yet another in the midst of his triumph. A senseless and excessive reliance on Government teaches all orders of men to hold that Government responsible for every misfortune of every sort, however beyond human foresight and precaution the event may have been.

Thus derangement in commerce, failure in manufactures, disorder in finance, even a bad harvest, a scanty vintage, an overflow of waters, everything of a calamitous nature is ruthlessly cast at the door of the ruling power. Never having been accustomed to manage even the comparatively insignificant concerns of their own municipalities, except in passive compliance with instructions from Paris, and being consequently incompetent to comprehend, and much more to repair, the simplest portion of a complicated political machinery, the mass of the nation, yielding to momentary discontent, welcome the first occasion which offers for tearing a government to pieces, in the silly hope of substituting a new one, without spot or blemish, in its place. And there is not a doubt in my mind that the many never neglected opportunities for indulging this their methodical madness during the last three-quarters of a century, have contributed more to their material and moral deterioration than would have the loss of the same number of pitched battles upon fields as disastrous as that of Waterloo.

We all know that the original component parts of the French nation differed from each other as much as the English from the Scotch, and that a Norman, even in our days, no more resembles a Toulousian than does a Highlander a denizen of London. But it is a melancholy fact that, under the paralyzing effects of a uniform subserviency to an unscrupulous policy of centralization, the descendants of the several tribes which have peopled France, whether of German, Roman or Celtic origin, all alike agree in their utter incapacity to improve their political and social condition proportionally to the occasions enjoyed by them.

Charles X., for example, so far as any benefit derived from him was concerned, might as well have perished in his first exile. Of sovereigns, it need not be said, he was among the weakest. He had none of the hardy virility and stubbornness, however intermittant, which distinguished the first king of that name in England. Moreover, the times were all in favor of experimenting on the former. His reign and character, therefore, were peculiarly suited to be used in a legal and constitutional manner for regulating the bearings of different classes and for settling the bounds of Parliamentary rights. Yet no wise advantage was taken of all this. But a feverish impatience — a conspicuous flaw in the mental organization of his countrymen — rudely rejected him as a thing of no value, and took up with his successor, who for eighteen years gave them practical illustration of the difference between a legitimate Negative and an illegitimate Positive.

Inadequate, however, as that successor proved himself to be in directing the movement of the age, even he might have been converted to an instrument of much permanent good, if the Opposition had assailed him only on broad constitutional principles, instead of tormenting him with personal provocations, which may humiliate, but can never reform, an antagonist, especially if that antagonist happen to be placed high above other men. But, in his turn, he also went the way of all royal and imperial flesh of French lineage, and, a fair field for inventing a new form of government offering, a Republic followed. And now, likewise, the Republic, which lives but in name, must be numbered among the things that have been, notwithstanding that less than four years ago it was servilely recognized wherever proclaimed, unblushingly subscribed to by every party, and cordially accepted, as a matter of course, by all who held, or who hoped to hold, office at the public expense, — and their name in France, it is unnecessary to add, is "Legion."

But neither from this, any more than from the "Annointed" of the land, was that profit drawn which an adroit management of the strength and weakness of each must have produced, if those who by right and duty were the guardians of the nation's welfare, had exercised even an ordinary degree of wisdom and firmness.

Now, judging from history, which is but a self-repeater, and from facts within our own knowledge, to which its pages will some day bear record, one is strongly tempted to speculate, however unprofitably, on the probable duration and possible uses of that resuscitation of the Imperial *Régime* which is just beginning to assume a consistency and shape.

The Prince at its head may rest at ease for the present, I presume, so great is the irritability of French nerves on the score of social danger, and so uncordial are all political parties towards each other, notwithstanding the daily authentic stories that are told of a *fusion* between two of them. He may go on his way rejoicing, so long as the credulous and timid can be kept in awe of the phantom Socialism, and while the foremost men of State remain coldly indifferent to that unity of patriotic purpose, for lack of which their country's happiness is withering, and they themselves are wasting in obscurity. He need apprehend no serious check till the avowed enemies of order crouch beneath, or elude, the hand that has so sorely stricken them. But this they have already done or are now doing, if on no other account, because of their numerical weakness. For, though I do not with some contend that they were always few and powerless, there are good grounds for believing that their numbers have been exaggerated and their forces overrated by calculating fraud. But armed resistance being now at an end, the real difficulty of the task Louis Napoleon has voluntarily set himself begins, and that too without taking into account his foreign policy. For, among other reasons, the total suppression of overt violence will, by allaying the apprehensions of the community, greatly diminish his importance, and consequently the factitious portion of his strength.

It has been computed by trustworthy and sagacious men, well placed for observation, that there are, or rather were, a few months since, in France, about a million and a half of individuals infested more or less with the doctrines of Socialism, and acting systematically in opposition to law and vested rights. From these dupes of cunning demagogues and victims of bad government, whatever be their number at present, no serious catastrophe need be feared while an armed force of sufficient magnitude, ever on the alert, is kept ready to confront them at every point. But beyond this material and barbarous state of things, which cannot always last without relaxation, there is somewhat to be considered that should alarm even the boldest. There are ideas, false in the main, but mixed with truth, which even under the stern compression of absolute power will go on germinating and spreading in secret, unless supplanted by others of a healthier nature. They are ideas which, in common with those proceeding from a purer source, cannot be eradicated either by fire or steel. Besides, let the weight of external pressure be removed, if only for a moment, from the faculty of asserting them by word or deed, and the uncured humor will rush to the surface with tenfold malice. Less obnoxious remedies, therefore, than those hitherto applied it behoves the present Usurper to devise, or France must remain, as she now is, in battle array, at a ruinous cost, ending in revolution, beneath which he will be sure to sink, weighed down by the personal responsibility that has crushed so many of his predecessors.

The most obvious and indispensable of these remedies is to scatter the darkness of ignorance, which covers the land, by *commencing* the moral and religious instruction of the lower classes, and by increasing the means provided for their intellectual improvement. For it is a sad truth that the French heart has been allowed to lie fallow, while the little pains bestowed upon the poorer children of the soil have been chiefly directed to the cultivation of the understanding. This is the reason, for the otherwise inexplicable fact, that crime most abounds in those Departments where the greatest number of inhabitants have been taught to read and write. But who can wonder at morality and religion being of such secondary concern in France, when he is told that the government has hitherto provided so niggardly for even the intellectual necessities of the humble, that to two-thirds of the population printed characters are a profound mystery, and that the art of committing thought to paper is an acquisition beyond their proudest hopes?

Has he, in whom all power is now vested, sufficient virtue and intelligence to supply with true knowledge, if only in its elements, the wants of those whose ignorance can easily be thrown as a stumbling-block in the way of every one who, from selfish or higher motives, would elevate the condition of his country? I fear not.

Powerful, however, as would be the general education of the people to cure the evils of Socialism, it could not half accomplish its object, unless accompanied by another remedy, the design and result of which would be to supply the willing laborer with sufficiency of work at a fair recompense, with plenty of food at a moderate price, and, in a word, with the common comforts of a decent existence, free from the cruel anxieties of an unprovided future.

But to attain such important ends, the only effectual instrument to be employed is, unfortunately, such that most persons in France, though otherwise well informed, shrink from the bare mention of it, as school-boys do from the first strange look of the simplest problem in geometry. And yet a Free

Trade Policy, the means I would indicate, cautiously but firmly introduced, must, I am persuaded, be adopted in that country before she can be brought to a commercial and social level with other nations in which it now flourishes, and *before, too, she can become a permanent resting place for any ruler whatever.* For it is that alone which can increase her revenues so as to prevent enormous deficits, such as annually occur, which can diminish the amount of taxes, lately become almost insupportable, which can provide new markets or enlarge old ones, where her produce shall not be sold at a ruinous sacrifice, as has recently happened year after year, and which can create many legitimate wants, with the attendant ability to gratify them, whereby the common people will be humanized, and their hearts, now festering amid wild theories with envy, hatred and all uncharitableness, will be sown broadcast with wiser and better thoughts.

Now, as no one hitherto occupying the highest post in France, ever made a single important advance in this the only true conservative direction, and as it is too certain that no legislative body, however constituted, will of itself take the initiative in a measure so fraught with peril to the imagination of a majority of the population, to Louis Napoleon is offered the opportunity and privilege of conferring on his countrymen a boon which may, if granted, redeem him in the opinion of posterity from a portion of the odium heaped upon him by his contemporaries. He cannot, with any show of reason, plead ignorance on a subject that has occupied so much of late the public mind, nor want of further information after the many hours he is said to have devoted to the study of political economy while in exile and in prison. Neither ought he, I apprehend, so to insult his own understanding as to affect an insensibility to the force of argument in favor of the change proposed, which nothing but the absence of knowledge or deficiency of sense can withstand. If, then, with no concurrent Power to hamper or circumvent him, he, like those who have gone before him, continue to tax the many for the benefit of the few, by keeping the ports of France more than half closed through the operation of a high tariff, on him, as it did on them, will fall that same responsibility before described, with all its fatal consequences, which neither decree, nor sabre nor bayonet can ward off or remedy.

I have contented myself with noting only one or two of those causes *within* the country, which, if neglected, must inevitably lead the Prince President to his fall as soon as they shall have had time to make themselves thoroughly felt. But should he, in a moment of desperation at finding the ground suddenly crumble beneath him, be tempted to plunge his country into a continental war, hoping thereby to defer the evil day, his doom will only be the more quickly decided. For if, on the one hand, he leave the Capital to head the army in person, prompted by the genius for war which he fancies to be a portion of his imperial heritage, unless he prove himself a greater General than the Emperor, Paris will close her gates against his return, as she once shut her ears to the appeal of that bold, bad man, when misfortune had stripped him of his power. Or if, on the other, he remain within her walls while generals, even of his own choice, fight his battles, victory and defeat will be equally ruinous to him, — victory, because it will give him a master in some fortunate captain, — defeat, because the disgrace will fall on him and on him alone.

But the penalty, alas! will not all be his. And let France beware, or the fate which once threatened her in the Allied Councils of 1814, and which has befallen more than one State in ancient and modern times, may be her lot. Let her look well to herself, or the spirit of the age, which is not warlike but commercial, may thrust her from among nations of the first rank, as a common nuisance and an enemy to the world's peace, by rending her asunder, so that her disjointed parts shall never come together again.*

Paris, Feb. 14, 1852.

LETTER XXI.

You are too much accustomed in America to regard the affairs of foreign countries in a purely commercial point of view, or, what is worse, as matters of mere curiosity. This appears to me a mistake, and especially since the advent of Louis Napoleon to supreme power. In my opinion, there was less danger of a general war in Europe at any moment during the last four years, notwithstanding the many fearful outbreaks that took place and the ferocious suppressions that attended them, than there is likely to be within an equal space of time immediately before us.

There is, for the punishment of crowned heads, a sort of chronic plague pervading the world, producing much, though not unalloyed, good, which has had more than one crisis, and may be approaching another at an hour when it is least dreaded. This "King's evil" is a hankering after liberty, which must sooner or later be satisfied. When once you have killed a man, there is an end of him; but it is not so easy to dispose of the creature of thought. The question then becomes one of conversion by main force against conviction, and the

---

*In all which has been said by me respecting the Prince President, I wish it to be most distinctly understood that I have spoken of him only as a public man, and of his *political* character alone. From sources beyond question, and from individuals perfectly truthful, who are well acquainted with Louis Napoleon, I know him to be kind and gentle in all the private relations of life, obliging and generous to those around him, temperate too, notwithstanding slanderous reports, and strictly honorable.

story is not so soon told. This notion of liberty, vague it is true, possesses the European mind to the utter exclusion of all possibility of passive submission and indefinite endurance. And it must necessarily become more defined, enlarged and disseminated, because, on the one hand, of its very nature, and on the other, of the constantly increasing intercourse between nations which are most blessed with political rights and those which have yet to attain them. New and newly-strengthened relations also with the American Continent will tend to the same result. Promises, too, in high quarters, will not so easily again delude the multitude. Promises of an extended freedom, sometimes though not always, given under the pressure of circumstances, have been shamelessly broken, and yet these same promises, or even better, must be renewed and redeemed, or no throne on this side of the Atlantic will stand secure. For the memory of a people is as tenacious as the fold of the constrictor; it never relaxes; and a nation never forgives.

In times long gone by, the ignorant and priest-ridden masses were controlled with facility, because matter in the long run can always be made subservient to mind. But in our day so much intelligence of one sort or another is scattered among the inferior orders of society, or among those who, without belonging to the highest class themselves, direct the former and influence the latter, that the ruler and the ruled, the oppressor and the oppressed, have something like a fair field whereon to fight. And is it to be credited by any intelligent observer, that, in that fight, millions of sentient beings, after having tasted the delights of liberty and self-government, however sparingly, after having enjoyed a glimpse of constitutional freedom, however undiscerningly, and after having realized a material existence less brutal than that they were born to, will cowardly return to their first estate of degradation, like the heart-broken African to the hold of the slave-ship, when the hour of recreation is over, or like the sluggish swine to his stye when the whip of the hog-herd announces that his repast in the forest is ended?

The present Potentate of France, thus far, has proved himself the cleverest of demagogues. He perfectly comprehends the terror which is inspired by the ill regulated and exaggerated, but holy, aspirations of the people, and makes a skilful use of it in his own behoof. His power is founded on a popular favor, or a show of it, before which the other Powers of Europe recoil with trembling. What a tribute, however involuntary, is this to Democracy in its true sense! But let that favor, or the image of it, waver or wane, and he will turn his back on the people and throw himself into the embraces of the Princes of the North. And who will insure the continuance of what, in this country above all others, is proverbially fickle? True, he is the hero of the day, and this very day he is entering Paris an emperor in all things, save the decree of the Senate, which is ready, and the votes of the people, which are prepared. No one can compete with him. The heir of the Bourbons loves his ease, and will wait till he is called for, while no representative of Orleanism could get an answer were he to call ever so loudly. The Republican is nowhere, and the Socialist is banned. But by what means does he keep up the fire of an enthusiasm which he lighted on the 2d of December? By giving crosses and ribbons right hand and left, by granting whatever priests and parasites demand, and by bribing in all quarters with promises which a power unlimited and a treasury uncontrolled, will enable him to fulfil for yet a season to come. But when the novelty of the thing is worn off, when his budget of baubles is exhausted and when, though the cry shall still be, Give! Give! he will have nothing more to give, what then can he find to keep up the excitement upon which he is now, while I write, riding triumphantly? His countrymen are greedy of change, ravenous for glory, impatient of personal inferiority, and are always writhing under a traditional disgrace upon the greatest battle-field of modern times. War, then, must come, or the embryo Emperor must go.

Paris, Oct. 16, 1852.

LETTER XXII.

In a country like ours, and under a government chosen by the people, the best means perhaps of arriving at truth is to give ear to all men. And there are moments, it seems to me, when it is the duty of all men to speak their thoughts as well as to listen. Will you then permit one, who has heedfully listened until now, to say a few words on the subject which lies heavily at the heart of every American who loves his country?

Having resided long in foreign lands, I have learned to regard that country — that *whole* country as *my* country, and to merge in its common being the existence of each particular State; and it therefore sorely grieves me when I find that the "value of the Union" is daily becoming more and more a matter of *calculation*. The Value of the Union! Well chosen words, which it behoves every man who takes them on his lips seriously to consider, and conscientiously to weigh, before he give to any "thought its act."

The Value of the Union! What, then! have we fallen so low, have we so degenerated from our sires, that we must needs set about *calculating* the value of that for which they lived and died, — that for which they sacrificed scruples and prejudices, — that for which their daily prayer was raised and on which their dying blessing fell? Are we so glutted with the prosperity which *union* has brought us that we long to taste of its reverse? Are we already wearied of its fruits, counting our rank and station among the foremost nations of the earth, the respect of friends and that dread which *united* strength inspires where no love is, as vapid nullities and worn-out baubles? Is our vast and varied Continent, teeming with every produce which can add life to life, — is it, like that of Europe, destined to be parcelled out, till internal broils and feuds shall be its only tokens of vitality? Is our commerce, boundless as the seas and oceans to which it gives no rest, rejoicing under a banner, the sight of which afar from home makes the heart thrill with gladness, — is this world-wide — this world-envied commerce to be torn piecemeal, some unrespected flag marking each paltry nationality? In a word, are we bent on defeating the only fair trial that self-government by man has ever had? Forbid it, Heaven! should be the cry of every one who believes that humanity was never intended by its great Creator to stand still or to retrograde. Yet such is the natural consequence of every step which leads to the pass of Separation, to the dislocation of a thousand ties, and to the annihilation of that magic charm of union which in the world's eye adds greatness to our greatness.

Why should any party insist on what is, or appears to be, its extreme right? It was not in this way that the authors of our Constitution and their worthy followers fashioned and confirmed it. If those who set so lightly by the Union could pass a few years in the Old World, and see as I have seen, how, for lack of union, great things become small and small things perish, — how strength turns to weakness and the realities of well-being dwindle away; if they could witness the high esteem and admiring honor in which the *United* States are held, and the envy with which our *united* condition is regarded by those who live from day to day by chance's suffrance, in hourly apprehension of beholding society rent asunder, property despoiled and nationality extinguished; if they could see all this with their own proper eyes, then might they indeed calculate the value of the Union, and not without advantage to themselves and others.

But there are those who exclaim, "Let the Union be destroyed rather than that slavery should be extended beyond its present bounds!"—while others, in the same spirit of chastened moderation, proclaim their hatred and contempt for this same Union, if for its preservation they are to be prohibited from going where they will with their human chattels. Both parties, in their eagerness for immediate conquest, seem too willing to sacrifice future interest to present passion; for they must know that a peaceful solution of the difficulties which have lately covered the land with shame and sadness cannot be hastened either by insulting inuendoes, craftily dealt forth in the Senate Chamber, or by the natural but deplorable consequences of such inuendoes, personal violence. Let them remember that life itself is but a compromise, that precipitation breeds derangement, and that extremes lead to dissolution.

Such is the condition of all human associations, and so false is the estate of man, that communities and individuals are frequently forced into a course of conduct which, if the circle of their own free will were less circumscribed, they would avoid; but which, owing to acts of their predecessors, they are compelled to adopt. Now the institution of slavery is generally admitted, especially by the slave-owner, to be an evil, and an evil, above all others, to himself. But it is only in its political and economical bearing that the inhabitant of a free State has anything to do with it. Its moral tendency is none of his business, unless he can refer to a higher authority than that of the Founder of our Religion, who, so far from putting the slaveholder in the same category with the murderer, the adulterer and the thief, took the institution as he found it, and was content to regulate, *thereby sanctioning*, the relation between the slave and his master.

But suppose there were any moral blame fairly imputable to slavery as it now exists in the Southern States, the slave-owner of our day ought to be held harmless, wholly undeserving, as he is, of the black and loathsome hues with which the popular artist of the day has begrimed his presentment, and of the irritating abuse inflicted on his character by certain public declaimers, emulous apparently of the notoriety of that same artist. If the institution of slavery be indeed such a crying sin, such an intolerable crime against morality and religion, as some aspiring politicians and unconscientious guardians of others' spiritual interests pretend that it is, let the stone of condemnation be cast, not at those who are the chief sufferers — the white inheritors of the horrible legacy — but at our own ancestors in New England and in Old England, at the slave importers of Massachusetts and of Rhode Island, of Bristol and of Liverpool. Why, not many years ago, so notorious and admitted was the general guilt in this regard, that the famous actor Cook, on being hissed upon the stage of the last named place for some deed of disrespect, exclaimed with figurative, if not courteous, truthfulness, "Men of Liverpool, you dare to hiss me! — me, who at the worst am guilty of but a venial folly! *You* dare to hiss me, when there is not a stone in the pavement of your whole city which is not cemented with the blood and sweat of a negro!" And no one was bold enough to gainsay his words.

How the Kansas troubles are to terminate, whether in curtailing or extending the "Institution," Heaven alone can tell; but this we know, that whichever party sent the *first* man to try by force the question of slavery or non-slavery within the limits of that territory, is responsible to God and to posterity for all the evil which has flowed, and may yet flow from such a diabolical act. On whatever side, however, victory shall declare itself in the terrible conflict — terrible because partaking so much of the nature of civil, mixed up with religious, warfare — I trust it will not be where a defeat would endanger the Union of the States. Compared in value to this Union, three and a half millions of negroes, aye, and of white men too, seem to me of little worth. Yet it cannot long endure if the quixotic folly of the last few years be persisted in by those self-constituted interpreters of the Constitution, who, a law unto themselves, believe that they are wiser than their fathers, and hope to accomplish by indirect means what the sagest of a past generation failed to effect when the course was clear before them. I am quite aware that the "non-extension of slavery" is the party cry of such persons, but no one doubts, I presume, that their real object is to root out slavery, at every risk and cost, from the places where the Constitution is its protector and the law its guarantee.

If the extension of slavery can be prevented by legitimate means, and at a cheaper price than the sacrifice of the Union, most men of conscience and understanding will gladly aid in the cause. And that the cause may prosper there are many reasons for hope and more for prayer. But, according to my poor way of thinking, insults and injuries on one side, which indicate a lack of moral sense, and blows and stripes on the other, which prove no moral courage, had better be kept in reserve, till means more gentle and more worthy of the christian gentleman have been tried and been found of no avail.

Boston, Dec. 4, 1856.

Trieste

Trieste Publishing has a massive catalogue of classic book titles. Our aim is to provide readers with the highest quality reproductions of fiction and non-fiction literature that has stood the test of time. The many thousands of books in our collection have been sourced from libraries and private collections around the world.

The titles that Trieste Publishing has chosen to be part of the collection have been scanned to simulate the original. Our readers see the books the same way that their first readers did decades or a hundred or more years ago. Books from that period are often spoiled by imperfections that did not exist in the original. Imperfections could be in the form of blurred text, photographs, or missing pages. It is highly unlikely that this would occur with one of our books. Our extensive quality control ensures that the readers of Trieste Publishing's books will be delighted with their purchase. Our staff has thoroughly reviewed every page of all the books in the collection, repairing, or if necessary, rejecting titles that are not of the highest quality. This process ensures that the reader of one of Trieste Publishing's titles receives a volume that faithfully reproduces the original, and to the maximum degree possible, gives them the experience of owning the original work.

We pride ourselves on not only creating a pathway to an extensive reservoir of books of the finest quality, but also providing value to every one of our readers. Generally, Trieste books are purchased singly - on demand, however they may also be purchased in bulk. Readers interested in bulk purchases are invited to contact us directly to enquire about our tailored bulk rates. Email: customerservice@triestepublishing.com

You May Also Like

War Poems, 1898

California Club & Irving M. Scott

ISBN: 9780649731213
Paperback: 160 pages
Dimensions: 6.14 x 0.34 x 9.21 inches
Language: eng

Second Year Language Reader

Franklin T. Baker & George R. Carpenter & Katharine B. Owen

ISBN: 9780649587667
Paperback: 176 pages
Dimensions: 6.14 x 0.38 x 9.21 inches
Language: eng

www.triestepublishing.com

You May Also Like

On Spermatorrhœa: Its Pathology, Results, and Complications

J. L. Milton

ISBN: 9780649663057
Paperback: 188 pages
Dimensions: 6.14 x 0.40 x 9.21 inches
Language: eng

The Credibility of the Christian Religion; Or, Thoughts on Modern Rationalism

Samuel Smith

ISBN: 9780649557516
Paperback: 204 pages
Dimensions: 5.83 x 0.43 x 8.27 inches
Language: eng

www.triestepublishing.com

You May Also Like

Report of the Department of Farms and Markets, pp. 5-71

Various

ISBN: 9780649333158
Paperback: 84 pages
Dimensions: 6.14 x 0.17 x 9.21 inches
Language: eng

Catalogue of the Episcopal Theological School in Cambridge Massachusetts, 1891-1892

Various

ISBN: 9780649324132
Paperback: 78 pages
Dimensions: 6.14 x 0.16 x 9.21 inches
Language: eng

www.triestepublishing.com

You May Also Like

Three Hundred Tested Recipes

Various

ISBN: 9780649352142
Paperback: 88 pages
Dimensions: 6.14 x 0.18 x 9.21 inches
Language: eng

A Basket of Fragments

Anonymous

ISBN: 9780649419418
Paperback: 108 pages
Dimensions: 6.14 x 0.22 x 9.21 inches
Language: eng

Find more of our titles on our website. We have a selection of thousands of titles that will interest you. Please visit

www.triestepublishing.com